SPRINGBOARD TO VICTORY

C. E. Lucas Phillips

SAPERE
BOOKS

SPRINGBOARD
TO
VICTORY

Published by Sapere Books.

20 Windermere Drive, Leeds, England, LS17 7UZ,
United Kingdom

saperebooks.com

Copyright © The Estate of C. E. Lucas Phillips, 1966.

First published by Wm. Heinemann Ltd., 1966.

The Estate of C. E. Lucas Phillips has asserted its right to be
identified as the author of this work.

All rights reserved.

No part of this publication may be reproduced, stored in any retrieval
system, or transmitted, in any form, or by any means, electronic,
mechanical, photocopying, recording, or otherwise, without the prior
written permission of the publishers.

ISBN: 978-1-80055-269-2.

TABLE OF CONTENTS

PREAMBLE

NO FULL AND authentic account has yet been published of one of the most remarkable sieges of modern history, in which a scratch force of some 1,500 British and Indian troops held at bay nearly the whole of a fanatical Japanese division for a fortnight at a moment of extreme crisis for the Allied cause.

The exploit which at that time captured the imagination of half the world was to become partly obscured by the subsequent achievements of the big battalions that profited from the little garrison's stand and used Kohima Ridge as their springboard to victory. Much also remained hidden by the lack of written records of all those small, inchoate fragments of troops who were hurriedly assembled to meet a desperate situation.

Certain unofficial accounts that have been issued are not only travesties of the facts, but also grossly traduce the honour of very gallant men and those who served under them. This book, therefore, is designed to set the record right and to narrate the half-forgotten deeds of a handful of men whose resistance was the 'hinge of fate' that opened the door to the destruction of the Japanese armies.

For Kohima was to Burma what Stalingrad was to Russia and Alamein to the Desert.

In the search for the facts of this exploit much material that is extremely difficult of access has been placed at my disposal, particularly the War Diaries of the Indian medical units concerned, whose evidence materially illuminates the otherwise obscure facts in more ways than one and for which I am especially indebted to Professor F. A. E. Crew and the official medical historians of the Ministry of Health. Mr James Barratt, whose company of misabused Indian 'non-combatants' worked in close union with the heroic doctors and orderlies in this unique battlefield 'hospital', has also added much to the re-creation of the scene and Mr Donald Elwell has been good enough to allow me the use of the revealing manuscript that he wrote afterwards.

Sir Charles Pawsey and Lieut-Colonel Keene have briefed me very fully on the topography and *mise-en-scéne* of Kohima from their long and intimate association with it. Major-General N. C. Rawlley, Lieut-Colonel T. C. Coath, Major Tom Kenyon and Major David Lloyd Jones have been to infinite pains in assisting me to sift the confused incidents of the continuous day-and-night conflict and no account could have been complete without the co-operation of the commander of the gallant garrison, Brigadier Hugh Richards.

To these, and to the many other witnesses whose names are recorded in Appendix B, several of whom have devoted a great deal of time and effort to the investigation, I am much indebted.

I am also most grateful to Field-Marshal the Viscount Slim, KG, for allowing me to quote some sentences here and there from his own superb *Defeat into Victory* (Cassell & Company).

1: BEFORE THE STORM

The Sleeping Jungle

FAR REMOVED from the scenes of conflict in Europe and the Middle East between the British Empire and the German-Italian Axis that had been in progress for two years, Burma seemed in 1941 to be secure against all threat of war. Even when the Japanese attacked the Americans at Pearl Harbor on December 7th and enlarged the European and African conflict into a world one, it did not for the moment seem likely that her dark and sleeping jungles and her peaceful paddy fields would so swiftly be penetrated by a distant enemy.

As a member herself of the British Empire, Burma was in fact implicated. Beyond her wild north-western border she could see her Indian neighbour busily training and equipping new forces for service against the Axis forces in the Western Desert and in the Middle East generally. Beyond her north-eastern border also she could very distantly see the ramshackle Chinese State desperately engaged in an entirely separate war with the Japanese, a war that had already been in sanguinary progress for four years, but in which no other State had up to that time been directly involved.

All this fighting, however, was very far away. Except for some productive efforts for the common cause and except for a small expansion of their home forces, the people of Burma as a whole pursued their normal way of life: sultry, colourful, somnolent, unperturbed. Their disillusionment was to be sudden, harsh and bloody as, one by one, all their neighbours and, indeed, the whole of the Far East, were overwhelmed by one of the most savage, swift and totally unprovoked campaigns of aggression in history.

Associated with India in membership of the British Empire, Burma was also geographically welded in India by the wild hills and forests along and athwart the frontiers of Assam and the little State of Manipur, remote and aloof in its primitive beauty. These three territories — Burma, Assam and Manipur — for the purposes of our study must be seen as one and, indeed, despite many contrasts, they all shared in common several significant features: mountains, jungle, magnificent scenery, a very high rainfall during the summer monsoon, virulent malaria, indifferent and often non-existent communications and a built-in lethargy among most of the indigenous populations.

Burma, largest and richest of these territories, is long and slim in form, having much length but no great breadth and at its southern end tapering to a mere point at Point Victoria. For practical purposes, its long, quivering tail south of Moulmein, forming the province of Tenasserim, may be disregarded, although it was here that the first and totally unexpected act of war was in fact committed.

On her western flank, washed by the waters of the Bay of Bengal, is the wet, mountainous, densely forested province of Arakan, separated from the hinterland by the massive mountain stretch known as the Arakan Yomas, rearing their sharp pinnacles as high as 10,000 ft and clothed on their eastern slopes with splendid forests of teak. On the opposite flank is the long, tortuous boundary of Siam, running through difficult hill-jungle till finally it climbs up into the fierce and desolate mountains athwart the border of the Chinese province of Yunnan. Across the formidable mountains flew the American 'volunteer' forces at considerable hazard (although

America was not yet at war with Japan) to bolster up the forces of Marshal Chiang Kai-shek in his long struggle with the Japanese invaders.

Swinging abruptly south-westwards round the lonely British outpost of Fort Hertz[1] on this far north-east corner, the boundary then skirts dizzily along the rim of the superb mountains of Assam and Manipur, among rhododendrons, magnolias and primulas, through forests of oak, pine, alder and thickets of bamboo, haunted by the tiger and the elephant, till it joins up again with the razor-edged ranges of Arakan. These forest-smothered ramparts, sweeping in a dramatic arc for nearly 900 miles, and forming part of the Himalayan mountain mass of Central Asia, seem to forbid all intercourse between India and Burma.

To the adventurous travellers and to the lover of wild scenery, standing on some point of vantage, these mountains display themselves, range upon range, as a superb panorama of primitive grandeur. He may in imagination see himself alone in the world, looking out upon a scene that has been unchanged since the days of the first man and philosophic thoughts of the most romantic kind may resolve themselves in his speculative mind. The slumbrous evergreen forest, the scented pines, the scarlet flame trees, the rhododendrons and magnolias, the sumptuous orchids, the flamboyant butterflies, the barking deer calling to each other across the valleys present themselves as the idyllic scene of Earth's age of innocence.

To Slim's and Stilwell's armies, however, these grandeurs of nature were but a sore affliction. Through the barrier that they presented, the soldier had often to cut his way step by step, dragging mortars, guns and ammunition with him, preyed upon by mosquitoes and leeches, carrying his wounded painfully up and down steep and slippery hillsides, looking behind every

11

tree for a lurking enemy and having small occasion to admire the beauties of nature. Awakened from its long sleep, the jungle lost its aura of romance.

A Land of Rivers

Thus Burma is clasped within a great chaplet of mountains on three sides. Within the chaplet its topography is dominated by characteristics that govern the lives of the people and direct or embarrass the course of any military operations. The first and most widely spread is the hill-jungle, in which the peaks and ridges are clothed to their very crests and pinnacles with dense forests and thick undergrowth, considered 'impenetrable' until the British and the Japanese clashed within their mazes. The second is provided by the valleys of great rivers and uncountable tributaries and hill streams. Chief of these rivers, dominating the life and economy of the country, is the Irrawaddy, which is to Burma as the Nile is to Egypt and the Tigris and Euphrates to Iraq.

For centuries the main highway of traffic, a busy commerce in craft of all descriptions passes continuously for the greater part of its 1,300 miles. Every town on its banks is a port. Throughout its broad valley agriculture and industry flourished. From its chill mountain origins near Fort Hertz it emerges, broad, brown and muddy, into the flat and dusty plains of the ancient kingly city of Mandalay, entering the great Dry Belt that distinguishes it from the wet highlands, then curls in great sweeps round the gaunt derricks of the Burmah Oil Company of Yenangyaung — the city of 'evil-smelling waters' — and finally launches itself through an enormous delta into the Bay of Bengal.

By the banks of the Irrawaddy have passed the conquerors and the traders of many centuries. The Mongol hordes of

12

Kubla Khan passed that way in 1284, plundering and destroying. By its lower and middle courses the little, ill-favoured army of General Alexander was to retreat before the onset of the Japanese invader in 1942, and by the same route the avenging army of General Slim swept back to victory three years later.

More important for the events of this narrative than the Irrawaddy, however, was its chief tributary, the Chindwin. A large river in its own right and half as long as the Irrawaddy, in a military sense it was the effective tactical boundary between Burma and India for some 200 miles in the main zone of operations. It ran at the foot of the great mountain barrier between the two countries through some of the worst malarial country in the world and across its waters the rival armies faced each other and bickered for nearly two years of stagnation.

To the military eye, the arresting feature of the map is that the 'grain' of the country, as represented by its rivers and hills, and consequently also its few roads and railways, ran nearly everywhere almost due north and south. This factor points out at once the easiest avenues of march alike for armies and for traders and labels those to avoid, for nothing is more difficult than to travel across the grain of a roadless mountain country thickly matted with jungle.

As the soldier or the traveller journeys north towards the Indian frontier and reaches the Chindwin, however, the grain begins to veer a little. The great mountain ramparts of Assam and Manipur confront him and he is in a country of deadly malaria. There are no roads, no commerce, no activities beyond the simple lives of the hillmen. One is brought to a halt and the only ways of travelling between India and Burma are on foot or on horseback by difficult jungle tracks.

When the traveller at last succeeds in struggling over the Indian frontier, he finds that the lines of communication swing suddenly from a north-to-south orientation to a west-and-east one. For here it is the great Brahmaputra, lying at the foot of the Himalayas, that governs the direction of men's steps. The nature of the river, the huge rises and falls in the volume of water in it, the consequent absence of bridges, the frailty of the small railway that wanders along the valley and along the foothills, designed to carry no more taxing loads than boxes of tea from the great tea plantations of Assam, seem to point at once to the hopelessness of attempting any large-scale military operations with modern transport and equipment.

For these reasons the only means of intercourse in 1941 between India and Burma was by sea. From Calcutta or elsewhere ships landed all travellers and all goods at Rangoon, the administrative and commercial capital, close to the mouths of the Irrawaddy, and thence they were distributed up-country by the ancient river highway or by the few railways and roads. In the military sphere, this meant that Rangoon was the base. The peculiar danger of that situation was to become apparent only too soon.

From Rangoon only two avenues of traffic were open to the north. The main railway, British-built, ran up the valley of the Sittang to Mandalay and thence to the town of Myitkyina[2], also British-built, in the extreme north, for which Stilwell's Americans and Chinese were to have to fight so desperately. This, with several branch lines, was the only railway system in the country. Alongside it a road ran from Rangoon as far as Mandalay, then branched off with it to Lashio and thereafter pursued its way alone into the mountain fortresses of China and so to the far-distant Chungking, capital and headquarters of Chiang Kai-shek. This was the famous 'Burma Road',

14

Chiang's only land link with the outside world, and by that route, until the Japanese captured it, went all the war stores for the Chinese armies. Lesser roads branched off towards the border of Siam.

Secondary to this main rail-and-road system along the Sittang Valley was another all-weather road, accompanied by a railway for only a short distance, from Rangoon to Mandalay by the valley of the Irrawaddy, with some deviations. This was to be the hard and bitter road of the Retreat, along which General Alexander's half-trained divisions sought to impose delay upon the nimble veterans of a more numerous enemy.

The Rains

In all these territories the difficulties of movement off the few metalled roads were heavily multiplied when the country became drenched by the summer monsoon, which in these parts blows in from the south-west across the Bay of Bengal from mid-May to October. Its advent was advertised by tempestuous thunderstorms and lightning flashes. Then it fell in dense perpendicular sheets for days at a time, splashing up from the ground in little water-spouts, drumming on roofs and walls, crashing noisily on the vegetation and drenching the whole country. It turned the rivers into rushing torrents or spreading lakes, filled all the dry watercourses, put a stop to movement off a firm road, and made life a misery to any creature not under cover. Only the stilts on which they stood saved the bamboo houses from being flooded. When the sun came out after each deluge, clouds of steam rose up from the soil. In the moisture-laden air, leather mouldered and clothing was continuously damp. A day's rain often measured five inches — as much as falls in London in ten weeks. The effect was felt most in the hills and most of all on the western or weather side of each range of hills. Assam is among the wettest places on earth. In Arakan, where the monsoon clouds from the sea are flung straight against the coastal mountains, 200 inches of rain falls in five months. Until General Slim's time, military operations in such conditions had always been thought to be utterly impossible.

In the other half of the year, from mid-October to mid-March, a mild monsoon blows from the opposite quarter and for most of this time the weather is cool and pleasant in the hills, but in March, as the north-east winds die down, there develops a two-months season of damp, stifling, oppressive weather, hot as the breath from a furnace.

By contrast, a large Dry Belt extends throughout the central plain crossed by the Irrawaddy in its middle courses, where lies the strategically critical stretch of country from Mandalay to Meiktila, where General Slim was to win his greatest victory. Less than 40 inches of rain falls and for the rest of the year the land is dry, withered, harsh and scattered with patches of semi-desert plants.

Even when it is not raining, movement off a road in the hill-jungle was often impossible, particularly on what was to become the Kohima battlefield. With a precipice on one side and a cliff or steep hill on the other, densely forested to the verge of the road, guns and vehicles could not deploy or park away from the road nor dumps and camps be set up. These things therefore often had to be done on the roadside itself, to the considerable embarrassment of movement.

The rainfall map is followed fairly closely by the malaria map. The disease permeated all these and adjacent countries but was most prevalent and most virulent in the regions of heavy rain. The Kabaw Valley, which lies along the frontier between Burma and Manipur, and in which so many arduous patrollings had to be done in the defensive period, and the Hukawng Valley, far away in what was to be the American zone of operations, were two of the deadliest malarial areas on earth. Dimapur, where the main British base was to be built up in the hot, sweaty plains north of Kohima, was nearly as bad. In the early operations there was no antidote to malaria except quinine, which was scarce and severely rationed.

To malaria was added that other great scourge of the tropics, dysentery. A third killer was scrub typhus, a very dangerous and difficult disease of the dry season borne by the jungle tick, for which the only known treatment was complete immobility, a treatment that was often impossible during operations. Leeches were also a considerable trial; any attempt to knock them off while they were gorging themselves resulted in a large, venomous and troublesome sore.

How serious was the effect of these and other maladies may be gauged from the fact that, in the early operations, when medical officers and their orderlies were working in appalling conditions, the casualties from sickness exceeded battle casualties in the ratio of 120 to one.

The People

The peoples who inhabit these territories were as varied and as colourful as their hills and plains. In general, they were highly intelligent, easy-going, humorous, fond of sport, delighting in gay clothing, impulsive in temper, easily moved to violence and inheritors of a long tradition of banditry, which had been brought under control by British rule but was ready to break out again at any time (and did so when the British left).

As in many other parts of the world, however, there were noticeable differences, which were to have important influences when the fighting began, between the plainsman and the highlander. The plainsmen of Burma were Burmese proper: Mongolian by race, Buddhist by religion, having higher standards of living, literacy and hygiene than Indians, but, for the greater part, of very poor fighting qualities. Their women, with their black, agate-smooth hair and their gay sarongs worn tight to the body, were often seen smoking long, fat cigars. Their Buddhist priests in their yellow robes were very politically minded and ardent collaborators with the Japanese, skilled in the treacherous arts of betraying British and Indian soldiers into murderous ambushes.

The various hillmen around them were of very different mould. The Nagas, Chins, Lushai and associated peoples astride the India-Burma mountain barrier and the Kachins near the China border were mainly animists or spirit worshippers, hardy, strong, self-reliant and brave. Those of the north, of whom we shall in due course notice the Nagas in particular, were devoted to the British, for whose cause, knowing that the British were their friends, they ran the most deadly risks.

The habits of life all over this area followed a broadly similar pattern. Apart from the big towns of Burma, people lived for the greater part in bamboo huts which were roofed with thatch or the fronds of the attap palm and, in areas subject to monsoon floods, especially in Burma, were raised on stilts. The villages, or often large agglomerations of villages, as at Imphal, were embowered in palms, bamboos or the shade-giving rain tree, the saman, beneath the generous foliage of which man and his small, hump-backed cattle found relief from the heat of the day. The Nagas, however, lived in villages which, for defence purposes, were built on the hill-tops or on spurs running from the great mountain ranges, and around their houses little black, long-snouted pigs rooted for a living and skinny chickens fluttered and scratched.

The peoples of these territories differed in their political status also. Assam was a province of British India under the Viceroy at Delhi and was administered by British officials of the Indian Civil Service, an administration without peer in the world for its high principles and devotion to the interests of the governed. In this province of Assam we shall have special occasion in due course to notice the district of the Naga Hills, centred around Kohima.

Between the Naga Hills and the Chindwin lay the little semi-independent State of Manipur, under its maharajah, advised by a British Political Agent. Extremely remote and difficult of access, its mixed hill people and the small British settlement led an idyllic existence in the fruitful upland plain of Imphal surrounded by hills of romantic beauty, among which was to be fought one of the greatest and most arduous battles of history.

Burma, by contrast, was administered under a constitution which was not far off that of Dominion status within the British Empire. It was a status for which only a limited number of its people was then qualified. However admirable this separation from India may have been in theory, its practical benefits were less obvious and its consequences in the war disastrous. Militarily the country became a backwater. Politically it became the scene of fierce quarrels between self-seeking rivals and its stability and equilibrium, in the four short years of its separate existence, were seriously upset. There was opposition to all expenditure on defence and indeed, on the outbreak of war, the Thakin Party, the most fiery of the nationalists, consisting mainly of brash young students, actively sided with the Japanese, cherishing the vain illusion that under the iron fist of the Japanese they would have a better chance of gaining their personal ambitions than under the velvet glove of the British. The Japanese, however, had not the slightest intention of liberating anyone and used these misguided Burmese as instruments of their own aggression.

Interplanted among the natives of Burma were well over a million Indian settlers or temporary immigrants. They were cordially hated by the Burmese, especially the Indian moneylenders, who too avidly foreclosed on land. Of the 400,000 refugees whose safe passage out of Burma General Alexander secured when the Japanese invasion began, by far the greater number were Indians fleeing from the wrath that would have descended upon them when the British forces retreated.

No less significant than these was a colony of about 30,000 Japanese of the professional and commercial classes, nearly all of whom seem to have been directed by their government to act as spies or information agents for the colossal operation of aggression that they had been preparing for years. The terrain of Burma had been studied with remarkable thoroughness and the services of guides and intelligence agents arranged long in advance. The Japanese, in fact, knew more about the jungle tracks than we did and many of these were marked out ahead of the invading forces.

2: THE RISING SUN

Step by Step

THE EMERGENCE of Japan from a position of medieval obscurity in the last century to one in which, by 1919, she became recognized as one of the five Great Powers is one of the most remarkable themes of modern history.

As an ally of Great Britain and with a navy trained under British auspices, she had joined in the First World War on the right side and had come out of it very profitably at negligible cost. Militarily, industrially and commercially, she had very rapidly become a modern nation. Hardworking, thrifty, disciplined under an autocratic regime, her people still, however, remained oriental, acknowledging total obedience to an Emperor sanctified by his attributes of divinity as direct descendant of the sun. State Shintoism, which was merely an Oriental form of Nazism, was sedulously fostered by the military leaders and gave fire to the kindlings of impassioned patriotism, which very soon began to seek expression by the exercise of martial power. The pressure of a rising population within her island boundaries and a lack of many raw materials gave an economic excuse for such aggressive promptings.

By a 'step-by-step' progression, Japan expanded her power and her frontiers, either by force of arms or by diplomatic pressure and trickery. After war with China, Formosa was annexed in 1895 and Korea became a vassal. Ten years later Czarist Russia was thoroughly defeated by land and sea and a dangerous rival removed from eastern waters. The First World War gave her fresh acquisitions in the Pacific at the expense of Germany. A whole series of further aggressions against China followed and, by the time this record had begun, she had seized the whole of the long coastline and driven the rabble of the Chinese army far into the interior. Thus, with only occasional breaks, the Japanese had been practising the art of war for the greater part of the century.

By the time of the Second World War, Japan had already become the ally of Germany and Italy in an anti-communist pact. Swollen by her already considerable and easy successes over second-class enemies, and believing her soldiers to be unconquerable under her symbolic emblem of the Rising Sun, she was already planning yet further aggressions against all and every interest in the Far East, under the sham pretext of establishing a 'Greater Asia Co-prosperity Sphere'. So vast had become her ambitions. She was actively planning attacks on America and on British, French and Dutch possessions. Taking advantage of the prostration of France in Europe, she squeezed the Vichy government into giving her complete military, air and naval control of Indo-China for the furtherance of her designs. By different means she drew Siam also into her orbit, supporting Siam's ambitious claim for Burmese territory. To secure her rear, she contrived a treaty of neutrality with Soviet Russia.

Diplomatic pressure failed to extort any concessions out of the Dutch in Java, while against Britain and America, Japan was aware, diplomatic coercion would be of no avail. But, by December 1941, having concealed her treacherous intentions behind the facade of diplomatic discussions with the United States, Japan had ordered her forces, now built up to a strength of 2,500,000 men, to take part in the most spectacular act of aggression in history. This time, abandoning her previous 'step-by-step' technique, she had resolved with extraordinary audacity on a simultaneous 'centrifugal offensive' extending to a wide arc of the compass: Pearl Harbor, Hong Kong, Siam, Malaya, Burma, the Philippines, Guam and Borneo were to be assaulted or occupied at one sweeping blow. Numerous other territories were to be assailed within the next few days or weeks.[3]

Siam and Malaya were invaded on December 7th-8th. Siam offered only a token resistance to save her face and on December 11th, using Siam as a springboard, the Japanese invaded Burma.

The Japanese Soldier

The Japanese soldiers who carried out these invasions were of a sort that had never before been seen on the world's battlefields. They were very aptly described by General Wavell (who was then Commander-in-Chief, India) when he wrote that they combined the equipment and organization of a modern continental army with the qualities of the savage.

The Japanese soldier acquired his particular qualities from his indoctrination in 'Bushido', the code of the Nazi-style military caste who dominated national policy. The aim of this creed was to produce a tough soldier of fanatical valour, convinced of his own invincibility and superiority over other people and dedicated to the idea, chanted by the soldier from his earliest recruit training, that 'our highest hope is to die for the Emperor'. All wars were holy, since they were fought in the interests of the Divine Emperor, and to die for him was to live for ever with the gods and to be enshrined as a hero in the temple of Yasukuni.

As a result, the Japanese soldier of 1941 had a tigerish quality, a complete contempt for human life — his own as well as others — and he completely lacked all 'softer' feelings, including all feelings of humanity. He despised the sick and all

23

whom he conquered. He particularly despised all whom he took prisoner, for here he was touched on a very particular point of the Bushido code and one in which he was set apart from other soldiers.

If to die was for the Japanese soldier his highest hope, to be taken prisoner was the lowest degradation, however severely he might be wounded, or however desperate his situation. Until very late in the war, when repeated defeats at Kohima and Imphal had shaken his confidence in his invincibility, virtually no prisoners were taken except the severely wounded, who forthwith asked their captors to shoot them. Suicide was the common practice of those no longer able to fight; they shot or knifed themselves or clutched grenades to their stomachs. On one occasion a whole unit that was trapped marched into a river and drowned themselves. When Japanese field hospitals were overrun by the British, the patients were all found to have been shot in their beds. Likewise, the Japanese also shot, bayoneted or cut the throats, *en masse*, of the British, Indian and Burmese wounded in dressing-stations that they themselves overran. Against unwounded prisoners, as most of the world knows today, they practised the most barbarous infamies, one of their favourite practices being to tie them to trees and use them for bayonet exercises. Against the Chinese their behaviour was even more abominable.

These characteristics made the Japanese very difficult to dislodge when in defensive positions. They always got dug-in quickly, building 'bunkers' with overhead cover of logs and earth strong enough to withstand direct hits by shellfire. They sited or concealed these bunkers well, with interlocking fire and mutual support between one and another. In these bunkers, whatever happened in flank or rear, they were prepared to fight literally 'to the last man and the last round', and it was impossible to shift them until every man inside had been killed, or until, their ammunition expended and all hope lost, they hanged themselves. Thus to overcome the Japanese in a defensive position it was often necessary to kill every man.

In attack the Japanese soldier went in with all the ardour to be expected of his training, but his methods were often very crude. He often attacked with small units believing that no troops could withstand the ferocity of his own, and he sought to terrorize his enemy before attacking by following the precepts of Henry V to 'imitate the action of the tiger' and 'lend the eye of a terrible aspect'. This he did by uttering loud, piercing, high-pitched yells, blowing bugles and often letting off fireworks, and he followed up this overture with a mass charge, shouting battle cries and uttering misleading commands in English. He used similar noisy tactics to unnerve his enemies and provoke them into disclosing their positions by opening premature fire. Thus his attacks were well advertised. These terror tactics had served him well in the past against the Chinese, but they failed when he came up against good-class troops who could not easily be rattled.

In keeping with his indoctrination, the Japanese soldier was brought up on a Spartan regime. Indifferently clothed in cotton tunic, trousers and peaked cap, poorly paid, savagely treated by his officers, required to undergo arduous marches and tactical exercises in the most severe weather, accustomed to maintain himself for five days merely with the rice he carried himself, he had no 'comforts' and little to look forward to but the glory of dying for his Emperor. In operations he presented few problems to the commissariat, for he was expected to maintain himself by capturing his enemy's supplies. He was untrammelled by military niceties and did not scruple to fight in civilian clothes and in the uniforms taken from the dead bodies of his enemies.

In weapons the Japanese troops were generally well equipped. They made great use of mortars and hand grenades, the grenades often being launched to a considerable distance by a small discharger operated in the hand. Grenades and mortar bombs burst with loud reports ('the angry bang' of the grenade, as one officer of the Royal West Kent expressed it), but they were thin-walled and much less lethal than our own. So also were their aircraft bombs. Officers went into action with long swords, which they used whenever they could get near enough. Their tanks were of poor quality and no match for ours, but one weapon they handled very adroitly and to the great discomfort of British and Indian troops was their 'infantry gun' of 75 millimetres.

Thus the Japanese soldier was a tough adversary. As Field-Marshal Slim has said to the author: 'If you have good infantry, you have a formidable enemy and the Japanese infantry, as fighters pure and simple, were superb.' Yet they were vulnerable. Their tactical methods, were often faulty, their marksmanship poor, their artillery generally indifferent. They were noisy and careless about protective dispositions and an enterprising enemy could make them pay heavily. They easily became confused when confronted by an unfamiliar situation, particularly when their enemy did not react as expected. Surprise confounded them. They were ill at ease when attacked in the open and often ran away when in danger of being enveloped. Thus the secret of success against the Japanese, when one had the means, was to take and keep the initiative.

At command levels, the Japanese were marked by a queer rigidity of mind. Their plans were often audacious and imaginative, but they were based on the expectation of a quick and easy success, and if that success did not follow they seemed incapable of restoring the momentum by a change of method or direction and, like Rommel at Alamein, went on battering their heads against the wall to their own destruction. They preferred to reinforce failure rather than admit failure. And they would let slip golden opportunities simply because they were not provided for in their orders, as when they had General Alexander himself and all his headquarters virtually 'in the bag' outside Rangoon, and as when they missed a chance at Kohima.

The favourite manoeuvre of the Japanese, executed at night, was to make a deep penetration through the British front, which jungle conditions so often favoured, block the line of supply and withdrawal and then attack on the main front in a hammer-and-anvil manner. They were also fond, in accordance with their 'terror' tactics, of beating up divisional and brigade headquarters, so that generals and brigadiers had several times to fight, like subalterns, weapon in hand. These incursions became known as 'jitter raids'.

A Japanese army in the field was organized in much the same way as an European army, but differences in nomenclature require some explanation for an understanding of the events to be related. The division was a very much stronger formation than a British one. An infantry 'regiment' (as in most armies other than British ones) was the equivalent of our brigade, consisting of three strong battalions. If the division was a 'triangular' one, it had three such regiments, plus, of course, artillery, engineer, cavalry, reconnaissance and service units. If it was a 'square' division, there were two brigades, each consisting of two infantry regiments, so that there were twelve battalions in the division, whereas British and Indian divisions had no more than nine. The division was commanded by a lieutenant-general and a special feature in it was a major-general commanding the infantry, who in operations had a very important forward tactical role.

A Japanese 'army', on the other hand, was the equivalent only of our 'corps', having two or more divisions under command and having also, of course, many other troops under its command beside the divisions. In these pages, for the purposes of comparison and convenience, the Japanese 'regiment' will be termed a 'brigade'.

The Japanese air forces, which were also organized in divisions and brigades for army support, were imbued with the same qualities as were inculcated into the soldier on the ground, but they were destined to play a much less spectacular part. The Japanese fighter machines were not quite the equals of the British and American, except for the Navy O, known as the Zero. Their pilots were never the equal of the British and American and although, by superior numbers, they drove the Allied forces clean out of the field in the opening campaign, the ball was to be returned very sharply into the other court when the British and American squadrons were eventually in force. The basic weakness of the Japanese in the air was that their factories did not have the capacity to sustain a long war against first-class powers and were unable to replace machines as fast as they were shot down.

Burma off Guard

To meet these 'savages with modern weapons' who so suddenly burst in upon them out of the trees in December 1941, the British and Burmese were quite unprepared.

Though Britain had an overall responsibility, fundamentally Burma's unpreparedness was due to her new separate political status. The Burmese politician took small interest in defence, since it was a matter little related to party advantage or personal ambition. Planning was further bedevilled by the frequent changes in operational responsibility and it was not until practically all the rest of the Far East had been lost that Burma was at last placed unequivocally in the hands of Wavell as C-in-C India.

Furthermore, Burma was a very long way from Japan and it seemed out of the question for the Japanese to attack it until they had first conquered the intervening territories and won command of the sea and the air. To the British Chiefs of Staff at home the defence of Burma seemed a purely academic matter and Britain was far too heavily committed in the struggle elsewhere with Germany and Italy to spare troops and aircraft for so remote a possibility. This of course was a perfectly logical appreciation and no one but the Japanese themselves could have been expected to foresee events so extraordinary as those which occurred in that December, events which were to paralyse the whole of the Allied position in the Far East at almost one blow.

Even after the blow had fallen, however, Burma continued to be at the bottom of the queue for all requirements — men, weapons, aircraft, vehicles and stores of every sort. Not the least remarkable feature of all the events to follow is that the British forces, both on the ground and in the air, fought their battles, built their roads, crossed their rivers, tended their wounded and sick, with the barest minimum of weapons, equipment and supplies of every sort, straining their meagre resources to the utmost, making-do with equipment that any other army would have written off as worn out and improvising their gear (even parachutes) from makeshift materials.

In consequence of this assessment, the military forces in Burma when the shooting started were hopelessly inadequate. The two good British garrison battalions had been reduced by 'milking' to only a company or two each and the only formation in the field was 1st Burma Division, commanded by Major-General J. Bruce Scott, whose troops were poor in quality, less than half-trained, very ill-equipped and in no condition to face a serious enemy. To support them in the air, there were only No. 67 (Fighter) Squadron, RAF, and the American Volunteer Group (AVG) under the able command of Colonel Claire L. Chennault.

This poverty of force was strongly emphasized by the entirely inadequate command structure. The C-in-C, Burma (Lieut-General N. K. McLeod, followed very shortly by Lieut-General T. J. Hutton), had merely a static, peacetime, War-Office type of headquarters in Rangoon, with no operational staff. A particularly serious deficiency, which was to embarrass the whole of the future operations, was the total absence of any external Intelligence service. McLeod and all his successors had to plan and fight entirely in the dark, except for such scanty information as could be gathered by an extemporized scouting force in the jungle.

Burma's military unpreparedness was even surpassed by the total unpreparedness of the various civil authorities. Even after hostilities had begun people in general seemed incapable of realizing the implications of a modern war and that a way of life that had been so easy for so long could be so swiftly and so completely wrecked. In spite of the efforts of the Governor and his senior officials, the civil administration collapsed almost immediately after the first bomb.

A few British and Burmese officials did splendid work in a desperate situation, but the majority showed themselves unequal to the unexpected, their confusion being worse confounded by the panic and flight of their Burmese subordinates. Thus it was upon the army that fell the heavy burden of shepherding, feeding and doctoring, as best they could, the 400,000 refugees who were soon fleeing northward from the approaching terror.

There were, of course, honourable exceptions. One of these was the Burma Posts & Telegraphs, who, like their military counterparts, Burma Army Signals, remained steady and did good service.

The First Blow

When the first blow fell on December 11th it was at the extreme southern tip of Tenasserim, not at all where anyone would have expected an invasion of Burma to begin. Here the Japanese quickly overran Victoria Point and its important but indefensible airfield. The blow, however, was only a gentle rap, for the operation had been undertaken by the enemy merely to protect the flank of his forces then invading Malaya.

A long pause followed, during which the Japanese were pursuing their conquests in the Far East with startling rapidity, and it was during this period that the legend spread throughout India, Burma and far beyond that they were troops greatly to be feared. No further significant penetration of Burma took place and the staff assessments of the probabilities of invasion seemed justified. Rangoon and other towns, however, were heavily bombed several times by the Japanese 10th Air Brigade, achieving the enemy's purpose of spreading panic among the Burmese civilians.

On January 9th, 1942, 17th Indian Division, commanded by Major-General J. G. Smyth, VC, began to arrive piecemeal.

This division was in due course to win a great name under its emblem of an angry black cat, but, at the start of things, pitchforked suddenly into a nasty situation while still incomplete and imbalanced, it showed little promise of its later prowess. Its state of training was 'low'. Some 25 per cent of the men were very young recruits, many under eighteen years of age, with only a few months' service. It was very short of artillery.

Worse than this, however, was the fact that the division had no knowledge whatever of jungle fighting and no equipment for it. This deficiency was common to all British-Indian troops. They had been in training for desert fighting and were equipped accordingly with motor transport. In consequence, when in the jungle, they were unable to move off roads or good tracks and the men were bewildered by the jungle and not a little fearful of it, particularly at night. They could not keep direction easily, lost contact with one another and imagined a Japanese behind every tree.

This state of affairs was not overcome until there had been some hard thinking and some hard lessons learnt from the enemy himself. Although there was a very small school of jungle training, no one had dreamt that large modern armies could fight a war in jungle conditions with virtually no roads. The Japanese, however, had carefully prepared for the campaign long before, their tactical methods for jungle warfare had been carefully thought out, the substitution of animal transport for motor vehicles prepared for, and the very tracks through the jungle selected. Tactical surprise dominated their thinking and for this purpose they adopted the jungle as their ally.

For the benefit of readers not familiar with these matters, a brief note on an Indian Army division, to the elements of which frequent reference will be made in this narrative, is given in Appendix A.

The passage of time and the course of recent events, however, make it necessary to remind ourselves first that, at this period, before the grant of independence by the British government, the sub-continent of India was not divided into the new states of 'India' and 'Pakistan'. Pakistan did not exist and the term 'Indian' applied to all parts of the subcontinent. The Indian Army of that time comprised some regiments that are now in the Pakistani forces and others that are in those of Delhi. The glory of the old Indian Army as it used to be known is fading away into the mists of a golden history but its traditions are at least in part maintained by its more distinguished regiments under both flags.

Invasion in Earnest

The five-weeks' calm after the seizure of Victoria Point was broken on January 19th, 1942.

Through lack of an external Intelligence Service, General Hutton remained in ignorance of the Japanese intentions. Though he made a shrewd enough assessment, his two divisions had to be strung out over several hundred miles while the Japanese 15th Army, under the bland-faced General Shojino Iida, was converting from motor transport to mules in Siam and while Siamese labour was making good the rough tracks over the precipitous frontier mountains higher up in Tenasserim to confound British expectations.

He crossed first with his 55th Division, following soon afterwards with 33rd Division who, wearing their emblem of the white tiger, were in the years to come the constant opponents of the 'black cats' of 17th Indian Division. The British forces were thus heavily outnumbered almost from the start. In the first serious fighting, which took place near Moulmein, the Japanese made rings round the raw brigades of 17th Division and continued to do so, repeatedly and swiftly, cutting in behind them and forcing them to withdraw by tactics that became only too familiar. In little more than a month Smyth had been forced back some eighty miles by these tactics to the line of the River Sittang, the last natural defensive position before Rangoon.

It was a very black hour for Britain and her Allies. All over the globe their fortunes were at the lowest ebb. A few days before had come the terrible news, galling to the British and calamitous for all her Allies, of the surrender of the fortress of Singapore on February 15th. The whole treasury of the Far East seemed within the grasp of the plunderer. A new blow was about to follow in Burma.

On the banks of the wide, swiftly flowing Sit tang, near its mouth, took place one of the most dramatic battles of the war. It was fought immediately to the east of a long railway bridge, planked over for motor transport, by which 17th Division was to withdraw. The Japanese, attempting to cut in ahead of them by a flank movement (using jungle tracks already marked for them), failed to secure the bridge, but, by a grievous misunderstanding, it was blown up prematurely and nearly the whole of the division was trapped on the wrong side.

The exultant Japanese fell upon them and there followed a grim two-days battle in sultry heat and clouds of choking dust, with the troops' water-bottles empty. Vehicles, the whole village of Mokpalin and the very jungle itself were on fire as the Indians and a few British troops held off repeated attacks by day and night and the gunners of the 28th Mountain Battery fired over open sights in the moonlight at an enemy often a few yards away.

When all hope was lost, the trapped brigades, under the command of Brigadier 'Jonah' Jones, took to the water, faced with a swim of one and a half miles across the swollen and swiftly flowing 'River of Death'. Bamboo rafts were extemporized for the wounded and for those unable to swim. In that terrible ordeal about two men out of three were drowned or shot by the Japanese machine-guns while in the water, yet there were men who swam the Sittang again and again to help over the wounded and those unable to swim. The remnant who reached the west bank struggled ashore without boots, without arms and nearly naked.

Two companies of the King's Own Yorkshire Light Infantry, with 8th Burma Rifles and elements of two Indian battalions, whom the withdrawal order did not reach, hung on to their fighting positions until 7.30 in the evening, their gallant defiance materially assisting the safe withdrawal of their comrades. When it became evident to them that there had been a general evacuation, they retired to the river.

In this disaster — a disaster partially redeemed by many acts of courage and devotion — 17th Indian Division lost eighteen guns, all its medical equipment and nearly all its mortars, automatics, signal equipment and vehicles. For the time being the division ceased to exist as a fighting force. Worse still was that its morale, already low, was severely shaken and did not improve during the long months of retreat still to come — except among the Gurkhas, whose cheerful resilience seemed to thrive on the conditions that depressed the spirits of others.

The Hard Road

It was in this desperate situation that a new commander for the Burma Army arrived at Rangoon by air ten days later (March 5th) to take over from General Hutton. This was General Sir

Harold Alexander, one of the foremost British soldiers of his time, very much admired for his military skill, his personal character and his disdain for the perils of the battlefield. He had been in command of the evacuation at Dunkirk and it was now again to be his lot to preside over an evacuation for, even before his arrival, that course had become almost inevitable.

A fortnight later, after the Retreat had continued for another 140 miles, there arrived a figure that, for the Burma war, was to have an even greater significance. Alexander, with very wide responsibilities, needed a corps commander and staff for his Indian and Burmese divisions and other troops and Wavell sent him the remarkable figure of Lieut-General William Slim, who arrived on March 19th to command the newly founded 1st Burma Corps, known shortly as Burcorps.

Bill Slim, a Gurkha officer, had risen rapidly since the war had begun in 1939. He was perhaps not a tactician of great genius, except as displayed in his ultimate great battle in the plains of Mandalay and Meiktila, but he had other splendid qualities that were to bring him out as the greatest military figure of the Burma war and second only to MacArthur in the whole of the Far East. First and foremost, he was a great leader. His bulldog face and jutting chin were an index of the tenacity and drive that were his mainsprings. His presence gave men confidence that here indeed was a fighter. Behind his John Bull appearance, however, lay an alert, inquiring and very shrewd mind. He understood men and sized them up as quickly as he did tactical situations. Perhaps, like some other Indian army officers, he understood Indian troops better than British ones. With the exception of Alexander, whose stay was short, he was virtually the only British commander from whom the bitter Anglophobe American Lieut-General 'Vinegar Joe'

Stilwell, who ambiguously commanded Chiang Kai-shek's troops, would accept orders.

Like Wavell and Alexander, Slim's instincts were all for aggression, though in the Retreat his offensive operations were repeatedly frustrated, usually by the Chinese. He had great mental resourcefulness in overcoming the difficulties presented by the terrain and the shortages of the tools of war from which the Burma troops always suffered. This resourcefulness was to be most brilliantly seen later on in his use of the air for transport and supply; the air-supply operations that he mounted were easily the largest and most spectacular of their kind and were to become the model of the future. By the same methods, as will be seen, he was soon to devise a means of beating the Japanese cutting-in tactics, by simply ordering the troops who were cut off to stay put while he supplied them by air. He was to be an innovator also in refusing to accept the monsoon as a compulsory ceasefire and to employ the appalling conditions it created to break the enemy through the guts of his own troops.

These things, however, were still hidden in a future that was anything but bright. The present field-marshal, in his own *Defeat Into Victory*, has vividly described the 'sinking of the heart' as the gloomy facts of the situation, particularly the low morale, the poor training, the absence of Intelligence and the shortages of equipment, crowded in on him when he arrived and as he surveyed the skin and bones of a staff which was all that could be spared him and the three vehicles and two motor-cycles that made up his operations headquarters.

For our purposes there is no need to record in detail the sorry tale of the great Retreat, conducted with considerable skill and its gloom illuminated from time to time by many gallant acts. Its importance for us is to paint the background of the picture and to emphasize the contrast with the subsequent events that are our main concern. Within thirty hours of his arrival, Alexander was forced to give the inevitable order for the evacuation of Rangoon and, as he left the smoking city, by the road to Prome, he and all his headquarters escaped capture by a hair's breadth as a Japanese column, in an audacious manoeuvre, cut across his front to attack Rangoon to the west.

The loss of Rangoon virtually decided the issue of the campaign. Not only did it permit the Japanese to bring in two more divisions — the 18th and 56th — not only did it deprive the Allies of Burma's valuable exports, but, over and above all, it obliged the Burma Army to withdraw away from its base. In future, it would have to carry its house on its back for the complete absence of roads from India made supply and reinforcement impossible, except for the very small effort that could be made by air.

Furthermore, the army was now left with virtually no fighter or bomber support, for the RAF and the AVG had been obliged to withdraw, some right back to India. The Japanese aircraft were free to bomb and gun the retiring troops at will, though the bombing was light-weight stuff compared to the Germans'.

The Retreat developed along the axes of two widely separated river valleys — those of the Irrawaddy and the Sittang — and here Stilwell's Chinese armies, who were allotted to the Sittang sector, came disastrously into the picture. With the exception of their 38th Division, which served most of the time under Slim, they were to prove a liability rather than an asset and were useless as a fighting force. Only one man in three had a rifle, only one division had any artillery (which it withdrew as soon as the enemy came within range). They had no administrative services whatever — no ration supply, no medical, no transport. All these Alexander had to provide for them out of his straitened resources. They had a complete contempt for the clock, could be relied upon never to keep an operational schedule, and had a total ignorance of staff duties.

After a good initial defence of the Toungoo sector, the Chinese in the Sittang valley broke, fled northwards in complete rout and disintegrated, refusing to obey Stilwell. It was not long before they had degenerated into regiments of terrorists who plundered the Burmese and, at the point of the bayonet, turned wounded soldiers and refugee women and children out of trains to speed their own flight. The loss of Toungoo was as great a disaster as that of the Sittang Bridge and the fate of Burma was sealed. Slim's corps retired up the Irrawaddy in a running fight step by step, shepherding the ever-swelling crowds of unhappy refugees. On Alexander's order the great oilfield of Yenangyaung, with its 5,000 wells, three gasoline plants and the biggest power station in Burma, was destroyed by Mr W. L. Forster in a gigantic conflagration while buildings crashed to the ground in one explosion after another. Under the great pall of black, oily smoke and amid the burning houses of the village of Twingon, Bruce Scott's Burma Division, cut off by another of the enemy's audacious deep penetrations, fought for its life and got through by a miracle when at its last gasp through the initiative of 2nd Royal Tanks. But they had had to abandon nearly all their vehicles (in which many of their wounded were butchered by the Japanese) and thenceforward one of their brigades was reduced to bullock-carts for transport.

BURMA and ASSAM
Burma Army's Retreat Routes ·······>···

SCALE OF MILES

Alexander now had no choice but to retire on to India as fast as possible. He rightly deduced that the Japanese plan was to cut him off at Mandalay and force him to a battle of destruction with his back to the Irrawaddy. The gallantry of a rearguard commanded by Brigadier R. T. Cameron and consisting of 7th Hussars, 414th Battery, RHA, and the Gurkhas of his own 48th Brigade, who broke the attempt of the newly arrived Japanese 18th Division to drive through to Mandalay, defeated the enemy's intention and enabled the whole of Slim's corps to cross the Irrawaddy safely on April 30th.

There was, however, one more river to cross — the Chindwin. There were now no more roads and no more bridges and still 225 miles to go before reaching the Indian border at Tamu, where other forces were at hand. The monsoon was only a fortnight away. There were 2,300 sick and wounded to be cared for. There were many thousands of Indian refugees, whom Alexander refused to abandon. The troops were on half-rations, their uniforms in rags, their boots worn out, their kits nearly all gone and their razor blades finished. But they could still fight and soon had to do so again.

On May 10th Burcorps experienced the last of its many hair-breadth escapes. As they were embarking in river craft at a rickety jetty near the little village of Shwegyin on the Chindwin, the Japanese seized the high ground overlooking them. Disaster was again averted by Cameron's rearguard brigade group and some other troops, who held them off until nightfall, when, having had one final fling at the enemy, they put a match to all their tanks, vehicles and ammunition and destroyed their guns. Then, the boats' crews having long ago refused further duty, they made good their own arduous withdrawal by a precipitous jungle footpath.

A few days later the monsoon rains burst to add to the discomfort of the troops and the refugees on the long foot-slog across the Kabaw valley. Many of the sick and wounded, jolted in lorries over the rough tracks for the last 225 miles, failed to survive the ordeal. Many of the refugees had died at the roadside all along the long trail. But the enemy, having reached the objective he had set for himself, did not now attempt to follow up.

The rearguard, now of 63rd Brigade, marched into Tamu on May 19th. Gaunt and haggard, they still kept their ranks under their officers and carried their arms. Slim watched them come in. 'They might,' look like scarecrows,' he wrote, 'but they looked like soldiers too.'[4]

Thus ended the longest retreat in the history of the British army. It had measured rather more than 1,000 miles and had lasted four months. It had resisted the Japanese longer than any other land forces. It had lost in all 13,463 men. The Japanese had won Burma, but they had failed in their intention to destroy the army that opposed them.

Many who had had to give way before them in that hard road were to return as victors. Among them were 17th Indian Division, who, under their new commander, Major-General 'Punch' Cowan, were soon to rise Phoenix-like from the ashes of Sittang and face their old foes of the Japanese 33rd Division for two long years in the precipitous mountains of Manipur and the fever-ridden Kabaw valley and finally defeat them.

The Burma Army as such, however, broke up. General Alexander went home, destined to become the leader of triumphs instead of the saviour from disasters. The Burma Corps and Burma Division ceased to exist. With some honourable exceptions, the Burmese troops had been useless, deserting in large numbers. The British infantry battalions, on the other hand, had in General Hutton's official words shown 'magnificent spirit'.[5]

Pre-eminent over all, however, had been those troops whom Slim himself described as 'that magnificent formation' — 7th Armoured Brigade, commanded by Brigadier J. H. Anstice.[6] Except for their infantry battalion, which joined them afterwards, they had disembarked in the fear-stricken docks of Rangoon just too late for the Sittang. Experienced, well trained, full of guts, they had come straight from Eighth Army in the Western Desert, where they had been fighting and beating Rommel's Germans and Mussolini's Italians for more than a year, and they were neither scared of the Japanese nor impressed by the quality of most of the troops they had come to support. They quickly adapted themselves from desert to jungle conditions and, serving frequently as an offensive rearguard, time and again held off the enemy and saved the situation, their cheerful and gallant spirit in the most critical situations being an inspiration to the whole army.

Unhappily these splendid troops were lost after the Retreat. They were whisked away to waste their excellence in static roles in the deserts of Iraq and Syria.

3: TWO LONG YEARS

Hard Thinking

THE LOSS OF Burma seemed to threaten the whole of the Indian sub-Continent and much else besides. In fact, the Japanese had reached the limit that they had set for themselves in their prosecution of their campaign for the 'All Asia Co-prosperity Sphere'. But no one could be sure of their intention and an invasion of India seemed an obvious and easy course. The fortunes of the Allies throughout the world at this period were at their lowest ebb. 'The crash of external disaster,' wrote Mr Churchill, 'fell heavily upon us.' All the Far East had been lost. The sinkings of Allied shipping in the seas of the world by Germans and Japanese reached enormous figures. The Royal Navy had suffered severe losses in Eastern waters and could no longer contemplate a major fleet engagement. A powerful Japanese attempt against Ceylon in April had been thwarted only by the skill and valour of the Royal Air Force. In the Western Desert Rommel began his Gazala offensive against Eighth Army. In Europe the Germans were trampling deeper into the heartland of Russia.

Before Rangoon fell Wavell had pressed the Chiefs of Staff at home for the immediate dispatch of his urgently needed reinforcements. In addition to his acute shortage of trained soldiers, he wanted 54 more air squadrons, 1,350 anti-aircraft guns and nearly 200 airfields. The War Cabinet in London promised to do what they could, but were desperately pressed in all the seas of the world.

Thinly he spread out his few troops and his meagre air squadrons and everywhere he ordered work to be pressed

ahead to improve the primitive roads and railways. He sent
Slim to command 15th Corps, strung out along the coast of
Bengal and covering Calcutta, where Slim improvised a soldier-
manned 'navy'. In Manipur, destined to become one of the
twin arenas of the great Kohima-Imphal battle, the romantic
terrain was held by the 4th Corps, wearing their emblem of a
trumpeting elephant and commanded from July onwards by
Lieut-General Geoffrey Scoones.[7] Here were to be found the
new 23rd Indian Division under Reginald Savory and the
remnants of Cowan's 17th Indian Division, decimated by
malaria and dysentery and without tents, bedding or cooking
gear in the drenching monsoon rains. Behind them, in the
sweating and fever-ridden plains, Dimapur began its build-up
as. a great advanced base. Beyond 4th Corps, in the far north-
east mountain of the China border, were Stilwell's American-
Chinese forces, known as Northern Area Combat Command,
with their operational base at Ledo.

Throughout India new divisions were training hard and all
commanders were thinking hard. Everywhere there were deep
heart-searchings on the cause of the Burma defeat. The
emphasis was now all to be on jungle fighting. Men must learn
jungle craft, jungle patrolling, how to live hard and move
quickly with the minimum of gear. Mule transport (already
much used in the Retreat) replaced a great deal of motor
transport. In artillery emphasis was placed on Mountain
Regiments, the crack troops of the Indian Army, equipped
with the 3.7-inch howitzer — the celebrated 'screw-gun' —
which could be taken to pieces and transported on mules.
Jungle regiments were created equipped partly with heavy
mortars. Certain Indian divisions, of which 17th was one, were
converted to light divisions, with mules and jeeps as the basis
of their transport. Wingate's celebrated 'Chindit' brigade was

formed for long-range penetration, under the cover title of 77th Indian Infantry Brigade. Indianization of the forces was accelerated.

To make good the lack of an external Intelligence service, a special jungle organization was created known as V Force. It consisted of a number of British officers, chiefly men with local knowledge, who worked far forward enlisting the help of local inhabitants and building up teams of agents behind the enemy lines. The Japanese created a similar organization but the local people usually preferred the British, particularly in the hills of the India border, where most of them were loyal to those who had for so long been their friends.

Above all, the crying need of the Indian army was to restore its normally high morale. The myth of Japanese invincibility had to be exorcized and the troops imbued with confidence in their power to win. Given good training first, the best method of achieving this aim was in quick victory and to this goal Wavell directed his energies. He was always a believer in the offensive, indeed, sometimes too sanguine a one, as in the Retreat, during which he constantly urged an offensive when none was practicable.

Lack of the necessary craft and warlike tools obliged him to put aside his first ambitious thoughts of a sea-borne attack direct on Rangoon itself and to content himself with a limited offensive in Arakan, to be mounted in the next dry season. His objective was to seize the horny-backed Mayu Peninsular and the island port of Akyab lying off the tip of it. Coordinated with this was to be an offensive by Stilwell's Chinese from their operational base at Ledo and a diversionary threat from Manipur by Scoones's 4th Corps. By these operations Wavell hoped to unbalance the enemy in any further offensive that they intended and to position himself favourably for more ambitious operations.

Far away in the north-east, on the Chinese border, Vinegar Joe Stilwell, no less offensively minded, was tackling similar but even more obdurate problems with his difficult Chinese. He had also to wrestle with the monumental task, now that the Burma Road was lost, of maintaining Chiang Kai-shek's forces within China by air over the Himalayan spur that became known as the Hump. Over this great mountain waste, rising to 15,000 ft and swept by air currents of the most violent turbulence, the United States Air Force, at great cost in gallant lives, built up one of the most remarkable air lifts in history. For this, as for operations on the ground, Stilwell was very largely dependent on the fragile rail and road communications of the Brahmaputra valley, of which more will be seen later.

Throughout the summer monsoon months of 1942 the preparations went on, often under extreme difficulties. The rains made life a misery for men out in the open, washed away newly made roads and made havoc of communications. With the rains came an enormous increase in tropical sickness, especially malaria and dysentery, with which the few field hospitals, especially those hurried forward to Manipur and Assam, were wholly unable to cope. In the tented wards and bamboo shacks the leeches crept into the makeshift beds to feed on the patients' blood, the beds themselves sank into the mud, big water-rats attacked the patients through the mosquito netting and had to be fought off by the less seriously sick, and doctors, nurses and orderlies tramped through the ooze in the deluges of rain.

The figures of sick and injured rose astronomically. The 23rd Indian Division was at one period 5,000 men short. One battalion was reduced to 120 men. To the sicknesses and injuries of the troops were added those of the great army of labourers building roads and those of the 180,000 refugees from Burma who passed through Manipur, many of them desperately ill, especially the women and children. In Manipur the build-up of sickness during the monsoon was such that, when at last the dry season allowed improvements to road and rail, 20,000 men were waiting to be evacuated.

The British were not the only people contemplating an offensive. The Japanese, watching the preparations being made — the pushing forward of roads and the active patrolling, the feeling southwards from Manipur across the fever-ridden Kabaw valley and down to the banks of the Chindwin, the construction of new airfields, the build-up of the great new base at Dimapur in Assam — drew the obvious conclusions.

The Japanese High Command therefore instructed 15th Army to plan a limited offensive during the next dry season to deny the Allies their opportunity and to stimulate the anti-Ally activities within India of Gandhi's All-India Congress. General Iida accordingly planned to invade Assam with three divisions and to occupy a line from Ledo through Dimapur to Arakan.

Thus both sides were, and not for the last time, planning simultaneous offensives against each other.

'First Arakan'

The British offensive in Arakan began at the end of 1942 and was entrusted to Major-General W. L. Lloyd, commanding 14th Indian Division. The Mayu Peninsular lay between two evil-smelling rivers, the Naf and the Mayu, where crocodiles wallowed in the oozy slime and mosquitoes swarmed in the steaming heat. Along the whole length of the peninsular ran a knife-edge mountain spine, with very narrow strips of flat country on either side. Thick jungle clothed the mountain range to its very ridge, and the whole craggy peninsular was traversed by only a few bullock-cart tracks.

After the stiff barriers to road transport had been overcome, the division had by 1st January 1943, successfully overrun nearly the whole peninsular. From that moment, however, everything went wrong. Unseasonable rain washed away the makeshift road behind the forward troops. In the resulting delay the Japanese rushed in reinforcements by sea from their Akyab garrison and rapidly built a formidable bunker system at Donbaik on the west coast. Further reinforcements followed as the enemy 55th Division crossed from the mainland. Lloyd's troops battered at the Donbaik position for some ten weeks without success. Though they may seem to have little relation to our main theme, we must take some note of these events, for they serve to illustrate the background atmosphere, the thorny problems to be overcome and the vivid contrast between 1944 and the years before it.

An audacious enemy manoeuvre then brought things to a climax. A column led by the remarkable Colonel Tanahashi, having landed on the east coast of the peninsular, scaled the precipitous mountain spine, descended on the west coast in the early hours of April 3rd, cut off the 6th British and 47th Indian Brigades and captured and killed Brigadier Cavendish.

The British brigade, its withdrawal covered in old-fashioned style by the guns of 130th Field Regiment, fought its way out, but on April 14th Slim arrived on the scene and ordered a general withdrawal to a position twenty miles back just before the monsoon rains began to pelt down.

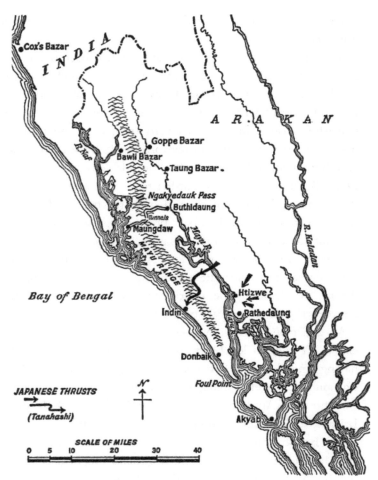

'First Arakan', showing the enemy thrust that cut 14th Indian Division in two.

Thus the hoped-for victory to restore morale collapsed in failure. Instead, it was merely another galling blow. Wavell had hoped that Stilwell's proposed offensive from Ledo would deter the enemy from reinforcing Arakan, but Stilwell's operation, through Chiang's intransigence, never even began.

On the other side of the balance sheet, though it was not known at the time (nor until very recently), this 'First Arakan' operation, together with Wingate's Chindit operation which had been taking place simultaneously, did succeed in one of Wavell's intentions; by drawing off the Japanese 55th Division it stalled the enemy's own proposed offensive into India at a time when the Allies were ill-prepared to meet it.

New Commanders

Wingate's first bold 'Chindit' operation, which had been launched in February, has only a slight bearing on our narrative and its adventurous incidents have been recorded by several pens. We may note, however, that, while it achieved no apparent tactical purpose, it was a very valuable exercise. It demonstrated that ordinary, unpicked troops could, after training, overcome the jungle, penetrate deep 'into the enemy's guts' (in Wingate's own phrase), beat the Japanese in combat and be successfully maintained in isolation from the air for up to three months. When the achievements of the brigade became known they acted as a marvellous tonic to morale after the gloomy depressive of First Arakan. Unknown to the Allies, Wingate's exploit also had a very positive result in stimulating the Japanese to the offensive that led to the great battles of Kohima and Imphal.

In the other fields and oceans of the world conflict the fortunes of the Allies had in the meantime changed dramatically. After the great victory of Alamein the forces of Montgomery and Eisenhower had united (under Alexander) to drive the Germans and Italians out of Africa. At Stalingrad the Russians had dealt the Germans a staggering blow. In the

Pacific the Americans had begun to turn back the tide of Japanese aggression. The Allies' greater inherent powers of recuperation were just beginning to assert themselves.

In South-East Asia, however, no light had yet appeared on the horizon. As the monsoon of 1943 broke, the rain pelted down like a cloudburst, the hill-tops were wreathed in mist, the chaungs and nullahs became rushing torrents and all land fighting stopped for five months. In the pauses of the rains there were a few brief encounters; the 1st Lincolnshires and the 1st North Staffordshires showed in two fine raids that the Japanese could be deeply penetrated and beaten up. In the air the RAF and Stratemeyer's 10th USAAF, now superior to the enemy in numbers, were beginning to assert their dominance. The first Spitfires, in the hands of 615 Squadron, had an electric effect.

At the top level, changes in the command structure of the utmost significance took place after a series of consultations between Mr Churchill and President Roosevelt on the need for unified operations. The young and brilliant figure of Lord Louis Mountbatten was suddenly exalted from his relatively junior position as an acting Vice-Admiral to become Supreme Allied Commander over all services of the new South-East Asia Command. Stilwell, adding further to the complex of his several and equivocal appointments, became his sarcastic and obstructive deputy. Wavell became Viceroy of India, having been succeeded as C-in-C India in June by General Sir Claude Auchinleck, whose distinguished and inspiring presence was known and admired throughout the Indian Army. The responsibilities of his post, however, became separated from the command of operations on the frontier, which passed to the new 11th Army Group under the wise and understanding command of General Sir George Giffard. Stilwell, old-soldiering everyone when it suited him, refused to accept orders from Giffard, but fortunately agreed to take them from Slim, who was now to become commander of the new Fourteenth Army, destined to share renown with Montgomery's Eighth Army as the most celebrated of British land-fighting formations. In the air, 3rd Tactical Air Force, under Air Marshal Sir John Baldwin, and Troop Carrier Command, under the US Brigadier-General William Old, became 14th Army's particular allies.

All through the 1943 monsoon, long before Mountbatten's arrival, the air between Delhi, London, Washington and Chungking had been humming with argument and counter-argument about future operations. Everyone wanted an offensive in the next dry season, but 'where' and 'how' were questions of wearisome long-range debate. The gear for ambitious projects was lacking. Britain and America did not have identical views on priorities. The Americans wanted to build up a powerful air force inside China and to prop up the rickety Chiang; the British wanted to deal a knock-out blow to the Japanese armies in South-East Asia. Auchinleck had to warn the combined Chiefs of Staff that the flimsy Assam transportation system, designed to carry nothing more sinister than boxes of tea, was incapable of supporting both projects, which made Mr Churchill very angry, for he seldom appreciated the administrative factors that govern large operations.

The outcome of the aerial tournament of words resolved itself into a plan that differed little from Wavell's earlier proposals: another attack in Arakan by 15th Corps, a limited southward advance by 4th Corps in Manipur, an offensive from Ledo by Stilwell's Chinese, and another Chindit operation, but on a far larger scale, to support Stilwell in the enemy's rear. This satisfied nobody except Wingate but more ambitious plans had to be put on one side for the time being. Or so it was thought.

Enemy Counter-plans

Meanwhile, the Japanese had also been reshaping their machine, strengthening their command structure and hatching their plots.

Over the head of 15th Army a new command had been established under the style of Burma Area Army Headquarters, with Lieut-General M. Kawabe in command. At the same time 15th Army was reorganized and put under the command of Lieut-General R. Mutaguchi, a ruthless fire-eater of the most exclusive Japanese military society.

After First Arakan and the first Chindit operations, the new command began, like the Allies, to shape their plans for the next dry season. There was ample evidence of the Allies' intention to launch an offensive and the enemy commander concluded that, with their present strength, they would be unable to break an Allied attack by standing on the defensive. They had been led to this conclusion specifically by the Chindit operations, which had demonstrated that good troops could easily penetrate their defence.

This exploit, which greatly impressed Mutaguchi, materially influenced the Japanese decision to forestall an Allied offensive by launching their own first, as they had intended in the previous dry season. The objective now, however, was a rather more limited one — to destroy 4th Corps in Manipur, to seize Kohima, the mountain gateway to India, and to establish themselves impregnably on the great mountain barrier that ran from the Naga Hills, through the Chin Hills down to the Arakan Yomas. This was to be the bulwark that would make their conquests in South-East Asia secure. Later on there was a great deal of talk, for propaganda purposes, of a 'March on Delhi' but there was never any such intention.

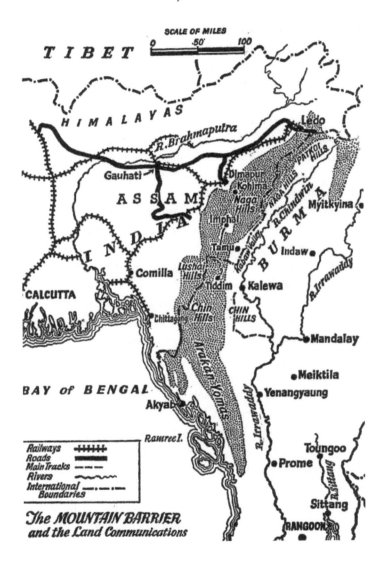

The MOUNTAIN BARRIER and the Land Communications

This offensive was given the code name of *U-Go* and entrusted to Mutaguchi's 15th Army. An integral part of the plan was that the main offensive should be preceded by a diversionary offensive in Arakan, code-named *Ha-Go*, and designed to appear to the Allies as an invasion of Bengal and so oblige them to commit their reserves. Thus both sides were proposing offensives in Arakan at approximately the same moment.

To carry out these bold and skilful plans Kawabe was sent three new divisions, plus an independent brigade, giving him a force of seven and a half divisions, with another in reserve in Malaya. A little later two new armies were formed: 28th Army for Arakan under Lieut-General S. Sakurai and 33rd Army opposite the Chinese. This left Mutaguchi free to concentrate all his fierce driving force on the Manipur offensive. Tokyo also sent large (but not large enough) reinforcements of engineers, transport and supply units, for, although the Japanese were fortunate enough to have excellent natural north-and-south communications nearly up to the Chindwin, beyond that point they would be faced with the same wide expanse of roadless mountain jungle as the British.

In addition to these good troops of their own race, the Japanese had the support of two traitor armies, both formed before the war as part of their long-term invasion plans, and much enlarged afterwards. One was the 'Indian National Army' under Subhas Chandra Bose, a former president of the Indian Congress Party, and the other the 'Burma National Army' commanded by Aung San under the puppet government of Dr Ba Maw, which the Japanese set up in Burma. Though they were of some use in relieving the combatant Japanese of certain duties, both 'armies' were useless as fighting forces and

56

their leaders were treated by the Japanese with the polite contempt that they merited.

The Japanese troops were frequently accompanied by detachments of the INA who prowled and howled round the Allied lines and, in both English and Urdu, tried to seduce the Indians and the British from their allegiance. Sometimes, as at Kohima, a loud-hailer was used. These gentry were contemptuously known as 'Jiffs'. Their methods were crude and their labours were in vain.

'Okydoke'

Mountbatten took the wheel of his triphibious ship in November 1943. The monsoon clouds and mists were evaporating and the dark earth had distilled its steaming vapours. All along the mountain frontier, from China to Arakan, the opposing forces closed up to one another, bickering and sparring in the hill-tops and the malarial valleys. The war with Japan had now been in progress for nearly two years and things in South-East Asia were still as they were. It was vital for the Allies that there should be no more disasters.

The Arakan campaign, the first to be launched, began in sparkling fashion. The 15th Corps was now commanded by Lieut-General Philip Christison. His assault divisions were 5th and 7th Indian, led by first-class commanders in Major-General Harold Briggs and Major-General Frank Messervy, both of whom had already distinguished themselves in the Eighth Army in the Desert. Christison sent Briggs down the western side of the mountain spine and Messervy down the eastern and to watch his open left flank he sent Woolner's 81st West African Division, who were accustomed to jungle and who carried their loads on their heads, away out into the Kaladan valley.

The Japanese had now built a very forbidding defensive system right across the Mayu Peninsular which they called the 'Golden Fortress', the core of which was based on a tunnel that ran right through the mountain ridge, buttressed by craggy heights honeycombed with bunkers. Here was posted the Japanese 55th Division under the grim-visaged Lieut-General Hanaya, with 54th Division in the island of Akyab.

By the end of January 1944, Briggs and Messervy had overcome all the enemy forward positions, had closed right up to the Golden Fortress and were preparing for the grand assault upon it when Hanaya, with a shrewd sense of timing, suddenly sprang his own *Ha-Go* offensive.

Under cover of the early morning mist of February 4th he slipped a solid column of 5,000 men, 16 abreast, led by local guides, through a gap between two units on Messervy's left flank.[8] By this extraordinary old-time manoeuvre the column penetrated six miles across country almost empty of troops, wheeled to the left behind Messervy's divisional headquarters and split up into four tentacles that swung south and west in an enveloping movement, while Hanaya began a northward attack from his main front.

In another dawn mist two days later one of the enemy tentacles burst in upon Messervy's own divisional headquarters. Another tentacle seized the pass across the Mayu mountain spine, known as Ngakyedauk Pass (or, to the British troops, 'Okydoke'). Seventh Division was trapped. Soon afterwards 5th Division's supply route on the western coast road was also cut. Hanaya intended to annihilate 7th Division where it stood and to cut 5th Division to ribbons. Every visible sign pointed to the imminence of a disaster even worse than that of the year before.

This year, however, things were different. Slim had given orders that in future the *riposte* to the Japanese encircling tactics was not for troops to fight their way out, but to stay put and to rely upon the air for supplies. The first example of these tactics was now seen.

Messervy and his headquarters staff, after a five-hours fight, broke out of their encirclement and made their way to an expanse of open paddy fields, surrounded by hills, in which lorries, mules, stores, workshops and all sorts of administration units were assembled. This became the celebrated 'Admin Box' round which the heart of the battle raged and in which clerks, mechanics, drivers and mule leaders fought with no less gallantry than the combatant troops of Geoffrey Evans's 9th Brigade, who, together with some gunners and some tanks of the 25th Dragoons, had hurried to their aid. For a fortnight the Japanese hurled themselves fanatically against the unsubstantial defences in day and night attacks, in one of which they overran the dressing-station and committed another of their appalling atrocities. Bombing from the air and bombardment by long-range heavy artillery made no difference to what Hanaya himself called the 'hysterical defence'.

The star heroes in this all-gallant cast were the 2nd West Yorkshires whose endless counter-attacks, together with the close-range blasting by the tanks of Frink's 25th Dragoons and the point-blank shooting of gunners of all sorts, saved the box.

Messervy's other brigades stood fast in similar fashion while British and American pilots of Troop Carrier Command flew in and dropped the means to continue the fight. The first mission was led by the American Brigadier-General W. D. Old in person, but had to be abandoned when half-completed in the face of heavy fire from the ground and attacks by enemy fighters, for the Allies had here not get command of the air.

Dropping by night and fighter protection by day overcame the difficulty, until at length the Japanese aircraft were drawn off to support the big operation impending on the central front.

The main enemy thrusts in the Battle of Ngakyedauk Pass.

After three weeks the enemy had been completely outfought and 'Okydoke' Pass was recaptured. The encirclers were now themselves encircled as Lomax's 26th Indian Division marched in from the north. Shattered, half-starving from lack of the rations they could not capture, the remnants began to steal away even before Hanaya gave the formal order for withdrawal, leaving 4,600 corpses on the ground.

Christison swung into the offensive again immediately and launched his divisions against the Golden Fortress. The gallant 5th and 7th were then relieved in the front line by 26th Indian and Frank Festing's 36th British.[9] After an entirely abortive attempt by Hanaya at another general offensive, the two new divisions plunged into the arduous and bloody battles for the craggy features and the honeycomb of bunkers that were grouped round the entrance to the tunnels. They captured the last precipitous height with the utmost gallantry on the moonlit night of May 3rd-4th, by which time all eyes had been turned to more critical situations.

Thus Second Arakan ended with the British as the victors on the tactical field. The Battle of Ngakyedauk Pass, the awkward official title by which the February fighting was known, was highly significant on two particular counts. It proved the feasibility of air supply in battle and set the pattern for future operations. It proved also that British commanders and their soldiers could keep their heads and could outfight the Japanese in the toughest situations. There was a terrific boost to morale throughout the whole of Slim's new Fourteenth Army, the effects of which will very soon be related.

Nevertheless, although Hanaya had been convincingly defeated in the field, he had fulfilled the mission assigned to him by the Japanese command: he had forced Slim to commit his reserves far away from what was to be the scene of the main operations. The results were to be immediately seen.

Chinese and Chindits

Very soon after Christison had begun his Arakan offensive, Stilwell put his American-Chinese forces of Northern Area Combat Command into motion from Ledo. His objective, to be captured before the 1944 monsoon broke in May, was

Myitkyina, key town of north-east Burma. Physically, it was a tough enough mission, requiring the crossing of the notorious Hukawng valley, but Stilwell, supported by American aircraft and artillery, had a large numerical superiority over the very weak Japanese 18th Division. In spite of this the offensive made terribly slow progress, the lackadaisical Chinese dawdling away weeks in desultory scrapping. The only bright spots were a fine exploit by Merrill's Marauders, American equivalent of the Chindits, and the Herculean road effort of the US engineers. Myitkyina was not taken until August, after a two-months siege ineptly conducted against a handful of Japanese.

On March 5th, when Christison's divisions were poised for their assault on the Golden Fortress in Arakan, the Chindits flew out on their second, greatest and last exploit. The bearded Wingate, breathing the phrases of the Old Testament, had now been given an enormous force of no less than 24,000 men — including the whole of the British 70th Division, fine, battle-experienced troops — and he was also given the cordial and gallant support of American and British air squadrons.[10]

Primarily, Wingate's task was to block and harry the communications of the Japanese opposing Stilwell. His gallant columns got off to an exciting and spirited start in the heart of enemy country and performed some brilliant exploits. Wingate was killed in an air crash fairly early. Not long afterwards things began to go wrong. Stilwell's advance still flagged, the Chindits were kept out too long and became exhausted and debilitated by malaria, dysentery, scrub typhus, jungle sores and hard rations. The whole exploit turned sour when the division was placed under the command of Stilwell, who expected the bearded scarecrows to carry out assault tasks for which they were not equipped, trained or fit. Finally they had to be flown back, most of them with their health ruined. It was a sad waste of splendid troops who would have been a godsend when the moment of crisis came on the central front.

These operations, as well as those in Arakan, we must imagine as continuing for some months as we turn to the vital scenes of Imphal and Kohima.

4: U-GO

The Imphal Battlefield

DURING FEBRUARY 1944, while 15th Corps was locked in its Arakan battle and while Stilwell was prodding his dilatory Chinese across the Hukawng valley, evidence began to build up of the impending Japanese offensive on the Manipur front. The lack of a sound Intelligence service and the difficulties of aerial photographic reconnaissance over jungle country were serious handicaps; but the watchful eyes of V Force, the accumulations of river craft on the Chindwin, the forward collection of herds of cattle, the clouds of dust on forward Japanese routes, the identification of new enemy units by fighting patrols of 17th and 20th Indian Divisions and the occasional captured document began gradually to develop into a pattern that conformed to the appraisal of enemy intentions formulated by the British general staff.

The analytical mind of Scoones, commander of 4th Corps, had, in fact, assessed the enemy's intentions with considerable accuracy (except on one significant point) and he had made a skilful plan for the disposition of his forces to meet them. Slim and Scoones regarded the prospect of the enemy offensive with equanimity, indeed with some satisfaction. Faced with the stiff problems that confronted their own proposed offensive into Burma, they welcomed the opportunity that would be given them of destroying the most formidable of the Japanese armies on the north side of the Kabaw valley, where all the difficulties of road communications would have to be borne by the Japanese and where they themselves, with tolerable communications, would be able to fight on ground of their own choosing.

Before we enter upon the great battles now about to start, we must have a quick look at the difficult and often confusing ground, confining ourselves as far as possible to the simplest essentials and avoiding the more forbidding names that sprinkle the map of that mountain country.

Within the borders of the little, semi-independent State of Manipur, lies a large, oval, upland plain which in ancient days had been the bed of a mountain lake. This is the Imphal Plain, so named after the agglomeration of villages which is the State capital. About forty miles long and twenty wide, it is completely flat and much of it is marshy, but it is closely girdled with mountains which here and there reach 7,000 ft, and which are covered to their summits with jungle. There are very few practical routes in or out of the Plain and none of them is easy.

The most important of these was the road that ran northwards, pursuing its dizzy way along the edges of precipices, through deep gorges and across treacherous shale slopes, passing through Kohima and thence plunging down into hot and sweaty plains to connect with the frail Assam railway system at Dimapur.[11] This was 4th Corps' life-line. Before the war it had been only a narrow lane, just wide enough for one vehicle in many stretches, but in the past two years, under appalling difficulties, in which large sections of the road were repeatedly destroyed in landslides, it had been widened and metalled.

South-eastwards from Imphal another new, fairly good road shot straight across the Plain to Palel, then climbed into the hills, swung through the Shenam Pass and so down to the frontier village of Tamu, aiming across the Kabaw valley to the

65

banks of the Chindwin and designed as one of the main arteries of the intended British offensive. At the extremity of this road, bickering along the fever-ridden banks of the Chindwin, was 20th Indian Division, under Douglas Gracey.

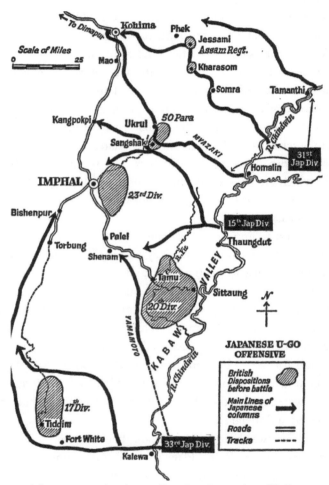

The enemy plan in outline for Operation *U-Go*.

Much rougher and tougher than either of these roads was the single-track way that, climbing and twisting vertiginously among the razor-edge crests of the Chin Hills, often at heights above 8,000 ft, led to the remote hill village of Tiddim, 162 miles distant from Imphal. Thence, a mere cat-walk now, the track struggled on for a few more hair-raising miles to a wild country where, among sumptuous magnolias and primulas, or stealing along elephant trails through thickets of bamboo, 17th Indian Light Division, still commanded by 'Punch' Cowan, were engaged in fierce skirmishes with their old enemies, the white tigers of the Japanese 33rd Division.

In addition to these three principal routes, there were two secondary gateways into the Imphal Plain, on both of which, as well as on the other three, sanguinary battles were to be fought. One, to be specially noted, came in to the north-east by way of Sangshak and Ukrul of fateful memory and the other was a poor track that led into Bishenpur from Silchar, ninety miles away in India.

Roads, however, were fortunately not Scoones's only communications. Within the Plain there were six airfields, though only two could operate in the monsoon. Supporting the corps, under Air Vice-Marshal Stanley Vincent, was 221 Group, RAF, with the equivalent of nineteen squadrons, though most of them had to be flown out after operations began to support the corps from farther back.

Within the large oval of the Plain large stocks of ammunition, rations, stores of all kinds had been built up, as well as the complete range of administrative units, including hospitals. Imphal was therefore vital ground. So also was Dimapur, 130 miles to the north in Assam. This was both railhead and road terminal. Formerly little more than a halt in the middle of a fever-ridden, hot and sweaty jungle, it had developed into an enormous hutted advance base. Moreover, the railway was the life-line for Stilwell's forces and its loss would have been crippling to Allied operations. In spite of this fact, no combatant troops were stationed at Dimapur. It was, after all, a long way from the enemy. The same argument applied to Kohima, the gateway to India and 46 miles from Dimapur.

With his foremost troops 180 miles south of Imphal and his railhead 130 miles back, Scoones's corps was strung out over a long, wriggling mountain line that had great length but virtually no breadth. Moreover, because of the grain of the mountains, this single and vital artery did not run at right angles to his 'front', which was the Chindwin, but roughly parallel to it; a position in which no military commander feels comfortable. All the country to the east of his life-line — between the road and the Chindwin — was an open flank. The terrain, however, was so forbidding, so covered with jungle on its steep hills and traversed by no more than a very few single-file footpaths, that it was considered impossible for any considerable force to make its way through. The jungle itself, it was felt, was sufficient flank protection for the rear areas and the dangers of surprise were provided for by the screen of V Force detachments thrown out far forward.

Scoones had decided just how he was going to fight the coming battles and Slim had approved his plans. He declined any attempt to forestall the enemy offensive by launching his own and he declined to oppose the enemy advance in the forward positions of 17th and 20th Divisions on the Tiddim and Tamu sectors. Either course meant accepting all the hazards of precarious forward communications and invited the enemy to defeat his divisions in detail, for they were too widely separated by a mountain mass to support each other.

Accordingly this was clearly a case for the classic manoeuvre of *recule pour mieux sauter*; his plan was to withdraw 17th and 20th Divisions right back to chosen positions in the rim of mountains surrounding the plain and then launch a counter-offensive with his reserve division, 23rd Indian, under Ouvry Roberts. To assist him both offensively and defensively, he had also the greater part of 254 Tank Brigade, commanded by his brother, R. A. L. Scoones, and to oppose an enemy flank attempt by the north-easterly route through Sangshak, Hope-Thomson's ill-fated 50th Indian Parachute Brigade was flown in.

What was done to provide against an unlikely descent upon Kohima we shall see very shortly.

Beyond the Chindwin, meanwhile, the Japanese commanders were experiencing administrative difficulties, particularly in transport, for the launching of *U-Go*, but Mutaguchi, inflexible and ruthless, was determined to drive forward the project of which he had been the most ardent advocate. To accomplish it Kawabe had given him three divisions — the 15th (not yet complete) commanded by Lieut-General Yamauchi, of Prussian caste and bearing, 31st, led by the plump, bull-headed Lieut-General Sato, and the veteran 33rd under Lieut-General Yanagida, who was a critic of the plans. In all, 15th Army mustered a little over 84,000 men, and was strong in tanks and artillery, particularly heavy artillery. Added to these were large numbers of Jiffs of the Indian and Burmese traitor armies.

Thus the land forces facing each other were at the start approximately equal in combatant troops, but the Allies held a strong advantage in the air.

In broad outline, the method by which Kawabe required Mutaguchi to execute *U-Go* was to attack with four groups of columns, many of the columns being splintered into an excessive number of smaller ones which would spread tentacle-like through the Manipur hills after crossing the Chindwin. Audacious in conception, it was not a good plan in detail, the effort too much dispersed, the emphasis in the wrong place and unlikely to succeed against good troops.

On the right, Sato's 31st Division was to make for Kohima, the undefended door to India. He was to approach it in three main columns from the south-east and east through the wild, ungarrisoned Somra Hills. Having seized Kohima, he was to hold it to protect the rear of the other two divisions in their assault upon Imphal and be prepared to send a brigade down to help them if necessary.

On Sato's left, 15th Division was ordered to move through the hills 'like a ball of fire' and descend upon Imphal by the north-east route through Sangshak; a dangerous move for Scoones this, though he anticipated it.

On the south 33rd Division, with a whole tank brigade under command and a large force of artillery, was to approach the Plain in three main columns. One, led by Major-General Yamamoto, commander of the divisional infantry group, was directed on Imphal by the Tamu-Palel road, where Douglas Gracey's 20th Division stood guard.

The remainder of Yanagida's division was to cut in behind 17th Division on the Tiddim Road, surround and annihilate it and then march on Imphal from the west.

Kawabe expected Mutaguchi to accomplish this conquest within five weeks of the first crossings of the Chindwin, which were to be made by Yanagida's white tigers on March 7th, the other two divisions crossing a week later. The columns were supplied with three weeks' rations, hopefully relying, in the usual Japanese method, on the capture of British stocks for their future needs.

70

In his Special Order of the Day on the eve of the offensive Mutaguchi declared that 'the army has now reached the state of invincibility', that it must 'reach our objective with the speed of wildfire' through 'the labyrinthine jungle' and achieve 'a victory of annihilation'.

Not Quite to Plan

Mutaguchi launched Yanagida's White Tiger division across the Chindwin against Cowan's Black Cats on the Tiddim sector on the due date. It was two days after Wingate's Special Force had flown in, not far from his right rear, but he was not put off.

Because of Slim's dislike of withdrawals, 17th Division hung on to its forward positions far too long and within a week was in great danger. Yanagida's troops, moving unseen along the wooded hill-tops parallel with the Imphal road, had planted no fewer than four road-blocks in Cowan's rear. At each block bunkers and well-concealed weapon-pits were quickly dug. The speed, dash and audacity of Yanagida's columns took everyone by surprise and completely altered the tactical picture. Scoones was obliged to send down nearly the whole of his infantry reserve from 23rd Division, accompanied by tanks, to attack the blocks from the north. It took a fortnight's stiff fighting to clear them out, the Japanese resisting always to the last man. Cowan's division, fighting back in the reverse direction for most of the 180 miles and carrying 1,200 wounded with them, reached the Imphal Plain on April 5th (the day that Kohima was seriously attacked) and was relieved by 23rd Division. Yanagida had failed in his intention to destroy his adversary, whose new fighting qualities shook his confidence, and he recommended to Mutaguchi that the offensive should be called off, for which lapse of faith he was soon afterwards dismissed. His successor was destined to batter fruitlessly at the south-west gate of the Plain in desperate encounters, in which Japanese officers, with drawn swords, drove forward their wounded soldiers, on crutches and even crawling on their bellies, against a defence that was often threatened but never shaken.

On the Tamu sector, the force led by Yamamoto, though stiffened by 61 tanks and much heavy artillery, similarly failed to shake Douglas Gracey's 20th Division.

Gracey withdrew a short distance in good order according to Scoones's plan, to a previously selected position astride the Shenam Pass, near Palel, where the Imphal road wound through jagged, mist-shrouded hills 5,000 ft high. There, for four long months, Gracey's division and subsequently Ouvry Roberts's, often separated from the enemy by only ten yards, fought an almost continuous battle among the hilltops, illuminated again and again by deeds of sheer heroism.

With brilliant artillery support, fantastic casualties were inflicted on the Japanese, as when 1st Devonshire, assaulting Nippon Hill, annihilated the garrison or as when 3/1st Gurkha Rifles, under Maurice Wingfield, killed 900 on 'Scraggy' in a desperate night battle and a single company of the same battalion slaughtered 300 at Sita Post. The stench of Japanese corpses was so foul that the British and Indians stuffed their nostrils with cotton wool and many of them vomited.

Far more dangerous than these offensives from the south were the thrusts made by the Japanese 15th Division and a column of the 31st under the redoubtable Miyazaki on the Sangshak avenue to the north-west of Imphal.

Here the inexperienced 50th Parachute Brigade, after a gory five-days battle close to an American mission church, on a bare and waterless hill-top, stinking with the crowded corpses of dead mules and men, was surrounded and defeated by

Miyazaki's superior force, but was able to escape destruction by breaking out at night, carrying with them all but 100 of their most badly wounded, whom they were obliged to leave to their fate. Though the brigade suffered a severe defeat, their stand saved both Kohima and Imphal. Miyazaki was delayed for a vital five days in his approach to Kohima. And 123rd Brigade, hurried forward into action direct from the aircraft that had flown them in from Arakan and now commanded by Geoffrey Evans, arrived just in time to stop the Japanese scarcely fifteen miles from Imphal.

Miyazaki then swung north to join his own 31st Division in the attack on Kohima, while columns of 15th Division pushed farther west, one to look straight down on to Scoones's headquarters and the main airfield on the plain, another to cut and block 4th Corps' life-line — the main road to Kohima — thirty miles north of Imphal on March 29th.

Imphal was now cut off from the world by land, with two divisions knocking loudly at three of its gates and a third in its rear. The long Siege of Imphal had begun.

The Great Air Lift

The arrival of Evans's brigade just in time to save Imphal was the first-fruits of the massive and historic air transport operations, far exceeding any such operations anywhere in the world, that was set in motion through Mountbatten's resourcefulness. Only these prevented the *Ha-Go* in Arakan from fulfilling its purpose of locking up Slim's reserves. The aircraft situation was, however, one of extreme delicacy. Mountbatten's powers as 'supreme' commander were severely shackled in this element, for he had no authority over the US air ferry operating over the Hump to China. That was part of Stilwell's ambiguous empire. When the Arakan emergency had arisen and aircraft had to be found for Wingate also, Mountbatten had had to wait for more than a week for Washington's permission to divert aircraft from the Hump, after three days of vain endeavours to get Stilwell's views.

The new crises in the Imphal Plain thrust upon Mountbatten, suffering from a painful eye injury whilst visiting Stilwell, an embarrassing dilemma. While the Chindit and Arakan operations were in full swing Slim asked him on March 14th, for not less than twenty-five Dakotas or their equivalent, to fly 5th Division out from Arakan to Imphal. Mountbatten, jeopardizing his goodwill with the American Chiefs of Staff, took the courageous decision of accepting responsibility to provide them. He treated the Imphal emergency as an extension of the Arakan one, for which he had already been given permission to divert aircraft, and in doing so he also saved the American life-line from imminent danger, for which he had not received permission.

Accordingly, Briggs's division, without a day's rest, pulled out of its offensive operations against the Golden Fortress as soon as it had been relieved by 25th and flew straight into action on the north-east of Imphal, except for 161st Brigade, which Slim fortunately diverted to Kohima. This was the first time in history that a whole division — 'horse, foot and guns' — had been moved by air. It was undertaken at a moment's notice and was carried through without a hitch by 194 (Transport) Squadron, RAF, and 20 US Commando aircraft, flying day and night for some ten days.

5: KOHIMA

A Place of Peace

KOHIMA, FIFTEEN MILES north of the Manipur State boundary, was a pleasant 'hill station' of British India at an altitude of some 4,700 ft in a country of great natural beauty. It stood at the summit of a broad pass or saddle between mountains that towered up to 8,000 ft on one hand and 10,000 on the other and from these heights cool winds sometimes blew to alleviate the fierce heat of lower levels. The same factor influenced the vegetation, with the result that the tropical jungle began to thin out and to give place to the oaks and conifers of more temperate climates. Southward towards Imphal the zigzag road climbed for another hair-raising thousand feet past skilfully terraced and irrigated ricefields before entering Manipur State. Northwestward, after an acute turn at Kohima itself, it plunged down through treacherous and shifting shale into a hot and fiercely beautiful country, cleft by deep chasms and enveloped in jungle, until it arrived at Dimapur, forty-six miles away in the hot and oppressive plains, where it ended but made contact with the flimsy Assam railway.

A place of peace and beauty, Kohima was the headquarters of the Naga Hills District of the province of Assam, administered by a Deputy Commissioner, who in 1944 was Mr Charles Pawsey. Here he had jurisdiction over a primitive, cheerful, brave and very intelligent mountain people who, before the coming of the British, had been engaged in murderous inter-tribal raids in which the most prized trophies were human heads.

The turbulence of the Nagas and their savage raids into the plains of Assam had obliged the British to penetrate into their forbidding jungle in the nineteenth century to establish law and order. This a slender British force had accomplished under rigorous conditions, but not before it had had to undergo the first Siege of Kohima in 1879.

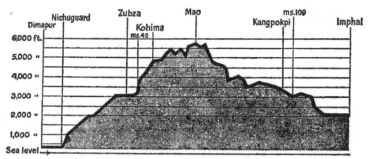

Profile of the road from Dimapur across the Mountain Barrier to the Imphal Plain

Adapted by kind permission of Lieut-Colonel O. G. W. White, DSO, and Messrs Gale and Polden from *Straight on for Tokyo* (the history of 2nd Bn The Dorsetshire Regiment).

Since those days, however, under the excellence of an administration that was founded on confidence and trust, the Nagas had become firm and devoted friends of the British. Many had become converted from their animist beliefs to Christianity by British and American missionaries. In due course they could beat a British team at football. But they still remained hillmen, with all the hillman's hardiness, and they still carried, in addition to a spear, a long, broad-bladed *dao* slung behind their backs, though it was no longer used for chopping off human heads. Their devotion to the British was to be severely tested when the Japanese invasion occurred, but they never faltered, risking death and torture to bring information

76

of enemy movements, to succour the British wounded and crashed American airmen and to serve as porters and guides. They had little respect for 'Indians', ignored the inflammatory anti-British pamphlets with which Gandhi's Congress Party flooded their villages, and when India was granted independence after the war were distressed to the point of tears and soon afterwards rebelled.

Pawsey, rather reserved but brisk in manner and independently minded, had a remarkable influence over the Nagas. He and they trusted each other implicitly. While he was at pains to protect their interests, he was able, when the war came, to employ their keen eyes and ears, their strong limbs and their stout hearts to the benefit of the Allied cause. Through them he had built up an excellent Intelligence system and without his influence operations might have been much handicapped. Pawsey had served in the First World War in the Worcestershire Regiment but never reckoned that he would one day have again to go into battle, this time in civilian clothes.

The locality of Kohima was divided into three parts. On the highest ground, sprawling over a lofty plateau and embowered in trees, stood the thatched and gable-ended huts of a large village, the largest in the Naga country but known simply as 'Naga Village'. Prominent among the native buildings was a large American mission.

On a slightly lower level stood the congregation of government offices known as the Treasury. Here Pawsey and his staff pursued their official duties and here was his court of law. The buildings stood within the ramparts of a fort, where the siege of 1879 had taken place, and thus the Treasury was also sometimes known as the Fort. A little to one side were the barracks of the 3rd battalion of the Assam Rifles, the armed police force of the civil authority.

When we go down from the Treasury to a slightly lower level we come to the third part of Kohima and the one that most closely concerns us. To do so, we must cross the main Imphal-Dimapur road as it writhes its way round the shoulders of the hills. At the critical hairpin bend where the road from the Treasury joins it the army had by 1944 established a Traffic Control Post. Beyond the road rose a bold, wooded ridge, the lower slopes of which had at this point been formed into a series of terraces, clasped within the acute angle of the road as it twisted round the shoulders of the ridge, and adorned with Australian blue eucalyptus trees, which were planted liberally through the station.

On these terraces were the government bungalows of the Deputy Commissioner, the Commandant of the Assam Rifles, a small club house and an asphalt tennis court. This was the tennis court destined to become of immortal memory, its playing lines to be marked out in perpetuity with white concrete to remind such passers-by as there may be of some of the most valiant of deeds. Not far from the DC's bungalow was a simple memorial to those who had fallen in the Naga war of 1879, a memorial to which in due time was to be added the gleaming monument, beside the tennis court, which now stands watch over the rank upon rank of British and Indian graves upon the terraced shoulders of the hill.

Above the tennis court, which stood on the highest of the terraces, the main ridge, of no less heroic memory, swelled up boldly. At this stage we need to look at it only in general outline, reserving its details, and those of the bungalow area, to later pages. Clothed with alders and fine oaks, with a tough undergrowth of tall grass and ageratum, which made walking on it hard going, it was in fact a series of small hills or large hummocks, like the knuckles of a giant fist, lying more or less north and south. It was this chain of little hills (see second and last photographs in gravure section) that was to become famous as Kohima Ridge.

Near the northern end of the Ridge, stood the highest of these wooded hills. Its domed summit had been cleared of trees but was covered with grass. In this rough, hill-top lawn stood a small thatched summer house, which gave the feature its peacetime name of Summerhouse Hill, soon, however, to be changed to Garrison Hill of historic memory. To this summer house, its beams carved with the names of many schoolboys, the British officials and their wives used to resort in the golden evenings to admire the magnificent views that lay spread before them on all sides. Below them the Ridge was girdled by a narrow bridle-path, known as the Ladies' Mile, where in cool weather in peace-time the British community were accustomed to walk or ride. Following a natural contour line, and connecting with the main road at its northern and southern ends, it was to become for a time more or less the perimeter line of the besieged British garrison.

Outside the well-ordered scene of pre-war Kohima lay some of the wildest, most rugged and most beautiful country on earth. To the south, dominating all else, rose the towering mass of Pulebadze, topping 7,500 ft, with the Aradura Spur, sloping sharply up to 6,000 ft, a little to its east, and both clothed in dense jungle which concealed their deep clefts and dizzy chasms. Thus it is particularly to be noticed that, from these southerly heights, from Naga Village, from the north and, indeed, from nearly all sides Kohima Ridge was overlooked by higher ground.

To the north and north-east of Kohima, there stretched enormous expanses of range upon range of steep wooded mountains dissolving in a blue haze where they met the horizon, their intervening valleys often dry for most of the year but becoming rushing torrents in the monsoon. These were the Somra Hills. Here oaks and alders covered the hills, diversified here and there by large stands of pines or with magnolias in the shaly soil of the valley bottoms. Here roamed the tiger and the leopard. Here flew the curious hornbill, whose tail feathers were much prized for the adornment of the Naga warriors' full dress. Here innumerable snakes slid and coiled among the undergrowth.

In these Somra Hills the Naga villages were few and scattered, lying on the crests of hills or along the shoulders of mountain masses. Their inhabitants cultivated rice on the hillsides, which they expertly terraced and irrigated. The only means of progress through the jungle were by a few pony tracks along the ridges used by the British administrative people or occasional elephant tracks or faint Naga footpaths which went straight down into a valley bottom and straight up the opposite ascent.

South-eastward from Kohima this rough country of the Somra Hills, considered impassable by any considerable military force, stretched right away past Ukrul nearly as far as the Chindwin. The important points to note in this difficult territory are two villages on tracks east and south-east of Kohima and lying on possible routes of penetration by a hostile force. These were Jessami, distant some sixty miles, and Kharasom, a little to its south. In the unlikely event of an enemy penetration through the Somra Hills, these were points at which he might be arrested or delayed. Accordingly, a narrow jeep-track, which followed the bridle-path used by the civilian administration, had been bulldozed by Captain Stephen Laing, adjutant of the engineer unit that will shortly be noticed.

When the Japanese overran Burma, Kohima developed into a large and important area on the lines of communication for 4th Corps on the Manipur front. Having a local Administrative Commandant, it constituted part of 253 Sub-Area, which was under the administrative command of Brigadier M. L. Hayne, whose headquarters were at Dimapur. He in turn was under the jurisdiction of 202 L of C Area, under Major-General R. P. L. Rankin, covering the greater part of Assam.

In the military, as in the civilian, sphere Kohima was no more than an administrative station. No combatant troops were permanently quartered there, for the front was a long way off. Here, because of the tolerant climate, were two large military hospitals. The 49th Indian General Hospital, commanded by Colonel Irvine, was accommodated in the barracks of the Assam Rifles near the Treasury. The 53rd, commanded by Colonel Wyndham Arundell, was situated on a long, sloping spur that ran north-westward from Garrison Hill (as we shall now call it), to become significant under the name of Hospital Spur. A third hospital was situated a few miles farther south of Kohima.

At Kohima also were large depots of supplies of every sort — rations, ammunition, petrol, ordnance and engineer — together with bakeries, workshops, a cattle drovers' unit, transport units, pioneers and a hygiene unit. Virtually all the troops in these units were merely civilians in uniform, without arms and without any training whatever in combatant duties. There was also a large force of native civilian labour generously supplied by the Assam tea planters, working on the vital task of road maintenance and improvement. These and other engineer duties were under the direction of the CO of 112 Works, who was Lieut-Colonel John Landor, a name to be noted, and whose adjutant was Captain Stephen Laing, later to become a vivid commentator on events.

Another typical L of C unit, many of whom were individually to play a gallant part in the forthcoming siege, was 24th Reinforcement Camp, quartered in tents under the command of Lieut-Colonel Malcolm Hepworth, seconded from 16th Punjab Regiment. Here were collected drafts from various regiments and corps, British and Indian, waiting to be called forward to replace casualties on the Manipur front. Many of them were convalescents from the local hospitals, together with drafts of non-combatant troops and civilian labourers. The combatant soldiers possessed rifles, but were not in formed organic bodies and they had no officers.

Permanently quartered at Kohima, which was their depot, were 3rd Battalion the Assam Rifles, under Major G. A. E. Keene (known to his friends as 'Buster' Keene), also seconded from 16th Punjab Regiment and awaiting an overdue gazetting to lieutenant-colonel. He had been decorated for his work in getting refugees out from Burma in the northeast under appalling conditions. The battalion, recruited mainly from Gurkhas and wearing Gurkha uniform, was normally a gendarmerie, or armed police, at the disposal of Pawsey, as the civil authority, for the maintenance of law and order among the hill tribes. Pawsey and the 3rd Battalion were thus old friends and associates. Keene (who was married to the matron of 49th IGH) was thus technically the 'Commandant' of the battalion and he occupied one of the two government bungalows at the foot of Garrison Hill.

Recently the Assam Rifles had been embodied in the Indian Army, but still possessed no other weapons but rifles and *kukris*. They were organized in platoons only, each platoon being fifty strong and commanded by a Gurkha VCO.[12] Seven platoons were in Kohima in March 1944. Thus they were not organized, equipped or trained for a pitched battle and their main duty was to provide protective detachments for the V Force ahead or for the American Air Force observation posts that were scattered through the hills. There was one such observation post on Kohima Ridge. There were only two other British officers with Keene at Kohima — Lieutenants Malcolm Smith and Donald Cleland. Like other Gurkha units, the battalion was accompanied by its 'line boys', aged from ten upwards, who were used as messengers and were the soldiers of the future.

One other unit present at Kohima when operations began has to be mentioned, but in these pages it will remain anonymous. This was a battalion of Native State infantry,[13] one of several similar units that were raised at their own cost by various princes partially or wholly independent of British rule, and some of which rendered good service. The unit at Kohima, after a period of L of C duties, had had a year's training in jungle warfare, but does not appear to have been of the best material and events were to prove that it certainly was not yet fit to be committed to serious battle. The unit was officered by men of its own State, but three British officers were seconded to it for training and liaison, without rights of command. These were Lieut-Colonel Gordon Borrowman, of 4th Gurkhas, who was Senior Supervising Officer (and a friend of Slim), and Captain Noel Lunn and Lieutenant James Hoyt. All were employed otherwise in the siege to come. This unit will be referred to, when necessary, as 'the State battalion'.

Such were the only troops at Kohima who could in any sense be termed combatant. All the remainder were administrative or ancillary troops, most of whom possessed no arms and had never been trained in their use. Although there was scarcely a square yard of flat ground anywhere, the whole countryside near Kohima became thickly sprinkled with store sheds, with the native bamboo huts called *bashas*, with tented camps, warehouses and parked vehicles. We should notice especially those on the lower and easier slopes of Kohima Ridge, with its many ration and stores bashas, and the large dumps of ammunition and petrol at the foot of Jail Hill, where also was the small, red, corrugated-iron civilian prison, looking oddly picturesque among the trees. There was an incessant coming and going along the road, as the lorries, guns, ambulances and tank transporters swung cautiously round the sharp turn by the DC's bungalow and passed onwards to creep along the dizzy edges of precipices and round the innumerable hairpin bends of the mountain road.

In February 1944, however, the war was far away. Though a few percipient minds were doubtful about that long, open, left flank parallel to the Chindwin and the enemy beyond, to most people it was unimaginable that Kohima could be in danger. All eyes were focused on Arakan, where the critical battle of 'Okydoke' Pass was being fought out, or, more distantly, on the sands of the Western Desert, where the campaign of Montgomery's 8th Army was nearing its victorious close. To the soldiers, the sisters of the Queen Alexandra's Imperial Nursing Service and the few civilians, off-duty life was agreeable enough, though the day's work was often hard. There was no black-out and the lights twinkled brightly among the trees. The nights were cold and a chill, wet mist spread over the hills, but it was wonderful in the morning to watch the mist gradually dissipate as the sun rose in its strength above the peaks, gradually disclosing village and hamlet and the wisps of wood-smoke from innumerable fires.

Away at Imphal, Scoones, assessing the slowly accumulating signs of the enemy's plans in February, took precautions to set a watch on the jungle tracks that led through the Somra Hills towards Kohima and Dimapur in case the enemy should attempt that unlikely route. He alerted the lonely posts of V Force, which had recently been much weakened, and he ordered forward the 1st Battalion the Assam Regiment from their training station in the Brahmaputra Valley to take post at Jessami and Kharasom, in place of the detachments of the Native State battalion. All his information led him to believe that this would be sufficient safeguard and with this view Slim agreed.

This Assam battalion was the first of a newly raised regiment. Its rank and file were partly Assamese plainsmen and partly Naga, Kuki and Lushai hillmen, so that many of them were now among their own people and their own villages. They had close links also with the Assam Rifles through their officers. They were commanded by a great individualist in Lieut-Colonel W. F. Brown, seconded from 8th Punjab Regiment and known to everyone as 'Bruno'. He was a small, sturdy, untidy figure, outwardly jolly, with laughing blue eyes and a puckish face, but very strict, physically extremely tough, able to march his battalion off its feet and demanding a very high standard from the young British and Indian officers who had come to him from civilian life and whom he expected, like himself, always to live rough.

His battalion had never yet been in battle, though it had had seventeen months of arduous patrolling on the banks of the Chindwin and in the deadly Kabaw valley. There malaria and dysentery had torn such holes in its ranks that it had been withdrawn to recoup and re-form.

Brown's battalion arrived in Kohima in the third week of February, welcoming its genial climate and cool breeze after the oppressive heat of the valley. All was still entirely calm, with no hint of danger ahead. On the night before going out on their mission the officers were invited by Pawsey to a party in his bungalow. It was typical of Brown, who always acted as though the enemy was at the door, that he required his officers to attend in battle order, which made them feel that the party was like the ball before Waterloo. The nursing sisters from the hospitals, however, took it all in good part.

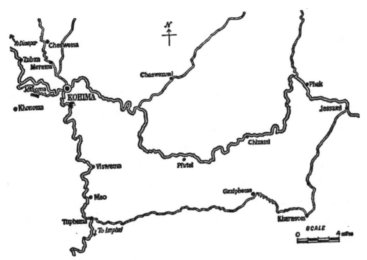

Kohima — Jessami — Kharasom.

In the early hours of next morning, in their Gurkha hats and new jungle-green kit, the battalion moved out, on foot, on its sixty miles march to Jessami, climbing and descending hill after hill in a country of incredible beauty. Four days later, after a final sharp climb, the Jessami ridge was reached. From there Brown sent A Company on to Kharasom, thirteen miles

87

farther south in Manipur State, under Lieutenant 'Jock' Young. Operationally, the battalion was under Ouvry Roberts, commanding 23rd Indian Division, a long way off on the north-east of Imphal.

Without any let-up, Brown set his men immediately to patrolling and to digging defensive positions for all-round defence, though there was no enemy within sixty miles and the Manipur front 'all quiet'. His officers thought that he was taking things much too seriously, but it was always his way to be ready for emergency action and it is fortunate that he was so. He had one Burmese company under his command at Phek,[14] nine miles to his left rear, and he left the greater part of his transport behind at Kohima in the charge of Lieutenant Donald Elwell, who, fortunately for the historian, afterwards wrote a long personal account of the siege to come.

Jessami, just within the borders of Manipur, was a 'black magic' village, shunned by most other villagers, but well known to British and Indians for its excellent native beer, or *zu*. About half a mile from it and at Kharasom, the Assam Regiment built strong outer and inner defences, well-bunkered and encircled with barbed wire, with cleared fields of fire and well stocked with ammunition and rations. At Jessami, be it especially noted, the battalion occupied a bivouac area outside the defences that they were building.

On March 8th, the day after the Japanese, unknown to the British, had begun the first two arms of their offensive, Brigadier Hope-Thomson arrived in Kohima with 50th Indian Parachute Brigade and the Assam Regiment passed under his command. This brigade, as we have seen earlier, was also under General Ouvry Roberts and the two commanders paid visits to Jessami and Kharasom.

A week later Hope-Thomson's brigade left Kohima for their ill-fated mission at Ukrul and Sangshak and Brown's battalion, though remaining under his distant command, were alone.

The next day, Lieutenant David (or 'Jonah') Lloyd Jones, a tall, dark, young Welshman, was sent out with a patrol of twenty men to reconnoitre the tracks ahead and find sources of water in case the battalion should be required to move.

After two days of stiff marching, he reached a V Force stockade on the Indo-Burmese border and encountered numbers of Nagas straggling up from the south-east full of tales that the Japanese had crossed the Chindwin and were advancing into the Somra Hills.

So far from his expectations was any notion of a Japanese offensive that Lloyd Jones assumed at first that the cause of all this agitation was merely some deep patrolling by the enemy. As the flood of refugees increased, however, he realized that something more was afoot. He sent runners back to Jessami with the news and got a signal direct through to Imphal by the V Force wireless. He decided not to complete his reconnaissance but to stay out, collect information and await events, remaining mobile and not occupying the V Force stockade. His was apparently the first news sent in of enemy movement on this sector.

Three days later the vanguard of the enemy appeared. By skilful jungle craft, Lloyd Jones kept contact, setting small ambushes, puzzling and delaying the enemy.

Brown reacted to the situation with energy and skill. He sent forward a company under Major Sidiman Rai, a plump and jolly Gurkha, to engage, delay but not become committed, and he pushed out other patrols on an interlocking plan. The volume of information thus built up rapidly. All through the hills the detachments of V Force were retiring. Gradually, after some useful small ambushes and some narrow escapes, most of the elements of the Assam Regiment drew back on to their strongholds, which they had been ordered by 50th Parachute Brigade to hold 'to the last man and the last round'. Brown at Jessami and Young at Kharasom now prepared to do so.

Meanwhile young Elwell, the battalion transport officer, had gone down from Kohima to Imphal for a MT course of instruction. When events brought him hurrying back he found the Kohima scene dramatically changed. All the bright lights were out, the hospitals packed up and gone and the even tenor of its life rudely transformed to the state of a defenceless town with the enemy at its gates.

Colonel Richards Arrives

In the third week of March the information reaching Scoones's Intelligence staff at Imphal painted the picture that two Japanese columns, perhaps being followed by a third, having crossed the Chindwin between Homalin and Tamanthi, were moving through the jungle footpaths of the Somra Hills that might bring them to Kohima or perhaps to Dimapur. The columns were reported to be of only battalion strength each and it was thought highly unlikely that they would be able to be supported by any artillery, so hazardous were the faint trails across the jungle hills.

This picture conformed to the appreciation that Scoones had made much earlier on the information provided him — that the Japanese might direct a force on Kohima-Dimapur, but it could be only a small one. He was in a difficulty. All his troops in Imphal were committed, either in defensive operations or in the counter-attack role by which he hoped shortly to defeat the enemy. In accordance with his appreciation, he had ordered the Assam Regiment to the Jessami area and they were therefore in the right place to oppose or at least seriously delay an enemy force of moderate strength. Hence the orders to Brown to fight to the last.

Scoones was aware that Slim would soon be assembling new forces at Dimapur and that 161st Indian Infantry Brigade was due to arrive there shortly by air from Arakan. The respective demands of Dimapur and Kohima and their relations to one another caused him some anxiety. Dimapur was vital. Kohima was not absolutely vital, but it was the gateway to India, an important nodal point on his L of C, and, if lost, would gravely prejudice the operations of new forces about to be brought forward.

Precautionary measures were accordingly taken. Orders were issued to set in motion a large-scale evacuation from Kohima, beginning with the three hospitals, and to prepare a defence plan. The first of these was the administrative business of Brigadier Hayne, the Sub-Area commander. The second was entrusted to the senior officer of the combatant arms on the spot, who was Gordon Borrowman, the senior supervising officer of the State battalion. Borrowman was a handsome, very tall, lean and greying Scot of great experience and a fine character, but he was in hospital recovering from a severe riding accident. Before the hospitals were evacuated he gave his orders from his bedside and entrusted their fulfilment to Malcom Hepworth, CO of 24th Reinforcement Camp.

Four 'boxes' were selected. One of these, known as Box C, was on Kohima Ridge and the other three were on the main road approaches to Kohima. In accordance with the orders that Borrowman received, they were located to protect the main stores and installations, and were intended to be manned by the non-combatant units on the spot. Accordingly two of them were not, and could not be, tactically well sited.

The whole task was begun in an atmosphere of complete unreality. None but the more prescient believed that the war would come here. There were no troops fit to man the defences. There were few troops fit even to dig them. The drivers, artisans, clerks and storemen had to carry on with their normal duties, which were urgent enough with the Imphal battle begun in earnest, and they had no stomach for digging. Their officers were equally non-combatant and had no knowledge of such matters. Their discipline was low compared with that of combatant units.

Attempts were made in some units to give a little combatant training, as in 19th Indian-Field Hygiene Section, where Captain Richard Glover trained his men in first aid and stretcher drill and had them instructed in small arms to the extent of firing a musketry course. But the lack of an overall command and staff in what was generally thought to be an unnecessary 'flap' resulted in confusion and a number of 'nonsenses'.

Scoones therefore needed an experienced senior officer to take charge and he asked for one. General Giffard at once sent him an officer whom he knew well and who was at that moment with him in Delhi.

Colonel Hugh Richards had originally been commissioned in the Worcestershire Regiment (the same regiment as Pawsey's, though not the same battalion). In the First World War he had been very severely wounded in France, had spent a year in hospital, had returned to the front and been again wounded and taken prisoner. Afterwards he was engaged in normal regimental duties before being given accelerated promotion, when he was appointed Second-in-Command of the 2nd West Yorkshire Regiment. He had later been seconded to the West African forces and until very recently had been commanding

3rd West African Brigade, which had become Chindit troops under Wingate, and he had thus had long experience in jungle warfare. When, shortly before they were due to fly out on their big operation, Wingate discovered that Richards had just passed his fiftieth birthday, he had told him that forty (his own age) was the maximum for anyone on Chindit operations and Richards had accordingly lost his appointment.

In person Richards was fair, of about middle height, not looking his age, very fit after his Chindit training; in manner balanced, not easily rattled and, as many were shortly to testify, in action completely composed and fearless. Moreover, to use an old-fashioned term, he was a great gentleman; Borrowman, who became his staunch and loyal friend until his death years later, in a report afterwards to the Official Historian, observed very pointedly that he was 'most courteous when others were being most offensive'. He was now to be tested in one of the most desperate situations and one in which he was to be confronted with problems of personal relationships of a nature totally unexpected in such circumstances.

Richards flew at once from Delhi to Imphal and was handed his orders immediately by Scoones's chief of staff (4 Corps Operation Instruction No. 83). These told him that he was to take operational command of all troops in the Kohima area, including 1st Assam Regiment in the Somra Hills. He was to hold Kohima and deny the area Jessami-Kharasom-Kohima by the use of the Assam battalion. He would be directly under the command of 4th Corps. His designation was 'Commander Kohima Garrison' with the code name Ephod. The 161st Brigade, on arrival, would be responsible for keeping open the road behind him to Dimapur, but exclusive of Kohima. Administrative responsibility in Kohima, however, was to remain with the commander of 253 Sub-Area (Brigadier Hayne).

Travelling by the mountain road, Richards arrived in Kohima in the afternoon of the following day, March 23rd. He was taken at once to Pawsey's bungalow (Pawsey himself being away in the hills) and there he met Major-General Rankin, commanding 202 L of C Area (who, to meet the emergency, had moved his headquarters from the Brahmaputra up to Dimapur) together with Hayne and Borrowman.

Richards was given a general description of Kohima and its embryo defences and met some of the senior officers. As Borrowman could still do no more than hobble about painfully, Richards went round the defences next day with Hepworth and also met Major Norman Giles, a Black Watch officer curiously attached to the Royal Indian Army Service Corps, whom he found to have sound ideas about ground and to be full of energy. Later, for that reason, he sent Giles out to take over command of the Burmese company holding Phek.

Richards did not much like what he saw. The country, difficult, broken and hilly, was dominated by yet higher hills. It was puzzling country in which to orient oneself. The maps were of too small a scale and unsuitable for military purposes. The trees limited observation and obstructed fields of fire. Some of the 'boxes' were tactically ill-sited and were too far apart to give one another mutual support. Manned by scratch troops who had never handled a rifle, they would each separately be easy meat for the Japanese wolves. Many of the weapon-pits were unsatisfactory and those dug by Naga labour, which Pawsey supplied, were too wide and open through lack of experienced supervision. With the exception of a single 25-pounder used for training in the Reinforcement Camp, there was no artillery and no prospect of getting any.

He met Landor, the engineer CO, and learnt that, with the exception of a very few rolls of wire, there were virtually no defence stores to be had either there or at Dimapur; all had gone forward to Imphal. He was very seriously concerned at the extreme shortage of any officers with infantry experience. Apart from the State battalion and the three officers of the Assam Rifles, there was only a handful of infantry officers in the Reinforcement Camp, and those junior ones. He assessed the Assam Rifles as good fighting material, but realized their obvious limitations for battle. He saw no reason at that stage to doubt the qualities or fitness of the State battalion, whose origins seemed to be a good guarantee, and he formed a good impression of their native CO.

As he went about, however, he noted that the other available troops, whom he was expected to command, instead of being trained to fight and to man their positions, were required, by orders of another commander, to carry on their administrative duties of issuing rations and stores, driving trucks and repairing roads for the support of the critical Imphal battles now being fought. Moreover, units and installations were being daily evacuated to the rear, so that men who were available to man the defences one day were ordered away the next.

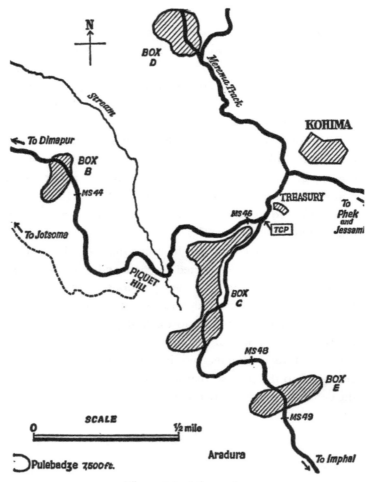

The original 'boxes'.

He was very much heartened, therefore, when, to his delight, his old battalion, 2nd West Yorkshire Regiment, arrived. They had just flown in from Arakan, where they had been the star heroes of the 'Admin Box' battle and Richards found that they were commanded by an old friend in the person of Lieut-

Colonel Gerald Cree, who had been adjutant in his own time with the battalion. Much concerned at the isolation of 1st Assam at Jessami, he gave orders to Cree at once to make contact with them and with the Burmese company at Phek, in order to be prepared to support them and to learn the ground. He also ordered the movement forward of four platoons of the Assam Rifles to be ready to give support.

The same day Richards was sent a small staff of junior officers hastily scratched up from various L of C formations. Unfortunately, with one exception, they were not experienced in the work they were called upon to do and he was very much handicapped. On the other hand, Richards luckily found in the reinforcement camp a man from his old regiment to serve as his orderly. Private Eric Wilson, of the West Yorkshires, was a little soldier of cheerful and gallant spirit, who became devoted to Richards and after the siege continued to correspond with him regularly until, to Richards's distress, he was killed in action some months later.

Rain fell on the first three days. Richards experienced the chill of the drenching mists that often crept over the hills during the night and he noticed how the dusk flooded in on the lower hills, while the tall peaks were still bathed in golden light. He reflected that the troops in their trenches would be very cold and wet and that the difficult lights of dawn and dusk would be dangerous hours. On Sunday he drove out by jeep over the stiff Somra Hills to visit the Assam Regiment at Jessami. On the way he met Pawsey in a hill village and had his first glimpse of the Deputy Commissioner's remarkable hold on the Nagas, who had fled from their homes at the advance of the Japanese. Richards felt for the first time that a clash was close at hand. The air was charged with the current of action. As if to add force to that current, the Royal Air Force had that morning bombed the head of the Japanese column approaching Jessami at the point where Lloyd Jones had encountered it.

At Jessami Richards met Bruno Brown and was impressed by his battalion's eager and confident spirit. He was no less impressed by the all-round defence works, with deep bunkers, cleared fields of fire, underground Regimental Aid Post, trenches for mules and petrol. He noted the barbed wire stretched uncompromisingly across the track by which an enemy would come and the bunkers closely commanding it. The battalion was now in occupation of the redoubt, having vacated their near-by bivouac. Brown told him that he expected to be attacked next day. He anticipated the enemy to be in battalion strength and was quite confident that he could defeat such a force.

He asked Richards if the order to fight to the last man still stood, and Richards replied that it must; he had no authority to countermand it. He added, however, that if Brown were by-passed, he was to take to the country, live on the villages and hit the Japanese in the rear.

Before leaving, Richards handed over a 101 wireless set that he had brought up to replace the battalion's broken set. He did not have time to visit Young at Kharasom nor the Burmese company at Phek and spent the night with Pawsey in the native village before returning to Kohima. He learnt that, as soon as news came of the Japanese advance, Pawsey had sent out his civil police and government interpreters into the hill villages to collect information and report to the nearest British military force. A stream of information was now coming in to Pawsey and for the next week he was able to inform Richards of enemy movements even before Rankin learnt of them.

A deep silence lay over all the jungle that night but Richards was conscious that in its dark and profound womb fierce convulsions were at any moment about to shake the stillness. He was worried about the 'last man, last round' order that Brown had been given. The circumstances in which Brown was placed did not seem to him to justify such an order. It would have been justified if the positions at Jessami and Kharasom covered some vital installation or if they were chosen battle-grounds that it was intended to reinforce. Brown had dug himself in for a serious battle, but Richards saw the two positions only as bases for extensive patrols or for a short delaying action. Nor could the order be carried out without an assured water supply within the perimeter, which the battalion did not have. The lack of artillery further severely limited the chances of prolonged resistance.

Having seen the quality of the Assam Regiment, however, he felt easier in mind. With them, his old West Yorkshire battalion, the seemingly good State battalion, and the Assam Rifles platoons, his forces should be sufficient to contain the two, or possibly three, Japanese battalions reported to be advancing. The absence of a proper signals set-up was an inconvenience and the lack of artillery a serious handicap, but apparently the enemy columns had none either.

He was, therefore, sorely disappointed when, on return to Kohima on the 27th, in company with Pawsey, he found a signal from 4th Corps telling him that the West Yorkshires were 'not to be used forward'. This was a heavy blow, as he intended to use them for the support of the garrisons at Jessami and Kharasom. Platoons of the battalion had, in fact, arrived at Jessami and Phek the day before. On the 27th, the very day that Kharasom was attacked, a further signal from Corps ordered the West Yorkshires to rejoin 5th Indian

Division at Imphal at once. They got through just before the Japanese cut the road north of Imphal on March 29th.

This unfortunate decision not only left the Assam isolated and committed but also imperilled the whole Kohima situation. Further to darken the horizon, Richards learnt that evening from Pawsey that information from his Nagas showed the force moving against him to be not two or three battalions but the whole of Sato's division. This was, observed Richards, 'a sobering thought'.

Since Kohima was now clearly of great importance, the move of this battalion, which the Corps could well have spared, was a great mistake. It was the severest blow that Richards experienced and occurred at a critical time. Had the West Yorkshires been retained, the whole aspect of future operations for many weeks to come would have been radically changed.

This was, however, only the first of a series of orders and counter-orders that Richards had to contend with during the next few days. The uncertainty of what troops he would have to fight his battle, and even what he would have to prepare for it, continued right up to the moment that the battle started. Thus Richard Glover, the doctor, who had been training his hygiene unit for medical duties in battle, was almost daily required to send off one squad after another to Dimapur, until there was finally no one left but himself and two orderlies. As the available troops changed, so had the defences to be changed. Trenches that had been dug had to be filled in and new ones prepared again and again.

Meanwhile, the Assam Regiment was marooned. On the very day of Richards's return to Kohima Young's company at Kharasom was attacked by the Japanese and on the following day Brown was attacked at Jessami.

6: 'LAST MAN, LAST ROUND'

Kharasom

LIEUTENANT[15] JOCK YOUNG, who commanded A Company of the Assam Regiment at Kharasom, was a happy, tough young Scot, full of high spirits, with a charming laugh, but a most conscientious officer. He spoke with a strong Glasgow accent. He was a good messmate and much liked by all ranks.

The position he had taken up was a small oval feature, perhaps 150 yards long, just to the north of the small village of Kharasom in a country of scrub and bamboo jungle. It commanded a clear view of much of the surrounding country and had a good water supply near by, but not within the perimeter. The ground to the east was open, sloping gently down to the track, only 40 yards away, which led to Jessami. About 80 yards from the northern end of the position this track was joined by another that led in from Ukrul, 25 miles to the south. Young was therefore well placed to watch both routes. To the west the ground sloped sharply down through thick jungle to a river.

The little strongpoint was well built, well stocked with rations, water and ammunition and surrounded by barbed wire. Having been reinforced by a platoon from another company, the garrison numbered perhaps 120 men. Young was the only British officer. As time went on, brother officers who spoke to him on the field telephone from Jessami could sense how lonely he felt.

While the defences were being built he kept patrols well out. On March 20th Jessami informed him that the Japanese had begun their advance. Young altered his garrison, called in his standing patrols and stood on the defensive, with small patrols watching the approaches.

At dawn on March 27th, Young's observation post on the Ukrul road came in and reported that a large Japanese column was approaching by that route. The garrison took post and Young ordered them to stay silent. He watched the enemy turn left at the junction with the Ukrul track in the early morning light and move along his eastern flank towards Kharasom village.

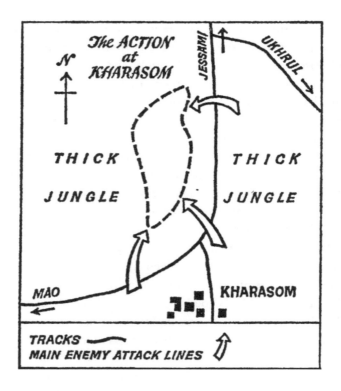

As they came abreast of him, Young gave the order to open fire. The silence of the jungle was shattered as the brens and rifles burst into a sustained volley. Taken aback, the Japanese momentarily stood bewildered, then broke away into the undergrowth, leaving the road littered with bodies.

Young reported by telephone to Brown's headquarters at Jessami, but shortly afterwards the line was cut. He had no wireless and was now cut off from the world. His only guiding light was the order to fight to the last man.

As the sun moved up over the tree-tops, the Japanese rallied and attacked under mortar fire. They were driven off with loss, but Young's second-in-command, a VCO of sterling quality,[16] was killed. They tried again and the fighting went on until the heat of midday. At dusk yet another attack was launched, but still no Japanese penetrated the defences.

For the next three days and nights Young's little company was repeatedly assaulted by greatly superior numbers. Each attack was repulsed with spirit under his inspiring personality. The casualties sustained were trifling; those inflicted, severe. At the end of that time he was distressed to see flames breaking out from the village of Kharasom, eighty yards to the south; the enemy, apparently in a fit of spleen, were wantonly burning it to the ground.

At the end of three days and nights of constant fighting, however, it was apparent to Young that his men were becoming exhausted. He did not think that they could long withstand further onslaught. And the water reserves were daily diminishing.

On the fourth day, March 31st, his attention was called to a new development on the track leading in from the south. There, beyond the ashes of Kharasom, was what a survivor described afterwards as a 'solid mass of soldiers coming towards us, with elephants, mules and carts'. This new force Young estimated as of battalion strength. He watched them go into bivouac some distance away in the jungle. He could not further observe their movements, but knew they would certainly soon join in the battle against him.

The young Scot was faced with an agonizing prospect. His orders were to fight to the last man, but it was inevitable that his little redoubt would before long be overwhelmed. There was no chance of replenishing his water, ammunition or food. He knew, also, that his position had already been bypassed by other enemy troops marching by the Ukrul track and making for Jessami. What possible good would it do to stay where he was? Alone in that remote jungle, he had no one to turn to. All his instincts told him that the right thing to do was to withdraw from an untenable position, now serving no tactical purpose, and save his company.

He called his platoon commanders together during a particularly heavy bombardment by the enemy artillery and mortars. He thanked them for the way in which they fought, but told them that the end had now come. They were accordingly to disengage that night westward through the jungle, make for the river, re-form and withdraw to Kohima. He ended by saying:

'I, however, shall stay here.'

There was an awkward silence and then one of the subedars asked:

'Why will you not come with us, sahib?'

'Because,' Young replied, 'my orders were to fight to the last man. I shall obey those orders and I shall be the last man.' He added after an uncomfortable pause:

'Nor would it be right for me to leave the wounded alone.'

Some of them offered to stay with him but Young replied: 'No argument' and he added the Indian Army term which in Urdu has so decisive a ring: 'It is an order.'

Darkness fell over the forest and the Japanese, put in one more assault, preceding it with a long mortar bombardment. The attack was expected and again decisively repulsed. After the enemy had recoiled, Young's company began quietly to withdraw, not all in the best order. Young went round and spoke encouragingly to the wounded, smiling as he spoke but knowing well what was to be their almost certain fate. One of them, badly wounded in the leg, dragged himself to Young's bunker, sat up, saluted and said, 'I will stay with you, sahib.'

The last scene was reported later to Donald Elwell at Kohima by a young jemadar with tears. Young was standing on the fire-step of his bunker, stacking tommy-gun magazines on the parapet, piling quantities of hand grenades around him and passing a bren gun to the wounded sepoy.

From that time onwards nothing certain is known. Villagers questioned afterwards reported that the Japanese launched another attack at dawn next morning. Finding the position deserted, they began to search the bunkers. There was soon a long sustained series of crackling explosions, followed by a burst of the high-pitched fire of Japanese machine-guns, and then silence.

Jessami

Jessami stood on a ridge at an elevation of 5,600 ft. From its crest a magnificent panorama was spread out of range upon range of wooded mountains stretching far away into Burma.

The position that Brown had fortified was a few hundred yards south of the village and stood boldly astride the junction of two tracks by which an enemy might arrive. One of these tracks led south to Kharasom. An enemy making for Kohima could not by-pass the position without negotiating precipitous slopes. The only drawbacks were that there was no source of water inside the perimeter and the fact that the position was itself overlooked by distant higher ground.

Brown's redoubt was fully manned and the bivouac area vacated on the night before Young was attacked at Kharasom. It was the day on which Brown himself expected to be attacked. He spent it making final preparations and seeing that his men had a hot meal. It was the last that most of them were to get for nearly a month. Then he settled himself in his command post with his quiet adjutant, Captain Michael Williamson. In his deep Regimental Aid Post, the medical officer, Second-Lieutenant Abdul Wahid, stood ready. All movement within the redoubt stopped.

Just before 9 o'clock on the morning of the 28th, Major James Askew observed twenty-five Japanese, led by an officer with his sword, approaching by the Kharasom track. Fire was held. The Japanese walked right up to the barbed wire stretched across the road and stopped, all bunched together, while the officer consulted his map. To the surprise of the garrison, few of whom had yet seen the enemy at close quarters, the Japanese were not the little men they had been led to expect, but tall, powerful men of the Imperial Guard, with whom Sato's division had been stiffened. At the given word, two bren guns opened on them at forty yards range. Twenty-three of the Japanese fell dead. The other two crawled away into the bush with wounds.

Kohima having been informed by telephone, an urgent request was received an hour or two later for enemy identifications. Two Kuki soldiers crawled out in an attempt to bring back one of the dead Japanese, but one of them was

106

killed almost at once. The other returned to the redoubt, armed himself with some grenades and made a second attempt, alone. Sidiman Rai then tried to take out a whole platoon but met with very heavy fire.

Later in the day the Japanese began a fusillade from all directions, in an obvious attempt to make the garrison disclose the positions of their mortars and light machine-guns. No reply was forthcoming and the fusillade served only to inform the garrison that the enemy had now worked his way through the jungle on all sides of them.

The first attack came soon after darkness had fallen over the jungle. The battle went on all night, the enemy attacking each sector in turn, trying to find a weak spot. He found none. Two or three Japanese managed to slip through the outer defences, but were killed at the inner. These provided the identification that higher command wanted, together with a flag which was later delivered to Richards.

When dawn broke on the 29th it revealed to the garrison a quantity of dead Japanese outside the perimeter and several hanging over the wire. It also showed the ground within the perimeter to have been showered with intact British hand grenades, which the Japanese had not known how to arm and were thus a useful addition to the garrison's own armoury. Brown's battalion had not suffered a single casualty that night and its morale was tremendously high.

Such was the beginning of the five-days battle of Jessami, in which 450 men held up an ever-swelling enemy who launched one attack after another with refreshed troops. The Japanese deployed what Williamson called their 'beastly little infantry guns' on the high ground overlooking the redoubt and with these and their mortars troubled the garrison all day, the infantry assaults being usually made at night with their usual wild yells and bugle calls. This was their technique to bring about the exhaustion of their adversaries by lack of sleep; most of their own infantry took their sleep by day.

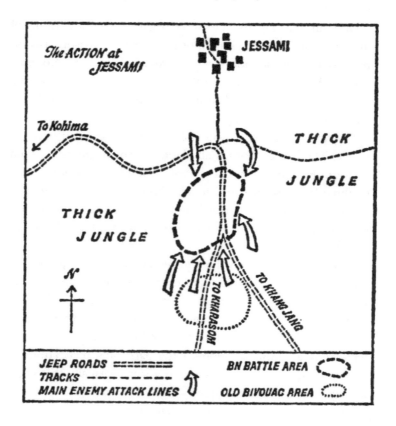

Some time early in the battle the garrison was very much surprised and impressed at receiving a telephone call from the Corps Commander in person. Speaking to Williamson on a very faint line, Scoones inquired how things stood and gave his encouragement to a gallant stand. Almost immediately afterwards the line went dead.[17] The wireless set that Richards had brought up was already out of action.

On the third day — March 30th — the Japanese pressure mounted in intensity and Brown's men began to feel the strain. The Japanese appeared to have been reinforced. Mortaring and shelling went on all day and the garrison could get no sleep. A few enemy again penetrated the outer defences but were again quickly disposed of. The most serious occurrences were the loss of all the garrison's mortars. Although in well-dug pits, their flashes had been observed from higher ground and all were knocked out. This was a serious blow, for it was the garrison's only form of artillery. From then onwards the lack of artillery support was keenly felt.

In the stress of the day's events, no one seems to have noticed an American light aircraft fly in from the north-west and drop a small object a few hundred yards to their south — an object that was of vital concern to them.[18]

The night that followed was the worst so far. A new impetus seemed to be impelling the Japanese, who made repeated attempts to break in with showers of grenades. Their well-built defences and their own determination enabled the garrison to survive the night with few casualties, but it was what Williamson called 'Very tiring indeed'. Everyone was now suffering from lack of sleep and Brown's ban on washing and shaving, to conserve water, did nothing to lessen the sense of fatigue.

All day on the 31st the pressure was again maintained by the Japanese with what seemed to be renewed vigour, with much excited shouting and screaming. In the midst of the din two disheartening scenes were enacted before the eyes of all the garrison. The first was a flight of RAF aircraft bringing supplies. Like the unobserved light aircraft of the day before, they overshot the redoubt and dropped their loads to the Japanese in the battalion's old bivouac area.

A little later a small light aircraft again approached from the north-west. This time it was seen and all eyes turned to watch it. It circled the area repeatedly, coming in lower and lower on each, obviously observing with great care and disregarding the Japanese small arms fire.

Brown watched its course and saw it drop a message. To his chagrin, he saw the message fall some fifteen yards outside his perimeter wire. There was a brisk fire fight, but the garrison had no chance of seeing that which was intended for their eyes alone. It was the Japanese who read, for the second time, Richards's order to the garrison to withdraw.

Mercifully, however, other eyes were turned towards Jessami from outside the box.

Lloyd Jones, the young Welsh subaltern who had made the first contact with the enemy near the V Force stockade, had been cut off on his withdrawal route to Jessami and he had made a wide circuit through pine forest to approach it by the north and west, befriended everywhere by the staunch Naga villagers. On the way he had joined forces with a patrol led by Lieutenant Peter Steyn, an exceptionally tall South African, very young, very cool and well-balanced, and another patrol under Lieutenant John Corlett, a stocky little Ceylon tea planter, athletic, courageous and stubborn.[19]

Together, these three young officers made their way to the small Burmese garrison entrenched on a hill at Phek, commanded by Giles. Reporting to Brown by telephone, they learnt that the battle had begun and were ordered to remain at Phek.

The Phek garrison, now much swollen by retiring V Force detachments, was itself making ready to resist attack.[20] It was therefore a great surprise to everyone when, on the 29th, Richards's IO, Lieutenant Peter Mountstephen, arrived from Kohima with orders for all the three outlying garrisons to be ready to disengage and withdraw two nights afterwards (March 31st/April 1st). Mountstephen explained that the reason for his arrival at Phek in person was the failure of the telephone line from Kohima. He now learnt that Phek was also cut off from Jessami. The problem of informing Jessami and Kharasom became acute. To the young officers of the Assam Regiment, cut off from their friends, it became very acute indeed. That night, across the intervening five miles of jungle hill-tops, they could see the distant gunflashes that told of their friends' struggle.

On the morning of the 30th, having received permission from Giles, Lloyd Jones and Corlett set out with a patrol of platoon strength. Keeping a sharp look-out for the enemy, they reached a hill-top from which they could clearly see the Jessami ridge in profile less than two miles away.

While they watched, a light aircraft, wearing American colours, approached in the strong sunlight, dropped down to a few hundred feet, manoeuvred over Jessami and made a steep dive just beyond the ridge. It then swiftly made height again and returned to the north-west.

Corlett is said to have been able to see the aircraft drop a message, but felt certain that it had overshot the redoubt. Whether that was so or not, he and Lloyd Jones learnt on return to Phek that Richards had in fact arranged for an aircraft from Dimapur to drop a message on Jessami with withdrawal orders. This was the aircraft that was apparently not observed by the garrison.

Very concerned, Corlett felt sure that the message had gone amiss. No means existed of knowing one way or the other and on so vital a matter it would not do to have any doubts at all. Accordingly he asked and was given Giles's permission to attempt to get through to Jessami the next night by himself.

At 4.30 PM on the 31st the Phek garrison withdrew, just as the first Japanese ranging shells began to fall. Corlett waited until night fell. Then, wearing gym shoes, carrying nothing but his revolver and accompanied only by his orderly, he stole out on his daring mission. He went by a circuitous route and chose intentionally the most precipitous hills, to lessen the risks of meeting any Japanese. But Corlett was tough and skilled in jungle craft and he took the sounds of the battle at Jessami as his compass bearing.

As he judged that it was time to swing in for the final approach he was faced with the steep escarpment far below the Jessami ridge. He and his orderly clambered up with extra caution. The sounds of battle had now died away and, as the two men reached the top, they found themselves, as Corlett had intended, in their old bivouac area. The Japanese were everywhere around, but there was little activity and most of them seemed to be asleep.

Corlett was a very cool hand and took everything in a matter of fact way. He was anxious to find his white Naga dog Kuku. He made his way almost casually to his old dug-out, furious to find a Japanese officer asleep in his bed. There was no sign of Kuku.

Evading the last of the Japanese, he reached the perimeter wire of the redoubt and here met his first check. The garrison was much more alert than the Japanese and fired on him. The whole redoubt was alerted and it was not until after a great deal of shouting and shooting that Corlett's voice and lisp were recognized and he was admitted.

It was after 10 o'clock when he at last reached Brown's command post and broke the news to him that he was to withdraw that night. Brown would not accept the validity of the withdrawal order until he had cross-questioned Corlett closely. He decided, moreover, that it was now too late to withdraw that night. His own orders required that anyone seen moving at night was to be shot at once without challenge and he had no means of communicating orders to every post. He therefore decided to defer the withdrawal till the next night and at dawn on April 1st he summoned his company commanders and gave orders accordingly.

He intended, of course, a properly controlled and orderly disengagement, but the events of that fifth day defeated him. Primed by the aircraft messages in their possession, which had not been in code, the Japanese made repeated and determined efforts to overcome the exhausted garrison. The defences were breached several times and savage close-quarters fighting took place. The garrison hung on tenaciously and the Japanese were obliged to draw off.

A further attack at 5 o'clock, however, tore a large hole and the situation deteriorated. The garrison had almost reached the limit of physical endurance. Brown was obliged to revise his plan for an orderly withdrawal. He went round himself giving orders for small groups to evacuate as soon as darkness fell. Some of the bunkers were cut off or so closely invested that the men got away only by a hair's breadth.

The withdrawal itself was perilous. In anticipation of it, the Japanese had laid heavy ambushes on all likely routes and these had to be fought through or evaded, while the night was made horrible as the Japanese ran howling and screaming through the empty redoubt and the surrounding jungle in search of the prey that had eluded them and murdering the wounded.

Among 'those missing' was Kuku. His master had found him in the redoubt and they had made their withdrawal together. But they had been caught in an ambush and Kuku was never seen again.

The five-days stand of the 1st Assam Regiment at Jessami and Kharasom, in which they had been opposed by greatly superior numbers, was their baptism of fire and won them immediate fame. Their stand saved Kohima and a great deal else besides. Had they broken or been overcome, the Japanese 138th Brigade would have arrived at Kohima at a time when there were virtually no troops of any quality to oppose them. The delay imposed was of priceless value.

The first of the battalion to arrive back at Kohima, on April 1st, were those from Phek, including Lloyd Jones and Peter Steyn. They immediately reported to Richards their fears that Jessami had not received the order to withdraw. Richards thereupon sent Lloyd Jones to Dimapur, whence he was to be flown out in a third attempt to drop a message on the Jessami redoubt.

At Dimapur, where Rankin, who had gone to bed, turned out in pyjamas to see him, Lloyd Jones learnt that the American Air Force colonel who had piloted the first aircraft two days before was terribly upset to hear of the error in dropping the previous message, but the fault was not his; the British officer who had flown out with him knew only of the old bivouac position, with its uncamouflaged diggings and had dropped the message there. The American and Lloyd Jones were about to take off again when news came that the battalion had been observed from the air marching strongly on their way back.

Brown himself and the leading elements from Jessami, having been gunned by their own aircraft on the way, reported in to Kohima on April 3rd, and others came in later, to a final number of about 280. Though worn out, they bore themselves well and each man carried his arms. They were to have only twenty-four hours rest before becoming involved in a yet more desperate affair.

7: ORDER AND COUNTER-ORDER

'The Duke of York's Own'

WHILE 1st Assam Regiment was fighting its delaying actions at Jessami and Kharasom, confusion, uncertainty and counter-orders impeded Richards's preparations at Kohima. Captain Stephen Laing, adjutant to Landor, in a report afterwards, declared that 'new orders came in torrents, countermanding, amending and substituting' and that 'units were moved in all directions at short notice'. The crisis was approaching.

Richards preserved his equanimity, however, and on the day after he returned to Kohima from Jessami, which was the day that Jessami was attacked, an entirely new picture was painted, which seemed suddenly to resolve all problems.

Rankin, the Area Commander, came up that day for a conference with Richards in Pawsey's bungalow and with him came Brigadier D. F. W. Warren, Commander of 161st Indian Infantry Brigade. This brigade, after having been flown in from Arakan, was due to arrive at Kohima the next day.

For, farther back in India — at Slim's 14th Army headquarters at Comilla, at the Commander-in-Chief's and Giffard's 11th Army Group Headquarters in Delhi — the situation in Assam was causing the greatest anxiety. Slim has said that he had rarely spent more uncomfortable moments. The enemy move through the footpaths of the Somra Hills in such strength had completely upset all plans. Slim, blaming himself for his mistaken assessment, had few fears for Imphal, but if Sato should descend on Dimapur, the Allied forces — British, American, Indian and Chinese — would suffer a major disaster. The situation was very tense.

The senior commanders and their staffs responded with speed and energy. Very large and complicated troop movements were put in hand over long distances. Fresh troops were put at Slim's disposal. The 2nd British Division, wearing the emblem of the two crossed keys and then training for amphibious warfare far away in Southern India, was ordered to move and placed under his command. Perowne's 23rd Long Range Penetration Brigade, which had not gone out on Wingate's Chindit operations, was sent forward to act as a mobile force to cover the railway to Ledo. To command operations in the new and vital sector, Lieut-General Montagu Stopford, an able and experienced Rifleman, was flown in with his 33rd Corps headquarters.

Never had air transport been so valuable and never yet had it been used on so large a scale. Without air supremacy it would not have been possible. British and American aircraft were flying almost continuously, with scarcely any let up, between Arakan, Dimapur and Imphal.

Slim himself flew in to Dimapur towards the end of the month. The situation there was deplorable. Of the 45,000 men at the great, sweating, malaria-ridden base, there was scarcely one who had ever fired a rifle. Slim's immediate problem was whether to attempt to hold Kohima or give it up and concentrate on Dimapur. Dimapur, lying in the hot Assam plain, had no natural defences. Kohima had. If there were not enough troops to hold Kohima, it was even more certain that there were not enough to hold the wide-open Dimapur. Kohima, therefore, seemed to be the best place at which to resist a threat to Dimapur, but there was the grave risk that the enemy might by-pass it. What Slim was manoeuvring for was 'the most precious element in war' — time. If the enemy could be held off while his reinforcements were concentrating, the crisis would pass. To do that, Kohima offered the best chance. Like the soldier that he was, he placed his faith in 'the stubborn valour of my troops'.

Such were Slim's thoughts as he considered anxiously what to do with 161st Indian Infantry Brigade. It was the last brigade of 5th Indian Division to arrive and in other circumstances it would have rejoined that division, which, as we have seen earlier, was being flown in to Imphal. Slim had already decided to hold it back and he now ordered it to Kohima and to go there at once. He felt pretty confident that this brigade could hold the enemy there, at least until the arrival of 2nd British Division, who, he hoped, even if the Japanese did by-pass Kohima, would have begun to arrive at Dimapur before the enemy. At the same time Slim transmogrified Rankin's administrative command into an operational one, with responsibility for the Kohima-Dimapur operations pending the arrival of Stopford. Kohima thus passed out of the jurisdiction of Scoones, who was at that date just about to be cut off in Imphal.

The 161st Brigade, which will occupy a large part in our narrative, was a battle-tried formation of high quality. Originally, it had been an English Territorial brigade based on Colchester, but the transmutations of war had turned it into an Indian one. Before going to India it had served in the Western Desert and had taken part in the Battle of El Alamein. It had done fine service again in Arakan. Like most troops who had come straight from that campaign, officers and men had their tails well up, confident in their ability to outfight the Japanese.

Wearing on their shoulders the celebrated 'Ball of Fire' of the 5th Indian Division, the brigade was composed of 4th Royal West Kent Regiment (Lieut-Colonel 'John' Laverty) of whom we shall see a great deal, 1/1st Punjab (Lieut-Colonel Neil

Brodie) and 4/7th Rajput (Lieut-Colonel Jack Cargill). Grouped with these battalions and under Warren's operational command was 24th Mountain Regiment (Lieut-Colonel Humphry Hill), equipped with 3.7 inch howitzers, 2nd Field Company Indian Sappers and Miners and 75th Indian Field Ambulance, where we must particularly note its remarkable 'tactical doctor', Lieut-Colonel John Young. The gunner regiment had, in part, been one of the gallant band that had held the 'Admin Box' in the Battle of Ngakyedauk Pass in Arakan.

The commander of this brigade, 'Freddy' Warren, was an able and experienced officer who had been through both of the Arakan campaigns. He was a thinking soldier and had the faculty of attracting the confidence of those above him as well as inspiring it in those below. His constant pipe, his spectacles, his 'khud stick' and his quiet manner gave him a paternal appearance, so that among the British troops he was known as 'Daddy' Warren. It was an appearance, however, which scarcely concealed the energy and determination that enforced his wisdom.

Before going forward to the Kohima Conference on the 28th, Warren had had a long personal talk with Slim himself at Dimapur, walking up and down a path, as Slim himself describes.[21] Warren, therefore, when he met Rankin and Richards at the DC's doomed bungalow, was fully alive to the extreme sensitivity of the situation.

At this conference Richards put forward his view that the 'last man, last round' order that the Assam Regiment had been given was not warranted in the circumstances. With this view Rankin and Warren fully concurred and a decision was made for 161st Brigade to disengage the Assam as quickly as possible and then, with them, 'to withdraw to a closer defence' around

Kohima itself.[22] Richards's spirits rose. Never was a reinforcement more welcome.

Almost immediately after landing from their aircraft at Dimapur, Warren's brigade began to move out of the hot plain and climbed the crooked mountain road into the genial air of Kohima. They completed their concentration on the 30th. No time was lost. Warren's orders for the disengagement operation had been issued on the 29th. Jessami and Phek were to be relieved by the Rajputs and Kharasom by the Punjabis, each battalion to be accompanied by a section of guns of 24th Mountain Regiment. The operation was to be completed in two days, the relieving forces moving forward part-way on the 30th and assisting the withdrawal of the Assam on the night March 31st/April 1st. The Royal West Kents were meantime to occupy the Treasury and when the relief was completed the other battalions were 'to cover the occupation of the outer Kohima defence line'. Since the brigade was very short of transport, Warren asked Richards for 'every additional jeep you can let me have'.

He also informed Richards, who now came under his command, that 'I have passed word to Phek and Jessami of the impending operation' and 'am arranging to get word to Kharasom'. What these arrangements were does not appear, but what is clear is that word did not, in fact, reach any of them. Richards, however, took his own steps. When he was informed that both the telephone and the wireless to Jessami had failed, he arranged with Rankin for a Captain Wemyss, who was confident that he knew the location of the Assam at Jessami, to be flown out from Dimapur and to drop a message with the withdrawal order.

On return from his flight, Wemyss reported that he had dropped the message on the Assam's bivouac site, which he knew, and not on the well-camouflaged redoubt. Richards sent him out a second time and the message fell outside the wire. Richards also sent out three local men of the Assam Rifles who knew the country, but they never arrived. Finally, with the result that we have seen, he sent out Lloyd Jones.[23]

The relief operation by Warren's brigade duly began on the 30th but was never completed. On the long route to Kharasom, Major Tom Ware's company of Punjabis ran into Miyazaki's brigade swinging up to Kohima after the Sangshak battle, was ambushed, and lost twenty-three jeeps and three lorries. More seriously, on that day another and even more critical conference took place at the roadside in Kohima, between Rankin, Richards, Warren and Pawsey. To the dismay of his hearers, Rankin called off the whole disengagement operation and ordered 161st Brigade back to defend Dimapur.

The reason for this precipitate reversal of policy, when the relief was on the eve of being carried out, derived from a written directive that Slim had sent to Rankin. In this Slim laid down the priorities of Rankin's task and the first of these was the defence of Dimapur. Subsidiary ones were the defence of the railway, the maintenance of a mobile striking force and, last, the defence of Kohima. This directive was routed through Stopford, who was now on the scene, though his Corps headquarters was not yet operative. Stopford personally handed it to Rankin and told him that, because of the danger that 161st Brigade might be cut off from Dimapur, now prescribed as Rankin's prime responsibility, he was to get the brigade back 'as soon as possible'.

This dangerous prospect was further coloured by RAF reports that Japanese parties, walking in single-file, had been observed on hill tracks leading in the direction of Dimapur.

Warren, Richards and Pawsey were horrified at Rankin's new orders. They were appalled at the idea of abandoning the Assam to their fate. There was time, they urged, to relieve them and get back to cover Dimapur before the Japanese could threaten it. Stopford's 'as soon as possible' did not necessarily mean 'forthwith'. Pawsey said he was certain that the parties on the northern tracks seen by the RAF were not Japanese but Naga villagers returning from their fields, who also walked in single-file. Had they been Japanese, he would certainly have been informed by his Naga scouts.

Rankin, himself very perturbed, felt obliged to overrule these objections. In view of his orders, he could not accept the risk that the enemy might cut the road behind Warren's brigade. The most that he would allow was that one battalion should stay one more day in an attempt to extricate the garrison.[24]

Warren's brigade, therefore, taking it very hard, went immediately into reverse. The Punjabis (who in any case would have been too late to save Young's company at Kharasom) disengaged from their action with Miyazaki. The Rajputs stayed one more day, unaware that Brown had not yet received the withdrawal order, but by the evening of the 31st, the whole brigade, twisting downhill by the mountain road into the plains again, was some thirty-six miles in the rear. Warren, contemplating the rapid uphill-and-down-again manoeuvre, dubbed his brigade 'The Duke of York's Own', which earned him a reprimand from a humourless higher command.

The Vital Decision

Richards now had precious little left in the way of troops competent to fight. He could not count on seeing the Assam again. Kohima was in utter confusion, with troops coming and going. The evacuation of stores, workshops, transport and

122

units was still in full flood, an operation in which he had no say. He was harassed all day by every kind of problem and every person and everything had to be improvised. The Garrison War Diary records:

> One of the greatest difficulties experienced in preparing to meet the enemy was the constant fluctuation of the garrison. Many units were moved without reference to Garrison HQ and the size of the Box and the number of troops available to hold it were therefore almost impossible to compute.

Notwithstanding the loss of Warren's brigade and the confusion of movements, what was left of the garrison remained, for the greater part, perfectly calm and self-possessed. They accepted the facts and got on with their jobs cheerfully as best they knew how. They were more concerned for news of the gallant Assam Regiment than for anything else at that moment. Accounts that were later published of a state of 'despair' and 'despondency' were totally untrue. Steyn, historian of the Assam Regiment, just back from Phek, recorded that 'hopes and spirits were high'. James Barratt, coming up from Dimapur as a reinforcement officer, found everyone 'cheerful and light-hearted'. Elwell, with his transport platoon of the same regiment, wrote: 'The men were alert and confident.' Glover, the surgeon, entered in his little diary: 'Things are not too bad' and a little later, when he had set up his Aid Post on Jail Hill: 'I feel reasonably calm.'

This air of calm was strengthened by a decision of the first importance that Richards made and one on which the very foundation of the great battle to come rested. Now alone, he surveyed again the four dispersed 'boxes' that had been selected before his arrival eight days ago and decided that it was futile to attempt to hold them. He appreciated correctly that the vital ground was Kohima Ridge. This controlled the approaches both from the south and from Jessami. This was ground that the enemy must have and therefore it was ground that must be denied him.

Richards therefore scrapped all the other three — one with regret — sent their units packing off to Dimapur, concentrated what was left on the Ridge and ordered new works to be put in hand at once. Time was running out and he assessed, from the information that was streaming in to Pawsey, that he would be attacked in four days' time.

Kohima had first been saved by the stand of 50th Parachute Brigade at Sangshak. It had been saved again by the Assam at Jessami. It was saved finally and for good by this sound tactical decision and by the providential arrival of some good troops, as will shortly be related.

A second decision, without which the garrison would never have held out in the battle to come, reinforced the validity of the first. Whatever Kohima lacked, it had quantities of ammunition, rations and stores of many kinds immediately at hand. Richards therefore ordered fourteen days' rations to be distributed in all weapon positions throughout the ridge. He drew up a table of arms for every weapon-pit and distributed ammunition to all in generous quantities for the same estimated period. These orders were promptly executed by his able Staff Captain, Captain W. Greenwood. In fact, there was sufficient of some commodities in the weapon-pits for nearly three weeks and ample supplies of most commodities were at hand along the ridge itself.

The estimate of fourteen days — which turned out to be almost exactly the duration of the coming siege — may appear to be an act of prescience, but Richards, though he had little but guesswork to go on, hardly expected to have to hold out more than a few days, for he knew now that 2nd British Division was due to begin arriving at Dimapur on April 5th. Knowing the propensity of the Japanese for cutting in, however, he took the opportunity of stocking up well for whatever other troops might occupy the Ridge and he foresaw that, whatever happened on the Ridge itself, a long and difficult battle would follow against Sato's Division.

With his headquarters in Pawsey's bungalow, Richards held daily conferences, during one of which a Japanese aircraft appeared, came down low and flew in a leisurely fashion up and down the road. He was worried by many problems — the lack of artillery, the shortage of defence stores, the acute shortage of trained infantry officers and the unsatisfactory signal services.

He was not worried, however, about medical services. On April 1st the staff of 53 Indian General Hospital (having evacuated the nurses and patients a few days before) packed up and left, but Arundell, the CO, left behind one and a half sections under Captain J. A. Hunter, with three other doctors[25] and equipment for 150 beds. Arundell had also already sent out three other medical officers to act as RMOs for Supply Hill, the State Battalion and Workshop Ridge.[26] In addition, a section of 80th Parachute Field Ambulance (belonging to 50th Para. Brigade) had been left behind under Captain W. Thomson. Besides these Hepworth had his Indian MO for his Reinforcement Camp, the V Force detachments had two doctors[27] and someone had discovered that Glover, the OC of the Hygiene Section, was qualified not only in public health but also as a surgeon, so he also was retained and was to do gallant service. He fortunately kept a very small, blue, pocket diary, in which he briefly jotted down the events of each day. In all, before further arrivals, there were twelve medical officers and some seventy or more orderlies, all but seven being Indians. On April 2nd, however, as the hospital buildings could not be defended, Richards moved Hunter's detachment to the Bungalow Sector.

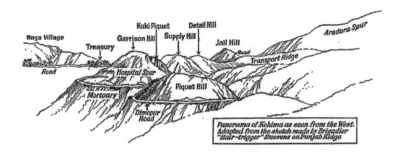

Panorama of Kohima as seen from the West. Adapted from the sketch made by Brigadier "Hair-trigger" Steevens on Punjab Ridge.

Water was the business of John Landor, the engineer. Kohima was supplied by a piped main that came in from a roadside reservoir just beyond Transport Ridge and emergency provision had to be made in case it was cut. After strenuous efforts, Landor was able to get six cylindrical steel tanks, of 500 to 1,000 gallons capacity. These and several large tarpaulins were filled with water. There was not enough time to fill all the tanks, nor to dig any of them in, but there existed already a large steel cistern in the bungalow area supplied from the main.

Richards hoped that the shortage of trained infantry would be in part made good by the troops in Hepworth's Reinforcement Camp. They included British, Gurkha and Indian troops, about 200 of each, many of them convalescing after discharge from hospital. They were not in formed organic units and had no officers of their own. The camp was now disencumbered of its unarmed troops, who were sent back to Dimapur. The remainder Hepworth organized into composite companies and platoons and Richards equipped them with arms. There was good material here and many of them were

126

individually to do fine service, but there was not time to make them into good units. Hepworth himself Richards sent to act as SSO to the State battalion in place of Borrowman, who could still only hobble about, and Richards appointed him as his second-in-command, for which his experience, his staunch character and his knowledge of the terrain suited him ideally.

Improvisation had to be employed in every direction at short notice. For lack of artillery, the solitary 25-pounder in the Reinforcement Camp was dragged up into Pawsey's garden under the command of Captain John Browning, a gunner officer from Hepworth's camp. There, standing naked and alone, the gun had all the appearance of a pathetic symbol of defiance; but, as others were soon to find, there was nowhere else on the Ridge to deploy a single gun.

The shortage of trained infantry officers was even more serious. There were very few in the Reinforcement Camp to take charge of the composite companies and none to direct the non-combatant units. Richards was therefore delighted when a very young and alert Indian major reported at the bungalow, announced himself as Naveen Rawlley and offered his services.

Richards asked him only one question: 'Are you infantry?'

Rawlley answered, '9/12th Frontier Force Regiment, sir.'

'Thank God. You will take command of Supply Hill and Detail Hill. Get up there at once and get things organized. There's no time to lose.'

On his way back from leave to rejoin his battalion at Imphal, Rawlley had gone down with malaria but when the hospital was evacuated he had elected to stay. At his sector, he found 'a queer mixture' of troops, with fifteen officers, only two of whom were infantry. These were good young subalterns named Carrington, of the Northamptonshire Regiment, and an Indian believed to be named Kuriyan. The latter was given a

127

platoon, which in these pages will be known as 'the Kuriyan platoon', although his own identity is not certain. Among other troops were about 50 Indian transport drivers and clerks under Captain Savoor, who had been a Wimbledon tennis 'ace'.

Rawlley found most of his garrison unwilling to work, but he quickly organized them into companies and platoons, sited new weapon-pits, formed a mortar detachment from two 3-inch mortars he found in the ordnance sub-park, established an extempore air post with some RAMC men and stocked the weapon-pits with ammunition and rations.

Very soon afterwards three or four young infantry officers, who had been returning from hospital or leave, were sent up to Richards from Dimapur. They included Captain Patrick, Lieutenant James Barratt and Lieutenant Gould (who was to be killed). Richards sent Barratt up to Rawlley, who gave him a company of 100 'odds and ends', wholly untrained to fight, and posted him on Kuki Piquet. We shall see much of them.

On April 1st, the day after the departure of the last of 161st Brigade, Richards received from Rankin a directive of critical importance. This told him, as he knew already, that the enemy force making for Kohima was the whole of Sato's 31st Division. In consequence, Rankin now gave Richards explicit authority to withdraw from Kohima at his own discretion.

Because of what has been said or omitted in other accounts, the relevant paragraphs of this directive (202 Area Operation Instruction No. 3) must now be published. These were as follows:

3. The garrison at Kohima will consist of: 1st Assam Regiment
   (if extricated from Jessami area).
   The Native State battalion.
   All other combatants at Kohima.

4. You will command the garrison of Kohima and will deny Kohima to the enemy as long as possible without being destroyed yourselves.

5. All unarmed personnel and all vehicles and stores which are not required for the defence and administration of Kohima will be dispatched to Dimapur immediately.

6. The decision as to the precise moment when it will be necessary to withdraw from Kohima must be made by you. You must, however, give me the longest possible warning of such an eventuality. It is emphasized that it is most important that Kohima should be held on to as long as possible, subject to the proviso in para 4 above.

There followed instructions on various steps to be taken on withdrawal, such as destruction of stores and documents and the safe escort of the Deputy Commissioner.

These, orders Richards disclosed to no one but Borrowman. From first to last, no thought of withdrawal entered his head; nor were any plans or preparations for a withdrawal ever made.

The Ridge

The time has now come to look more closely at the knuckly features of the famous Ridge, with which the remainder of this narrative will be exclusively concerned.

The extreme northern sector, pointing its sharp nose at the Traffic Control Post and the Treasury, constituted a sloping shoulder of the main ridge. Within the two arms of the hairpin bend that the main road here made, the ground swelled up boldly, with steep drops to the road on either arm. Its detail will be studied more closely at a later stage, but we may note here that the natural slope had been converted into a series of terraces on which stood the government bungalows of the Deputy Commissioner, the Commandant of the Assam Rifles, the famous tennis court and a small club house.

129

Parts of the area had thus been cleared of trees but on other parts there were plantations of eucalyptus as well as the natural forest growth. The whole area was completely overlooked from all sides, particularly from the Treasury and Naga Village. In operations at the time and in official accounts this sector was known as 'DC's Bungalow'. This is not a suitable name and in these pages accordingly it will be known as the Bungalow Sector.

At the southern end of this terraced slope the ground rose up boldly to form the main and dominant feature of the Ridge. This was Garrison Hill, crowned with its little summer house and fairly densely clothed on its flanks with oaks and with alders that were frequently pollarded for firewood by the Nagas. Beneath them was a thick, tough undergrowth of tall grass and ageratum.

South of Garrison Hill was a much smaller one, similarly clothed, known as Kuki Piquet, so called because the Kukis, who were hereditary enemies of the Nagas and who had taken service with the British in the Naga war of 1879, had been posted here as guard for the Deputy Commissioner's camp.

Southwards again was another fairly large feature but of indeterminate form, on which stood numerous sheds and bashas. This was the Field Supply Depot and the whole feature was therefore known in operations as 'F S D'. In this account, however, for the convenience of the general reader, it will be called Supply Hill. For the proper functioning of the depot, the feature had been partially cleared of trees and was traversed by several paths and vehicle tracks. There were thus good fields of fire, but, as the air photos show, there were still a good many trees to give cover alike to the defence and to an infiltrating enemy.

Next came a small, oval feature covered with the buildings, which included a large bakery, of the Detail Issue Store, or 'D I S'. This will be known here as Detail Hill. It was of modest height, was one of the features protected by a little dannert wire, and was to be the scene of some of the most heroic fighting. As on Supply Hill, the trees had been partially cleared.

Opposite Detail Hill, on the other side of the Imphal road — the only part of the defences on the east of the road — rose the high, sharply conical Jail Hill of evil memory. On the curving roadside at its feet stood the small civilian jail, an ammunition depot and a petrol depot. Jail Hill completely dominated Detail Hill and, after it had passed into Japanese hands, became the thorniest of the problems that confronted Stopford's troops.

South-west of Jail Hill and back on the western side of the road was a long feature, not as steep or well-defined as the others, veering approximately south-west and forming the southern extremity of the defences. This also was liberally sprinkled with bashas, cookhouses and so on. Here were located the General Purposes Transport Companies and it was accordingly known as GPT Ridge. We shall call it more simply Transport Ridge. Here oak and alder gave place in part to conifers and lantana bushes and here also some coils of dannert wire had been quickly laid out after Richards's decision to concentrate on Kohima Ridge.

Thus for the north, east and south. On the western side of the Ridge, the narrow bridle-path of the Ladies' Mile more or less marked the perimeter of the defences. Below it, on its west, the ground fell away very steeply in heavily wooded ribs or corrugations, forming a difficult but not impossible approach for an enterprising enemy. Before completing the circuit and returning to the Bungalow Sector, the Ladies' Mile

131

led to a sensitive sector which was the back door to the defences. This was the steep and wooded sector known as Hospital Ridge. Immediately below it, slanting away to the north-west, lay the long, treeless slope covered with the now empty buildings of 53rd Indian General Hospital, thus known as IGH Spur (and frequently confused with Hospital Ridge), but which for us will be Hospital Spur.

So much may be seen from a quick reconnaissance of the Ridge. It measured a trifle more than a mile in length and an average of 400 yards in width. Its rough and knuckly face was wrinkled by numerous vehicle tracks and footpaths and dotted with many small buildings. A few feet below the surface — sometimes only two feet below — lay hard rock, scarcely assailable by pick and shovel, which found even the root-packed top-soil difficult enough.

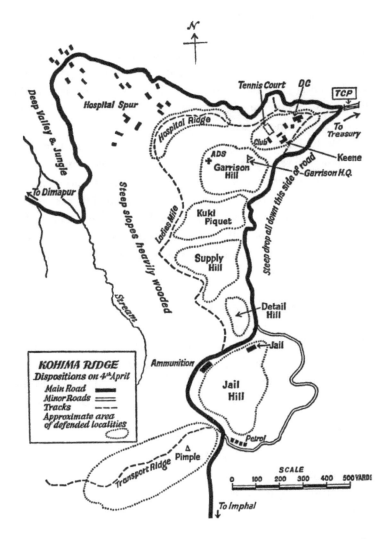

All down the eastern face, from the Bungalow Sector to the Jail, the Imphal road was cut into the hillside, forming cliff-like banks from 10 to 50 ft high. It was by no means unscalable and there were one or two dangerous inlets between the hill features. While it required watching, Richards regarded all this side as reasonably secure and the steeply wooded slopes on the west as tolerably so. He therefore appreciated that the enemy's probable tactics would be to attempt to roll him up from the south, biting off one feature at a time, or else to assault the Bungalow Sector and Hospital Ridge, which would strike immediately at his heart.

In all, Kohima Ridge was a very good position, certainly the best that offered for a small force. It closely commanded the main road at a critical point, as well as the tracks leading into it from the Somra Hills by way of Naga Village. The fact that it was overlooked by higher ground on nearly all sides, particularly from the hill features in and around Naga Village, from the crest on the north on which ran the road to Merema and from the majestic green eminence of Aradura, had to be accepted.

Richards chose a site for his battle command post about halfway between the tennis court and the summit of Garrison Hill. Dug by the Nagas, it was a simple trench of three traverses, roofed with corrugated iron and covered with a few inches of rubble. From here he looked straight down on to the Bungalow Sector on one side and out to Naga Village on another.

'Into Your Trenches'

The first days of April were, if anything, more full of bustle than before. The tense atmosphere that always precedes a great battle pervaded the hills. On Transport Ridge Donald Elwell and Noel Lunn engaged in deep heart-searchings, as young officers do before their first battle, wondering whether they would stand up to the test when the bullets began to fly and set the example that their men expected. The troops as a whole were in cheerful spirits as they cleared the decks for action and philosophically awaited orders. The few British soldiers chaffed one another light-heartedly and cracked their little jokes.

Outside a great silence pervaded the hills. From high Aradura, 'green, majestic, mysterious', a profound spirit seemed to Elwell to flow over the lesser eminences, telling of great events to come. More prosaically, Glover noted in his diary that it was 'the calm before the storm'. Everywhere the hillmen had stolen away from their habitations before the approach of the enemy. Naga Village, nearly a square mile in extent, was almost completely empty. Nearly all the transport companies had now left Kohima and the road back to Dimapur, so recently thronged with a busy traffic, was deserted throughout its forty-six miles, the villages vacated and many of the houses burnt to the ground. Looking back along its tortuous length from Kohima Ridge, not a sign of life was to be seen. No wood-smoke rose now from the green hills. No men worked on the terraced paddy fields.

Some little military movement there was into Kohima itself. Detachments of V Force, withdrawing from the Somra Hills, were drifting into its protection. The Burmese company from Phek and the remnants of the Assam Regiment from Kharasom and Jessami began to march in. Brown himself arrived with the main body on the 3rd, marching in good order, having extricated themselves without any of the help arranged for them. All that came back were 260.[28] They were exhausted and hungry and possessed nothing but what they stood in. There was just time to get them re-kitted before the enemy arrived. Brown himself borrowed a polo sweater from Pawsey and wore it throughout the forthcoming siege — and indeed until he was killed in later operations.

To Pawsey there came in a steady flow of Nagas with information of enemy movements and Richards knew with considerable accuracy when he might expect to be attacked. On the 3rd he learnt that the Japanese 58th Brigade, having reached Mao, twenty road miles to the south, were moving up the road towards Kohima from the south. Later in the day Japanese patrols were reported only ten miles away in the south.

These troops were the left-hand column of Sato's division, led by Miyazaki, who, according to plan, were swinging up north after their battle with the Parachute Brigade at Sangshak and who had ambushed Ware's company of Punjabis attempting to relieve Kharasom. Others from the same column were making towards Naga Village.

On receipt of this news Richards sent out a patrol of the Assam Rifles to get more exact information. Then he called together his sector commanders and told them:

'Collect your bedding and get into your trenches.'

To those who had been long stationed at Kohima this order was like the shock of someone violently shaken out of his dream. Though the march of events was known, what was inevitable still seemed impossible in those peaceful parts. Elwell recorded that a 'large silence' possessed the surrounding hills and Landor said afterwards: 'We never believed that it could really happen.'

Most of the motley garrison were already at their stations, now damp from the recent rain. When all was complete, the general dispositions were according to the following pattern.[29]

BUNGALOW SECTOR. 200 British NCOs and men from
the Reinforcement Camp, with the 25-pounder gun.

GARRISON HILL. Headquarters and B Company of the State battalion, the remainder of the battalion being on patrols or manning ambushes.

KUKI PIQUET. Barratt's composite company.

SUPPLY HILL. About fifty drivers, mule leaders and clerks of the Royal Indian Army Service Corps. A composite Indian company from the Reinforcement Camp. The Kuriyan platoon. No. 1432 Company Indian Pioneer Corps, unarmed. A few other small details also, including the staff of the adjacent ordnance field park.

DETAIL HILL. Two platoons 5/27th Mahratta Light Infantry (apparently) and V Force detachments. These and the garrison of Supply Hill were under Major Naveen Rawlley.

JAIL HILL. Two companies of Burmese troops,[30] and a platoon of the Assam Regiment, the whole under Major Reginald Lowe, commanding the Jail Hill-Transport Ridge sector.

TRANSPORT RIDGE. A composite Gurkha company from the Reinforcement Camp under Captain Douglas Frew. A composite company of Indian infantry. The transport platoon of the Assam Regiment under Elwell and another platoon under Steyn.

HOSPITAL RIDGE. Assam Rifles under Keene and the main body of the Assam Regt under Brown just arrived from Jessami.

Several Regimental Aid Posts.

Other oddments included persons of the Kohima administration, such as the Administrative Commandant, the Garrison Engineer and various signals details. V Force detachments were on various sectors.

Such was the mixed bag of troops that was expected to resist an onslaught by the world's toughest soldiers. Their total strength amounted to about 2,500, of whom 1,500 were, either actually or theoretically, combatant soldiers. Separate fragments as they were and for the greater part untaught in battle practices, there was little coherence between adjacent units and sub-units and no established chain of command. There were no lateral communications and the only links that Richards himself had with each sector were by field telephone; it was therefore very fortunate that he had a small squad of particularly brave Sikh linesmen who, in the siege to come, worked day and night under fire to keep the lines alive.

Well outside the perimeter Richards had sent out several patrols, road-blocks and ambushes on all approaches to Kohima. The most important of them were a road-block about half a mile south of Transport Ridge, manned by Gurkhas, and an ambush farther down the Imphal road, manned by the State battalion. It was by this route that he expected the first enemy troops to appear. In this locality we should specially note a feature known as Workshop Ridge, a mile and a half south of Transport Ridge. Here had been situated one of the boxes that Richards had to abandon. He had done so with regret in this case, for it was a strong position, but he had no troops fit to man it and no artillery for its support. As he anticipated, it was to be a source of trial to the garrison when it passed to enemy hands.

It was now vital for Richards to take matters into his own hands and get rid of as many as possible of the non-combatant Indians who were encumbering his garrison, including the remainder from the boxes he had just closed. Even at this hour many continued their normal duties. Ordnance clerks were still demanding issue vouchers for urgent stores. A considerable labour force still remained.

With the object of preventing weapons from falling into enemy hands, Richards issued small arms from the ordnance stores to as many of these troops as possible and sent them off on the deserted Dimapur road, in vehicles or on foot. As they went these men, who were merely civilians in uniform, many of them no more than coolies, carried all manner of panic rumours, such as refugees always spread. By the troops of 161st Brigade whom they met on the road farther back they were egregiously mistaken for 'deserters' and 'stragglers' from the garrison, 'all too eager to give up their weapons' and created the impression that the garrison they had deserted was a rabble with no stomach for fighting. Further currency was later given to this notion by later commentators who grossly corrupted the facts and who thus wantonly slandered a garrison of whom a great many, if not all, were entirely staunch and who were soon to prove their courage and steadfastness.

First Contact

As dusk closed in on that night of April 3rd, everything was very quiet. The troops were at their posts and the sentries alert. 'Our sleeves,' wrote Elwell, 'were rolled up.' Only the chink of picks on Transport Ridge, where his transport platoon were digging far into the night at their new positions, interrupted the silence. A brilliant moon sailed in the heavens, flooding the jungle with a light as bright as day.

First contact was made that night by the patrol of Assam Rifles that Richards had sent out to the south. They came in early on the 4th, reporting that they had met the Japanese six miles south of the road-block on the Imphal road and killed fifteen of them. A patrol of the State battalion also came in, bringing with them the ears of three Japanese as evidence of another successful encounter.

Richards went round all sectors that day, paying special attention to those on the south. On Transport Ridge he found Frew and his Gurkhas quietly confident and on Jail Hill, though there was a motley collection there, he hoped that the Assam under Lowe, supported by Corlett's mortars, might have a steadying influence. On Supply Hill and Detail Hill he found that the energetic young Rawlley had taken a firm grip and he felt confident that his men would give a good account of themselves.

Then, at 5 o'clock in the afternoon, Richards moved from Pawsey's bungalow into his command-post trench. With him went Borrowman, still walking painfully, his small staff and his West Yorkshire orderly, Private Wilson. He tested the telephone lines laid to all sector commanders and found them in order, but he was worried at the continual nonarrival of a charging engine for his wireless set, which he knew could not last long.

Anxious to take some offensive action on the southern sector, he sent out two platoons of British soldiers under Norman Giles at dusk, accompanied by Maclachlan of the Burma Regiment, with orders to occupy the high ground above the road on the Aradura Spur and to find and harass the enemy. This little mission Giles accomplished with mixed results. In the bright moonlight he waited expectantly for signs of the enemy but found none until the time came for him to return. He then found that during the night he had become surrounded. His platoons attacked forward, and fought their way through at daybreak.

This small success was, however, heavily outbalanced by less creditable events.

At about midnight the patrol of the State battalion that Richards had sent out to set an ambush a mile south of Transport Ridge were encountered by the enemy. They broke in disorder and fled through the Gurkha road-block behind them.

This in turn led to one of those senseless fusillades that are often the mark of raw troops at the approach of their first battle. It started on the lower slopes of Transport Ridge. Hearing shots in the distance and seeing Elwell's platoon digging in the bright moonlight, some troops behind him 'fairly blasted' Transport Ridge with automatic fire, causing the Assam to dive for their trenches. Very soon wild and purposeless firing was going on everywhere with tracer from bren guns scoring the night sky with coloured streaks.

One small incident out of many similar ones will serve to illustrate the temper of events. Landor, the sapper, seeing a sepoy firing aimlessly up at the stars, asked him, 'What are you shooting at?'

The soldier replied: 'I don't know, sahib, but I'm shooting.'

This ebullition was not, as commonly reported, merely a display of 'jitters'. The sepoy's reply to Landor, as many survivors testify, summed up exactly the instincts of men who, throughout the operations to come, were willing enough to fight, but did not know how.

None the less, the events of that night were a bad beginning and worse was to follow. Richards now knew that the Japanese were in possession of the Aradura Spur, which he always expected,[31] but when the morning mist cleared away on the 5th, it was found that the composite company of Indian troops posted on the western end of Transport Ridge had gone, abandoning their arms.

141

The discovery was made by Elwell, when he sent out contact patrols, and his experience on this occasion is illuminating. The Japanese had closed up to the lower slopes of Transport Ridge, which was now under the fire of their mortars, as well as from the bren guns of his own friends behind him. By the desertion of the troops on their right and front the Assam transport platoon was thus left high and dry. Leaving it in charge of his little jemadar (whose normal business was to lead mules, not riflemen), Elwell made his way, under fire from friend and foe alike, to the foot of Jail Hill, where he asked Lowe for orders. Lowe gave him a reinforcement of a platoon of the State battalion, which had just arrived, under a good subedar whom Elwell knew.

Elwell led the platoon across the main road and up on to the lower slopes of Transport Ridge, picking his way through the scrub and the lantana bushes. Half-way back to his position three mortar bombs burst in quick succession near by and at the same time a bren gun from his own friends on the Ridge opened up again. With the exception of the subedar and a naik, the whole platoon 'vanished as if by magic'.

Telling the subedar to rally his men and bring them on, Elwell went ahead by himself, while the State battalion bren gun was still raking the bushes and scattering their leaves. He climbed up the last slope and reached his defence position, which lay on either side of the ridge, some on the forward slope in view of the enemy.

In the bright morning sunlight he darted from bunker to bunker and from trench to trench under fire that grew heavier every minute. There was not a soul to be seen. He called out and no voice answered. The little jemadar, he learned afterwards, believing from his long absence that Elwell must have been killed, had withdrawn the platoon to Jail Hill.

Fixing his bayonet, slinging a bandolier of ammunition over each shoulder and holding a grenade in either hand, Elwell dropped down the slope behind him, spattered with pebbles from mortar bursts and pelted by small arms fire. He made for the shallow gulley where he had left the State battalion platoon. They were gone, too. Here the bren gun from the Garrison picked him up again. He dived down under a lantana bush, panting and exhausted.

As he lay recovering his breath, there was a stealthy movement below him. Someone kicked a tin can. He saw a bush move. He slid forward the safety-catch of his rifle. He was about to fire when the branches of the lantana parted and there, behind a pistol pointed towards him, was the rubicund face of John Corlett, sent by Lowe to find him.

They exchanged jests and together crawled back to Jail Hill.

The eastern end of Transport Ridge still held, though its right flank was in the air. Here were posted good troops in the composite company of Gurkhas commanded by Douglas Frew and a platoon of the Assam Regiment under the tall Peter Steyn. These troops stood firm under the fire that was sprinkling the ridge. Enemy pressure mounted during the day, the mortar fire increased and a series of attacks was launched by the Japanese. They now had possession not only of Aradura Spur but also of Workshop Ridge, the feature that Richards had reluctantly abandoned; and on this ridge they had mounted their infantry guns, which blasted Transport Ridge under open sights. The attacks were resolutely held, with the aid of the Assam mortars under Corlett, until he was accurately ranged by the enemy guns and obliged to move. Heavy casualties were suffered and inflicted.

With no artillery support, and with their right flank exposed, Frew and Steyn were in no shape, however, to withstand an attack by night, nor to prevent infiltration. Richards accordingly gave them orders to withdraw, which they did after nightfall with bitter feelings.

Transport Ridge was lost.

The sequel to the flight of the mixed Indian company from the ridge had been witnessed very early that morning by Barratt, with his own mixed company on Kuki Piquet, and by the Indian subaltern believed to have been Kuriyan, whose platoon was just in front of him on Supply Hill. They saw coming towards them a mass exodus and feared that their own men would become infected. Accordingly, ordering their companies to keep to their trenches, the two young officers walked forward and, with drawn and levelled revolvers, halted and turned away the rabble.

8: FAS ET GLORIA

HELP, HOWEVER, had now providentially arrived.

On April 2nd Stopford's 33rd Corps headquarters had begun to operate and Slim had given him his tasks. Though Stopford did not yet know full details of the enemy's dispositions, the prospect with which he was in fact faced was that Sato's division was advancing with two brigades towards Kohima — the 58th Brigade from the south along the axis of the Imphal road under the celebrated Miyazaki and the 138th from the south-east through the Somra Hills. Both brigades were moving in mixed battalion groups by different routes, converging on Kohima: thus illustrating Napoleon's maxim 'divide to march, unite to fight'.

Sato himself moved with 138th Brigade by the Jessami route. His third brigade — 124th — was in the rear in reserve. His task was to capture Kohima, hold the great mountain barrier through which Kohima was the principal pass and be prepared to send a brigade south to assist the other divisions in the assault on Imphal if need arose. He was not authorized to descend into the Assam plain, but his operations would involve cutting the road leading down into it from Kohima.

Stopford naturally expected, however, that Sato's intention was to invade the Brahmaputra valley and the primary task that Slim had given him was to prevent such a disaster. He was none the less very sensitive about Kohima, the loss of which would itself open the door for a descent on Dimapur, and he took the earliest opportunity to send help to the meagre garrison.

On the 4th the leading brigade of 2nd British Division began to concentrate near Dimapur and that evening Rankin suggested to Stopford that one battalion of 161st Brigade might now be sent up to Richards's assistance. Stopford decided boldly to send the whole brigade.

'Proven Warriors'

Accordingly at dawn on the 5th, just as the Japanese 58th Brigade was beginning to worry Transport Ridge, a battalion group of Warren's brigade set out once again from the sultry plain to climb the now silent and deserted mountain road to Kohima. It was in motor transport and consisted of:

> 4th Battalion Royal West Kent Regiment (Lieut-Colonel 'John' Laverty).
> 20th Mountain Battery, Indian Artillery (Major R. de C. Yeo).
> A platoon of 2nd Indian Sappers and Miners (Lieutenant John Wright).
> A platoon of 75th Indian Field Ambulance under Lieutenant Aiappa to assist the medical officer of the RWK (Captain Alec Wattison).[32]

Warren himself, with his brigade headquarters and a battalion group of 4/7th Rajput, followed a few hours later.

Before we proceed further, we must take a closer look at the men of Laverty's column, who were to provide the garrison's doughty mainstay, though by no means its only prop, during the long trial ahead.

The Queen's Own Royal West Kent Regiment, wearing the county emblem of the white horse rampant, was the 50th Regiment of Foot. Its 4th Battalion were Territorials who had already seen much service during the war in very diverse and far-flung fields. They had fought in the Battle of France in

146

1940, in the Desert at Alam Haifa and El Alamein and in the jungle in Arakan. Everywhere they had done creditable service, but Kohima was to set the crown on their laurels. Their Kentish element had been somewhat diluted in the passage of the years, particularly by drafts from South Wales and Durham, but they had remained essentially Territorial and essentially Kentish.

The battalion came into Kohima, according to the statistical records of 33rd Corps, with a strength of only 18 officers and 426 men, since they had received heavy casualties in Arakan and since certain of their elements, such as their vehicles, mules and administrative elements, had not yet arrived from Arakan or had been left at Dimapur. But they were the one and only coherent, organic and fully integrated infantry unit at Kohima, the only complete fighting machine with all its essential components, including excellent signal communications, and with its structure inviolate. Their spirit was high and their performance was to be, in Richards's word, 'magnificent'. They were very fit and they had just given the Japanese a licking in Arakan. In the words of Donald Elwell, of the Assam Regiment, they were 'proven warriors'.

In the kind of 'soldiers' battle' now to be fought Laverty was particularly fortunate to have under his command a group of company commanders who, all observers agreed, were 'outstanding'. Shaw the stockjobber, Winstanley the medical student, Kenyon the lawyer, Easten the young City clerk and Harry Smith the schoolmaster, Territorials all, were fine and natural leaders. They in turn were supported by some excellent junior officers and by many staunch NCOs, such as Company Sergeant-Major Haines, Sergeants King, Tacon and Brooks, the Welsh Sergeant Williams and many more.

The CO of this battalion, we have briefly noted, was Lieut-Colonel Laverty, known to his friends in the brigade as 'Dan'. A Regular Service officer, he was not himself a Royal West Kent, but had come from the Essex Regiment. A thoroughly competent professional soldier, he was concerned that his battalion should also be professionally efficient. He had taken it over at a difficult time a few months before and had quickly moulded it into a good fighting machine which had passed a severe test in Arakan and had gained confidence in itself and in him. In person, Laverty was of soldierly presence, somewhat slight and wiry of figure. He had won the Military Cross ten years before when serving on the British Military Mission to the Iraq army.

Unfortunately, the relationship between Richards and Laverty was not at all clear. Though Richards was, of course, the senior in rank, Laverty considered himself to be under the command of his own brigadier rather than of Richards, whereas Richards had received no orders in modification of Rankin's very specific Operation Instruction and naturally considered himself in command of the Kohima Garrison until the arrival of a more senior officer. Laverty, of course, commanded only his own battalion group (which he did extremely well) and had no jurisdiction over other units, who took their orders from no one but Richards. As a result a certain strain unfortunately crept into the relations of some of the senior officers but did not spread further.

There is no need for this narrative of a very gallant action to be dimmed by emphasizing this difference, but its existence has to be recorded, not only as an historical fact, but also because it ennobles all the more the valour of the junior ranks in the companies and platoons of more units than one. For, as the siege progressed, it developed more and more into a soldiers' battle, with both Richards and Laverty exercising less and less personal influence on the fierce local fighting, in which the commanders of companies, platoons and even sections largely decided the course of events. In the words of Captain Tom Coath, who was to command one of the companies in one of the very toughest sectors, 'the siege was primarily a privates' battle and our success was due mainly to the very high morale and steadiness of the NCOs and men'.

Laverty's second-in-command, also a regular officer originally from the Essex Regiment, was the rotund and genial Major Peter Franklin who, without respect to unit, was on good terms with all and was to render many valuable services of those sorts which are in the special realm of a second-in-command. He admirably complemented the qualities of his CO.

With Laverty and under his tactical command came a subunit of the first importance, joint holders with the infantry and the doctors of the honours of Kohima. This was Yeo's battery of artillery, one of the batteries of 24th Mountain Regiment. It was a four-gun battery[33] of 3.7-inch howitzers. These 'screw-guns' were normally taken to pieces and mule-borne, but on this occasion were motor-transported, the mules not having yet arrived from Arakan. They were exceptionally fine and handy little guns to serve, of remarkable accuracy but of short range. They were manned by Sikhs and Punjabi-Mussulmans. Yeo brought in with him two other officers in Captain Peter Kendall and Lieutenant Dickenson. By an apt and happy coincidence, the Royal Artillery British officers shared with the Royal West Kents the same proud regimental motto, *Quo fas et gloria ducunt.*[34]

The guns of Yeo's own battery, as will shortly be related, were in fact themselves to prove of no value, but the presence of Yeo himself and his brother officers enabled the garrison, though not immediately, to have the support, through the battery's wireless, of the other three batteries of 24th Mountain Regiment under Humphry Hill — 2nd, 11th and 12th Batteries — from positions outside the perimeter.

Deployment under Fire

Laverty's column reached Kohima Ridge only in the nick of time. They had not expected to be put to any severe trial. The apparent remoteness of the enemy in any strength, the erroneous rumours that they had heard, the quiet skies undisturbed by aircraft and perhaps the romantic beauty of the countryside seemed to foretell a simple holding operation against light enemy forces as the brigade vanguard, for it was Warren's intention to reoccupy, with his whole brigade, the positions around Naga Village and the Treasury, that he had previously chosen.

They were very soon disabused. D Company, commanded by Captain Donald Easten,[35] was in the van when, as they passed Hospital Spur late in the afternoon, they came under small arms fire. In accordance with orders, they at once dismounted from the vehicles and took up fire positions. The rest of the battalion followed, however, without immediate incident, while Jail Hill and Transport Ridge were under attack.

The first to deploy, after dismounting a little short of the Traffic Control Post, was Major Tom Kenyon's A Company. Richards had a guide waiting for them and they were directed at once on the Garrison Hill, where they displaced the headquarters company of the State battalion. It was about 5 o'clock, with the evening sunlight golden in the tree-tops.

Kenyon found a good field of fire to the south, a protected east flank and ample water in tarpaulins (which, however, was exhausted too soon, either by over-use or by enemy fire). He also found plenty of trenches, many well sited, but some were merely large, round holes dug by the Nagas and he had to dig afresh. Providentially he ordered his second-in-command, Captain John Steddy, to bring up the company cookhouse, where, regardless of the mortar bombs and shells, his cooks kept open house, as best they could, to all and sundry for the rest of the siege.

On the heels of A Company, Laverty arrived with his battalion headquarters. Richards went down to meet him at the roadside and had guides waiting for his remaining companies. Winstanley went to Kuki Piquet with B Company, Shaw to Detail Hill with C, Easten with D in battalion reserve and Harry Smith with Headquarters Company in the locality of Richards's command post. Captain Stephen Laing, Landor's adjutant, and his British RE sergeants, having no sapper task, armed themselves with rifles and served with the Royal West Kents throughout as privates. The V Force and most of the other oddments previously on Kuki Piquet and Detail Hill appear, except for Barratt's composite company, to have remained there, but nothing more is heard of them.

The later companies came under fire from the moment of their arrival, for the lorries of these companies halted nose-to-tail on the road on the south-eastern side of the Bungalow Sector. Here they were in view of the Japanese 4-gun battery on Workshop Ridge, which at once opened on them and set several lorries on fire. Most of the men lost their kits and their blankets, a loss they were to feel keenly in the cold, drenching night mists.

The garrison watched their arrival with relief, but Rawlley and three other officers, incautiously standing up on top of

Supply Hill to do so, paid the penalty when a shell burst a few yards away and wounded all but Rawlley.

In a gallant attempt to cover the deployment of the Royal West Kents as they dismounted, the lone 25-pounder near Pawsey's Bungalow under Captain John Browning, opened fire on the enemy battery. It was an unequal contest. After firing a round or two the 25-pounder was knocked out and Browning was wounded in the head; when being evacuated later he was killed by a burst of machine-gun bullets in the stomach.

Despite this hot reception, Laverty's companies deployed in good order over ground that was being swept by fire. A machine-gun from Naga Village was playing on the sector of the Assam Regiment and fired some small vehicles of B Company trying to get through on the Ladies' Mile. Sharp fighting continued on Transport Ridge and at the foot of Jail Hill. The burning petrol and the flames of bashas fired by the Japanese shells told of a battle already in full swing. The battalion quickly realized, as Harry Smith recorded later, that 'we had come to a hotter spot than we had been led to believe', but they counted on having only to hold their ground until Warren and the bulk of his brigade came up next morning.

Laverty himself set up his battalion command post a trifle below the crest of Garrison hill on its northern side, a little higher up the hill than Richards's. It was a trench about 9 ft long with a niche at one end for the wireless set to 161st Brigade and another at the opposite end for the wireless to his companies. Telephone lines to each company and to Richards's Garrison command post were run out. Throughout the siege the battalion's signals, both wireless and line, were maintained remarkably well and Laverty was nearly always well informed of what was going on in his own sectors. Though the lines were frequently cut, the battalion signallers never hesitated to go out over the shell-torn hills to repair them.

In his command post Laverty was normally accompanied by his tall, auburn-haired adjutant, Captain Douglas Short, his Intelligence Officer, Lieutenant Brian Dungay, and his signals officer, Captain John Topham, who was wounded during the siege and then mortally wounded when being evacuated. Franklin was frequently there also.

Yeo, having first reported to Richards and discussed artillery tasks, set up his main Observation Post close alongside Laverty, within easy speaking range. For the artillery support of other units in the garrison, Yeo had a telephone link direct to Garrison Headquarters, from which Richards was able to call for, and unfailingly to receive, immediate and highly effective fire.

Yeo's guns received an even hotter reception than the infantry. They were taken to pieces, carried up and brought into action in the Bungalow sector — the Right Section just behind Keene's bungalow and the Left Section close to Pawsey's. No sooner had the detachments begun to dig in than, being in direct view of the same Japanese battery on Workshop Ridge, they drew fire. Richards was standing talking to Yeo about defensive-fire tasks about thirty yards from his guns when the shelling began. Both happened to be looking forward towards Workshop Ridge and saw the first flash. Yeo at once ran towards his guns with the intention of engaging the enemy, while Richards moved away to cover. It very soon became clear that the Bungalow Sector was as much too hot for Yeo's battery as it had been for the lone 25-pounder. They fired no more.

Chinks in the Armour

153

Soon after his arrival Laverty visited the Garrison Command Post in Richards's absence and suggested to Borrowman that the Treasury (where he himself had been posted during the brief stay of Warren's brigade) ought to be occupied. Its danger to the garrison, and to the Bungalow Sector in particular, which it overlooked, was obvious, but Borrowman demurred.

The War Diary of the Royal West Kents states, quite erroneously, that 'the Garrison Commander believed some of his troops were still occupying the Treasury'. Richards had intentionally rejected the Treasury, as it was 'out on a limb' and could not be supported and he did not have the troops to hold it. It formed a natural part of a larger scheme of defence, as it had done for Warren's brigade, but it had no place in the meagre scale of Richards's resources. However, on his return to his command post, while dusk was flooding in, having spoken to Laverty on the telephone, he agreed to send out a company, but was at fault in doing so.

It was by now almost dark and Richards sent out a company of the State battalion. Some time later rifle fire was heard from the direction of the Treasury and shortly afterwards most of the company came back, reporting to Richards that they had met strong resistance, but that an officer and a small party were still out there. A report made to Pawsey after the battle by a Naga schoolmaster stated that the Japanese had 'crept stealthily into the village', where they had a brisk fight with the State troops, and that the Japanese had then 'crowded in great numbers like rats in a field'.

At dawn next morning (April 6th) a message arrived from the officer to say that he had occupied the Treasury but could not hold it if attacked. Richards promptly sent the company out once more. They were not seen again, however, until after the siege was over — at Dimapur.

There is no doubt but that some of the troops of lesser quality had been badly shaken by the sharp opening clashes. While the better troops were collected and steady, others, through lack of sufficient and suitable infantry officers, were in some confusion. The numerous oddments, such as the V Force detachments, who had drifted in at the last moment, had no cohesion and no stabilizing organization such as exists in a battalion. Many troops, moreover, had not even any arms. They were thus at a loose end and uneasy. Many slipped away and fled back to Dimapur before the Japanese closed the ring and were no loss to the garrison. They had been asked to do what they had not been recruited nor trained for.

The case of the State battalion was not quite the same, but they were not fully trained troops, with inexperienced officers. One or two of their patrols did well, but the harsh fact is that all four of the battalion's rifle companies were lost to the garrison and, from the posts to which Richards had assigned them outside the perimeter, withdrew not on Kohima but straight back to Dimapur. Only the headquarter company remained, with Hepworth as a liaison officer with little power. It was believed at the time that all these absentees must have been taken prisoner and their unfortunate native CO was very much distressed.

On the other hand, most of the so-called non-combatant Indians, so much maligned in other pages, stayed loyally where they were, even those who were unarmed, and many of them performed disagreeable and dangerous tasks under fire which would otherwise have had to be performed by the combatants. Many, moreover, were to be counted among the dead and the wounded.

In numbers, the loss of the State companies was approximately made good by the arrival of the Royal West

Kents. The men remaining in the garrison capable of bearing arms with any degree of effectiveness still amounted to not more than 1,500. Those to be reckoned as non-combatants amounted to another 1,000 or so. Some of the units or detachments shown in the official Order of Battle were in fact not there when operations began.

9: THE RING IS CLOSED

The Morning Scene

THOUGH THE SUN illuminated the mountain-tops on the early morning of April 6th, Kohima Ridge still stood in deep shadow as the chilled and sodden garrison stood-to in their trenches, peering into the drenching mist. No attack had come in the night, and a brooding silence lay over the misty hills till the cocks began to crow in deserted Naga Village. Richards, having sent the State company out to the Treasury again, went round most of the sectors. He climbed up Supply Hill and found that Rawlley had got his mixed Indian troops in good order and his tarpaulin water tank half-filled. He noted that the company commanders of the Royal West Kents in other features had their soldiers balanced, steady, well in hand and well turned out. It struck him how good the Territorial code of discipline could be under the right officers and fine NCOs. He had a long talk with Shaw on Detail Hill, found him cheerful and confident in spite of his very exposed position at the foot of Jail Hill. He saw the 3-inch mortars deployed under the staunch Sergeant King. He regretted the loss of Giles, who had been wounded the day before.

As the sun rose in its strength the condensing mist fell from the trees like rain. Already the pines and lantanas at the southern end of the ridge had begun to lose their leaves under the shattering of shell and bomb. Broken branches lay on the ground. The alders, when hit by a projectile, split down the middle. The black smoke of the burning petrol still curled round Jail Hill and the charred remains of some burnt-out bashas stood grey on the lost Transport Hill.

As soon as Transport Ridge was lost. Jail Hill, roughly conical in outline, commanding and dominant in situation and stature, became closely threatened. It was being manned by about eighty men of the Assam Regiment who had not been at Jessami, under Major Reginald Lowe, and by some Burmese troops and various oddments. Lowe had his command post in the jail at the foot of the hill, where also Captain Richard Glover had set up a Regimental Aid Post. To this mixed force were now added elements of those who had withdrawn from Transport Ridge. This assortment of troops inevitably led to a state of disarray without any overall control and without cohesion. Furthermore, there was no support and little or no barbed wire.

In the dripping morning mist of the 6th, vision was limited to about thirty yards as the troops stood-to. The heavy silence was suddenly shattered by the crash of mortar bombs and the crack of shells from the Japanese infantry guns. One of several British officers killed was Noel Lunn, with whom Elwell had had his heart-searching talk the day before, and whom Richards had appointed to command one of the Burmese companies. The bombardment went on for some twenty minutes, and when it subsided was succeeded by the blasts of bugles and the high-pitched yelling and jabberings of the Japanese as they mustered for assault at the southern footing of the hill. Then out of the mist appeared an officer, brandishing a sword, at the head of a small assault force, shouting, discharging grenades and firing from the hip. The garrison met the attack quite firmly, however, with small arms only, and brought it to a halt as suddenly as it had begun. It had been only a probing attack.

The Japanese kept up a little desultory fire on the hill as the sun rose higher, quenching the mist and bathing the Ridge in golden warmth. Parties of Indian stragglers continued to drift in, taking shelter near the jail. They were soon spotted by the enemy and suffered multiple casualties from a cascade of mortar bombs. Too many troops were milling about purposelessly instead of manning defences.

At midday, after a sharp mortaring and shelling, the Japanese attacked again, in great strength. Superior in numbers, fire power and cohesion they secured a foothold, which they rapidly exploited. Elwell's Assam platoon on the crown of the hill and perhaps some other troops stood fast, but others withdrew in disorder, many making use of the vehicles parked near by, for the road was still in use. Lieutenant P. A. L. Brown, of the Assam, that moment returned to his battalion from a course, was preparing to take up a platoon to join Elwell when he was mortally wounded in the stomach.

Most of the hill was now in enemy hands and some mortar fire was plunging down at the foot of the reverse side as troops withdrew. Several small parties, however, were still holding their ground at or near the top of the hill, when, as Elwell records in his contemporary manuscript, they appear to have received an order, but certainly not a warranted one, to withdraw. They did so in reasonably good order, under fire that increased their casualties. Elwell himself was severely blasted by a close bomb-burst, which partially blinded him and rendered him non-effective for the rest of the battle.

Many of the Burmese troops absconded to the safety of Dimapur while they still had the chance. What was left of them Richards ordered to a position on the north-west flank of Garrison Hill,[36] and he also withdrew and disarmed all troops, who, by their indiscriminate firing, had shown themselves unfit

159

to possess arms. The various composite companies formed from the Reinforcement Camp ceased to be effective fighting forces once they had been dislodged from their allotted positions, as it proved impossible to re-form them, though some individually continued to do good service. Various oddments of troops collected near Richards's headquarters, calling themselves jocularly the 'Kohima Rifles'. Garrison Hill was beginning to get crowded and the area of the Box had been reduced to one of about 900 yards long by some 400 yards wide. The tempo of the battle was rising rapidly.

The losses of Jail Hill and Transport Ridge had serious effects. Jail Hill immediately dominated and overshadowed Shaw's company of the Royal West Kents on the small Detail Hill at very close range. The main road between the two features was not thirty yards away from Shaw's forward sections. Laverty, having been led to believe that the Japanese were not in strength and that a small British force was still holding out on the summit of Jail Hill, ordered D Company, which was his battalion reserve, under the soldierly figure of Donald Easten, to counter-attack.

The attack was put in quickly, but Easten, though he went himself, used only a platoon and no artillery support was yet available. He met far more opposition than had been expected. He got to within thirty yards of the top, but found the Japanese firmly installed there and could make no progress against their machine-guns. He reported by air to Laverty, who, having no troops to spare to press the attack and none to hold the feature if recaptured, called off the operation and posted D Company at the foot of Supply Hill, where they would be well placed to support C.

The Japanese quickly made good use of Jail Hill, developing it into a Gibraltar-like fortress, honeycombed with tunnelled galleries that were impervious to shellfire and aircraft bombs, and mounted on it their infantry guns, which soon began peppering Detail and Supply Hills at a few hundred yards range.

After its fall, Borrowman drafted a signal to Rankin's headquarters, saying that 'unless more than the balance of one brigade were sent it would not be enough to restore the situation'. It seems that, Richards's wireless being now useless, this signal was apparently never sent. But Borrowman's assessment was entirely right, for in the ensuing five weeks of fighting it took not only 'more than the balance of one brigade' but in fact more than a complete division to restore the situation.

Detail Hill now became the hot-spot. Shaw, with Kendall as his artillery FOO, made ready to receive an attack and Yeo came down to make a defensive fire plan. The Japanese began a fresh outburst of mortaring and Shaw dropped into a trench. A bomb burst in the trees above him and shattered his thigh. He was removed to a basha by Corporal Day, his stretcher-bearer NCO, and thus Laverty lost one of his best company commanders right at the start. Command of C Company passed to Captain P. E. Watts (who had won the Military Cross in the Desert). In his front-line trenches at the base of the little hill, his sections, led by particularly stout-hearted NCOs, peered down to the road below and the bigger hill beyond and braced themselves for the clash that they knew must soon come.

Warren Moves Up

On the previous night Warren had arrived at Milestone 42 on the Dimapur road. In addition to his headquarters, he had with him his supporting gunner (Lieut-Colonel Humphry Hill, commanding 24th Mountain Regiment), 2nd Mountain Battery of that regiment under Major Peter Hartley, 4/7th Rajput under the impressive and immaculate figure of Lieut-Colonel Jack Cargill, a company of 75th Indian Field Ambulance under Captain N. K. Mitra, and the remarkable CO of that unit, Lieut-Colonel John Young. Hill at once deployed Hartley's battery.

Warren spent the night in a roadside hut. On the morning of the 6th, as the mountain mist cleared, he could clearly see the burst of high explosive on Kohima Ridge, less than two and a half miles away across country, and his own headquarters also came under shellfire. At 9 o'clock, Franklin, second-in-command of the Royal West Kents, arrived and his report of the situation made it clear to Warren that there was little chance of his getting forward to reoccupy his former positions as he had intended, and to Humphry Hill it became clearer still that the guns would be of no use if he did, for there was nowhere left for their deployment. To Hill, therefore, it was a 'godsend' that the whole brigade could not get forward.

Having first weighed and rejected the notion of getting in behind the enemy by a wide 'hook' across the hills, Warren resigned himself to making the best use of what he had got for the time being. He was in 'good form' and not outwardly disturbed by the difficult situation. Hill suggested that the brigade position should be hinged to a suitable location from which his guns could give support to Kohima and he set off on foot to reconnoitre accordingly. Two days later, when he had been cut off from Kohima and knew that he was about to be cut off from Dimapur also, Warren moved to higher ground, with a superb mountain panorama spread out before him, about half a mile north-east of the village of Jotsoma, and Hill moved Hartley's battery and subsequently 11th and 12th

Batteries into an 'ideal gun position',[37] from which they were to fire night and day for the next six weeks. This position was 3,500 yards from Garrison Hill, so that all the defensive fire that was to be poured down in support of the garrison ahead was by good fortune at the optimum range for the little 3.7 mountain howitzers. With Yeo's battery now off the board, however, he had only twelve guns at his disposal — half the number that an infantry brigade normally had for its support from a field regiment.

When very shortly 1/1st Punjab came up under Neil Brodie (to be succeeded a week later by Harry Grimshaw) and completed his brigade, Warren formed what became known as the Jotsoma Box. It was not a good tactical position, being overlooked by higher ground, but fundamentally it was designed for the protection of Hill's guns, which Warren saw as the most valuable form of support he could provide for Kohima.

In the garrison, the halt of Warren's brigade created an uncertain situation on the 6th. There was nothing they could do but sit tight. They could sense the enemy moving all round them and closing in. The trees obscured vision in many directions, but the enemy, who took no pains to conceal his movements, believing that the fulfilment of an easy conquest was at hand, could frequently be seen. On that day two Japanese battalions marched into the Naga Village.[38] Sato himself arrived very shortly and established his command post on Point 5120 in the Village. The shelling and mortaring of the Ridge increased during the day but did not yet become serious. The Bungalow Sector was given a second buffeting; casualties were sustained by the Indian gunners and by the composite British company from the Reinforcement Camp manning it and the medical post there soon had its hands full.

On the other hand, the garrison itself received a small but valuable reinforcement this day. The Japanese had not yet quite closed the ring and a company of the Rajputs, commanded by the gallant Captain Mitchell, were just able to make their way in after an exchange of shots. They were posted at first in reserve behind Garrison Hill, but it was not to be long before they had their full share of very tough fighting. With them came another valuable little reinforcement in an OP party from 2nd Mountain Battery, led by Lieutenant J. S. Punia, a gallant young Sikh, whose battery had come into action in the Jotsoma position and whose four guns were for a day or so to be the only artillery support. He at once began shooting his battery from an OP on Garrison Hill, his main targets being Jail Hill, the Treasury and Naga Village.

The 'Tactical Doctor'

An even more important reinforcement, finally completing the muster roll of the Garrison, was the person of Lieut-Colonel John Young, CO of 75th Indian Field Ambulance. When Franklin had reported in to Warren at Milestone 42 early that morning he had said that the medical situation could become serious if the rest of the brigade could not move up. The exposed hospital buildings were under fire and there had already been large casualties, which ought to be evacuated. Even before the arrival of the Royal West Kents seventy-eight officers and men had been killed and well over 100 wounded. Young accordingly, with Warren's permission, went up himself with a small escort of Rajputs, arriving at Kohima at 2.30 PM of the 6th.[39]

Young was a remarkable character. As a surgeon, to quote a later medical Director-General,[40] he was 'neat, quick and daring'; but he was as well known for his military knowledge as for his medical. He was known as the 'tactical doctor' and indeed later became a General Staff Officer, abandoning medicine. In person, he was very fair, slight and wiry of figure, but an active athlete and, as events were to show, of extraordinary stamina and resilience. He had a firm and incisive manner and demonstrated the soldier in action as well as the doctor. He was quite fearless and his bearing, his example, and his devoted service made him an inspiration to everyone. Indeed, he was perhaps the most remarkable man in that gallant company.

When he arrived on the Ridge, the battle was in full swing. Jail Hill had just been lost. The buildings of 53rd Hospital, where there were still a few patients, were on fire and the mortar bombs were crumping in Bungalow Sector. Young reported first to Richards, saw Laverty and made a reconnaissance of the whole Ridge. He brought information from Warren that a relief was now not likely for 'four or five days' and on that account he recommended to Richards that all the dispersed medical detachments should be concentrated to form a Combined Advanced Dressing Station, except for a few Regimental Aid Posts that would remain with the troops on the main features. He would then be able to hold and treat casualties for a few days and carry out emergency operations.

In recording these facts, Young's War Diary, when read with others, makes it obvious that the ill-natured criticisms of the medical arrangements before his arrival made by other commentators, and clearly directed against Richards, are without substance and based on ignorance of the facts. The War Diary of 75th Indian Field Ambulance is a document to which it is exceedingly difficult to get access.

Richards gave his approval and Young set about his task with great energy and expedition. He sited his ADS among the trees on Garrison Hill and not far from the top, which at that time seemed to be the safest area. This was near Laverty's command post and close to a Royal West Kent cookhouse. By six o'clock, when the lengthening mountain shadows had flooded over the valleys, the stretcher-bearers, carrying under fire, had brought in seventy-eight cases and Glover, Abdul Majid and Young himself had begun operating. At this moment there came unexpectedly to their aid a company of those 'non-combatants' who were afterwards to be so basely disparaged.

One of the extempore companies that Richards had withdrawn and disarmed after the loss of Jail Hill had been the mixed Indian company on Kuki Piquet under James Barratt, who was an officer of 1/17th Dogras and belonged to the same division as the West Kents. His company, made up largely of drivers and clerks from the RIASG, had been one of the offenders in the indiscriminate shooting on the first day. Like others, they had not been 'jittery' and, in fact, when Barratt had dashed round his trenches to subdue them, a platoon pointed with pride to three dead bodies on the main road below. To his horror, Barratt saw that they were a British sergeant and two Gurkhas. He therefore was not sorry when Richards made his decision, for such men were clearly more dangerous to their friends than to their foes.

Richards ordered him and his company away to an apparently innocuous area on the western slope of Garrison Hill. Barratt at once set his men to work with pick and shovel and provisioned them for a long stay with tinned foods from the Field Supply Depot. He had at first to overcome resistance to discipline, but, after he had clouted a towering Pa than on the jaw for his mutinous bearing (breaking a bone in his hand in the process), he had no more trouble and his mixed bag of troops soon began to do sterling service. Barratt, his injured

166

hand in a sling for the rest of the siege, was joined by Lieutenant Wilson-Hoole, whose mixed company on Supply Hill had also been disarmed.

Now the site selected by Young for his ADS was a little above Barratt's new trenches. Seeing the wounded collected and lying on stretchers in the open, Barratt walked up the hill to Young and offered to dig trenches for them. At first light on the morning of the 7th Young visited Richards and asked if Barratt's company could be allotted to him. Richards gladly agreed and thus began the construction of this astonishing 'hospital'. Digging was very hard. The ground was full of tough roots and below them, often only two feet below, was rock. Many of the trenches that Barratt's men dug were thus very shallow and little more than the width of a stretcher. Other excavations were wide bays to accommodate a number of men. This trench digging went on continuously throughout the battle, as the numbers of wounded hourly increased and the ADS expanded farther and farther down the hillside; some of Barratt's men were very soon to be lying in the trenches that they had dug.

In addition, Barratt dug out two pits, each about 6 ft deep, to serve as operating and dressing theatres, one with a solid enough timber roof, the other covered by nothing but a tarpaulin, and each dimly lit by hurricane lamps. It was in these crude pits that the British and Indian doctors and their orderlies carried out all the terrible surgery that had to be done day and night for almost a fortnight.

No part of the Ridge, however, was completely safe and, in spite of the precautions, it was not long before many of the wounded were being hit again where they lay as the mortar bombs and shells plunged among them. In Young's War Diary fifty-six are recorded as having been so killed. Many others died from their wounds. When they died or were killed they had to be buried as quickly as possible. This service Barratt also undertook. Towards the bottom of the hill he found an area of reasonably soft soil and this he selected as the burial ground. Each night his Indians carried down the dead and interred them in a long, continuous trench, friend and foe together (for there were several enemy dead in the place), thanking Providence that the War Graves Commission would in due course of time come along to reduce to decency what had to be done in indecent haste. The burial ground was frequently under fire, often very severe mortar fire, but the behaviour of the 'non-combatants' was exemplary. Barratt himself was with them every night and, his own ears on the alert, soon taught them how to respond instantly to his commands for evasive action.

These were not the only services that Barratt's company rendered with no little devotion and self-denial, as will shortly be recorded. Barratt made sure that they were self-dependent and made no calls on anyone. They kept their nerve and behaved extremely well under constant fire and the most testing conditions. 'They did,' said Barratt afterwards, 'as well as anyone could have done.'

As soon as Barratt had begun work on the protective trenches on the 7th, Young began strengthening his medical service, building it up into something like a complete outdoor hospital, crude enough to be sure, dangerous rather than comfortable, but a hospital still and so called by the troops. He detailed surgical teams and organized his makeshift unit, with whom Barratt's company became integrated, into a nursing group, a stretcher-bearing group and an entrenching group. He was short of supplies and tools, however, and had no blood plasma for transfusions. Himself apparently impervious to fatigue, he drove his team hard day and night, but it was mainly this forceful authority and personal example and the services rendered by Barratt's company that caused what might have degenerated into a nightmare scene of blood, despair and horror to become instead a centre, not indeed of peace and orderliness, but at least of hope and heroism. For, as Young said to his doctors, the ADS had a morale value to the whole garrison scarcely less important than its primary task of saving human life and he records in his unit War Diary that the shelter of the trenches, slight though it was, at once raised the spirits of the wounded themselves. It was surely one of the most remarkable dressing-stations ever seen on any battlefield in history. The few doctors, three of whom were to be killed and two wounded while operating or dressing, and their no less devoted medical orderlies, worked without cessation on the stream of wounded who came into them to the number of nearly 500 and, in the words of the senior medical officer of 33rd Corps, carried out an 'immense amount of heroic surgery under shocking conditions'.

Not least poignant of the few records of the siege is the small pocket diary kept by Captain Glover, who each day, sometimes after having been at the opera ting-table all night, jotted down his thoughts in a few hurried words. In this he speaks of 'shocking wounds', of 'terrible casualties', of 'awful nights', of the stink of putrid flesh, of the seeming futility of saving a life that was soon to be extinguished at the crash of the next shell.

In battle the usual companion of the doctor is the chaplain and in the Rev. Roy Randolph, chaplain of the Royal West Kents, was to be seen another of the remarkable figures of Kohima. He took as his special care the walking wounded who were assembled in some covered trenches on the south side of Garrison Hill, near Kuki Piquet. Very tall and lean, with an ascetic face illuminated by a gentle smile, the scenes of blood and death around him were an agony to his spirit to be overcome only by his spiritual strength. He was not naturally fearless, but he subdued fear and forced himself into those situations where he knew his duty lay. His lanky figure, bending over the wounded or stumping among the trees to the men in the trenches, became a symbol of faith and compassion in the days of trial.

Water Supplies Cut

The Rajputs arrived at a time when a new crisis had developed. Though the loss of Jail Hill that morning was to have serious long-term results, of more immediate concern to the garrison was the previous day's loss of Transport Ridge; for across that feature passed Kohima's water pipeline from the reservoir at the foot of Aradura Spur. It was not until the 6th that the Japanese discovered the reservoir, when they promptly cut the supply. Flow from the comparatively high take-off on Supply Hill gradually ceased.

From Supply Hill the pipe dipped to a lower level and Landor, the sapper, caused a hole to be blown in the four-inch pipe. Water gushed out and was collected but in a few minutes the flow ceased. A trickle of water continued to come through to the steel cistern near the tennis court in the Bungalow Sector but the other tanks and tarpaulins that had been filled for emergency use on each sector became exhausted before long, or were holed by shellfire.

Richards accordingly (on the 7th) issued orders for controlling the drawing of water, rationing its issue to a mugful per man. Borrowman and Greenwood, Richards's efficient and courageous staff captain, provided a number of canvas water containers and a schedule of times was given for troops from each sector to draw supplies — a task of no little complexity when providing for the many small bodies and for the numerous unorganized non-combatants. Thereafter, under the supervision of Landor, Franklin or Greenwood, parties went to the cistern, an operation that became extremely hazardous when, two nights later, the Japanese overran part of the Bungalow Sector. Another source used by a few units was the small stream that ran in the valley to the west of the Ridge, but this required going well outside the perimeter and down the very steep and wooded slope.

Richards gave orders forbidding washing and shaving, so that officers and men soon became very dirty, shaggy and foul and, in the heat of the day, very thirsty. Some of the garrison, particularly Rawlley's men on Supply Hill, where all such things were at hand, were able to supplement the ration with tinned fruit and tomato juice. Private Wilson, Richards's orderly, with his friend Gunner Albert Appleby, on their own initiative, went frequently to and from the Supply Depot, despising the bombs and the bullets, to collect tinned fruit for the wounded, who were very soon in a deplorable condition.

A few days later someone remembered having seen some water running in a ditch between Pawsey's bungalow and 53rd Indian General Hospital. The garrison was by then closely invested, but Landor, at great risk, went out with a small party and, just below the sector manned by the Assam Rifles, found a weak spring issuing from the cliff formed where the road had been cut out of the hillside. He fixed a short length of piping and with this was able to fill a container. It was a hazardous source of supply, only usable at night and requiring men to scramble up and down the cliff with a rifle and a container. But the Japanese never discovered it and there were never lacking sufficient men to undertake the nerve-racking experience of drawing from it. A piquet from the Assam Rifles gave them protection. Fortunately the climate at this height was not hot enough to make thirst a very serious problem but the people to whom water was of paramount importance were the unfortunate wounded and the medical staff attending to them.

This service Barratt's Company at the dressing-station undertook to provide in addition to their other tasks. Barratt detailed a special platoon under a havildar and on the first night took them down to the water point himself. Thereafter, night after night, and all night, at great risk, the havildar silently led down his platoon and kept replenished a forty-gallon drum in the ADS. So that the wounded should have as much water as possible, Barratt allowed his own men none. To slake their thirst, he ordered them to puncture tins of peas and beetroot and drink the juice, the remainder of the tin being thrown away. Throughout the siege this company of men made no tea and had no hot food of any sort.

Detail Hill Attacked[41]

Soon after Young and the Rajputs had made their way in on the 6th, the Japanese blocked the road behind the garrison. Though the Ridge was not yet entirely surrounded, its investment was virtually complete.

That night the enemy, from his new vantage point on the dominating Jail Hill, launched a series of attacks on C Company of the Royal West Kents on Detail Hill, as Richards had expected. It was the beginning of a fierce and desperate battle, in which the battalion first showed the heroic mettle of which it was made.

Detail Hill was a small oval feature, running roughly north and south, about 160 yards long and 30 or 40 yards wide at its middle. Some of the trees had been cut down to make room for the numerous bamboo bashas, still full of ammunition, rations and stores, that occupied the ground. The feature was separated from Jail Hill, which rose high above it, by the main road to Imphal. At its northern end a minor service road ran through the gulley that separated it from Supply Hill.

The defences that had been provided before the arrival of the Royal West Kents consisted of a series of trenches and bunkers around the greater part of the oval perimeter and disposed in depth. There was a little dannert wire round at least part of the perimeter. At the southern end, facing Jail Hill and overlooking the main road at a distance of barely thirty yards, these defences were no more than twenty yards wide. Shaw, commanding C Company, had had most of the overhead cover removed as soon as he had arrived, to improve fields of fire and to prevent them from becoming mere refuges. The company, now commanded by Watts after the loss of Shaw, was occupying these trenches and a series of others on the west side of the feature, with company headquarters towards the southern end. The defences at the northern end were left manned by some troops of the original garrison, untrained in battle.

After the loss of Transport Ridge on the 5th there had been a continuous stream of Indian troops from Jail Hill across the road into Shaw's position. He had tried to hold them, but without avail. When Jail Hill fell at midday on the 6th, Watts knew that his turn would be next, but he faced the prospect with equanimity, with his platoons and sections, led by good young officers in Inglis and Phythian and exceptionally fine NCOs, steady, confident and well disposed. One of Yeo's artillery officers accompanied them as FOO.

On the night of the 6th/7th, with the moon still bright, the Japanese could be clearly seen assembling among the trees of

Jail Hill and moving down to the road preparatory to attacking. They did so without any attempt at concealment and advertised their intentions with all those rowdy demonstrations by which they thought to frighten their enemies — high-pitched yells, battle cries, singing and the blowing of bugles. They anticipated another easy success for the Emperor's invincible troops.

They were engaged as they filtered down Jail Hill by C Company's brens and their screams could be plainly heard as they fell dead or wounded. They were not deterred and fresh men came forward to take their places.

Judging the right moment, Watts called for mortar support and Sergeant King's bombs fell accurately on the road where the Japanese were forming up to attack. The bren guns joined in and the attack was broken up with heavy casualties. Other attacks followed, to be similarly repulsed. C Company held their positions confidently.

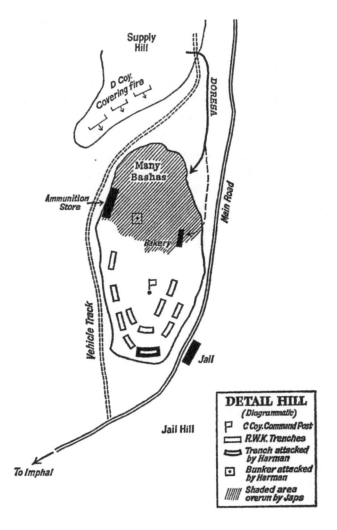

Supply Hill

D Coy. Covering Fire

DORESA

Main Road

Many Bashas

Ammunition Store

Bakery

Vehicle Track

P

Jail

Jail Hill

To Imphal

DETAIL HILL
(Diagrammatic)

P *C Coy. Command Post*

▭ *R.W.K. Trenches*

◣ *Trench attacked by Harman*

◉ *Bunker attacked by Harman*

▨ *Shaded area overrun by Japs*

Later in the night, however, finding frontal onslaught unprofitable, the enemy sent a company round by a left hook to come in from the westward, where the trees outside the perimeter were thick, the slope steep and an unseen approach facilitated.

They quickly seized the northern end of Detail Hill, where some of the original garrison troops had been posted, and barricaded themselves in the numerous bashas with bags of rice and flour. From these they began to snipe the Royal West Kents and were so close in some places that they could lob hand grenades into the trenches.

This was an exceedingly dangerous situation. C Company was cut off and threatened with a Japanese hammer-and-anvil annihilation. Watts accordingly reported by radio to Laverty, who ordered Easten to counter-attack with his D Company from the north and restore the situation. No artillery or mortar support was possible since friend and enemy were closely interlocked. There followed a brilliant minor infantry operation, in which the Japanese were to experience their first local reverse, and of which Rawlley was a keen spectator from the top of Supply Hill.

At first light Easten made a reconnaissance from the front slope of Supply Hill. He found the gulley between the two features to be under accurate fire from the Japanese battery firing in enfilade from Transport Ridge and a straightforward assault from where he stood was therefore out of the question.

Accordingly he ordered Lieutenant Peter Doresa to take his platoon round by the east, where he would have the advantage of some dead ground, and assault the northern end of Detail Hill from the north-east. To support Doresa's attack, he posted another platoon on a low ridge at the foot of Supply Hill in such a position that their fire would be at right angles to the line of Doresa's assault and he ordered them to keep the bashas under continuous fire until they saw Doresa's men close up to them.

The little assault went in soon afterwards with dash and precision. Doresa's platoon formed up quietly at the northeast foot of Detail Hill for the forty yards uphill attack. Easten, with Sergeant-Major Haines and others of his company headquarters, fell in behind them. As the men fixed bayonets and steadied for the assault, two Gurkhas appeared and asked Easten's permission to join in, which he readily gave them.

Then, at the word, the platoon went straight in with bayonet and grenade. As they reached the bashas, their supporting brens ceased fire, but their staccato rattle was replaced by an eruption of greater violence. Shouts, shots, the screams of the wounded, bursting grenades and the crash of Japanese shells in the gulley were augmented.by the roar of flames and explosives as an ammunition basha caught fire.

The lesser sounds, however, were quickly over. No Japanese escaped. All in the bashas were dead. Easten ordered Doresa to consolidate, brought in his second platoon and ordered his third to take over the positions of the second on the low spur of Supply Hill. At that moment the two Gurkhas came up to him, looking very happy, saluted and asked him to 'come and see something'. They led him round to a basha and, with wide grins, showed him the corpses of three Japanese whose heads they had cleft from crown to chin with their *kukris*.

Easten began to move off to make contact with Watts, but was stopped by some men of C Company, who warned him that there were still some Japanese in a large basha on the east side of Detail Hill that Doresa had bypassed. At that moment the enemy in the basha began to open fire on him and on Doresa's men. Easten decided that he would have to attack it, but something peculiar about its construction caused him to make a careful reconnaissance before taking steps to do so.

What in fact he found was a bakery. Its eastern face was solid brick, which constituted the back of a row of some six ovens. The other walls were of the usual bamboo, with a corrugated iron roof. The Japanese were shooting from between the ovens and from the doorways at each end of the structure, a machine-gun from the southern door having Watts's C Company headquarters closely covered. Clearly the garrison was no mere handful. An attempt to clear them out with grenades failed.

Easten thereupon asked Laverty by radio for engineer assistance and Lieutenant John Wright came hurrying down through the trees with his Indian sappers. A plan was quickly made. Having found an old door lying not far away, Wright fixed to it several slabs of guncotton, primed them and fitted an igniter or match.

Before all these preparations could be completed, the morning was far advanced and the Japanese in the bakery were making any movement in the area difficult. Easten decided that the placing of the charge was a job he could not delegate. He and Wright, carrying the door between them, made a dash uphill to the bakery, slammed it against the brick face and actuated the igniter or match. They turned, ran back and reached dead ground with safety.

A moment or two later there was an 'almighty explosion' and the bakery erupted in a cloud of dust and smoke, with bricks and pieces of metal flung high into the air. Out of the smother Japs ran out and bolted in every direction, to be met by the waiting rifles and brens of the British. There also ran out a number of Indians whom they had taken prisoner. One Japanese ran headlong straight at Easten, who shot him with his revolver at two yards range. Easten then went in with the platoon into the clouded havoc of the bakery and found no Japanese left alive except a badly wounded officer and other rank, the first prisoners of the campaign.[42] The officer died soon afterwards, but the private yielded a little useful information.

In the whole of the exemplary little operations of this morning, well conceived, carried out with dash and determination and a model of junior initiative, forty-four enemy bodies were counted; few if any of the intruders got away. Rawlley, however, saw a Japanese fall wounded while trying to escape and five British soldiers run to take him, when the Japanese pulled a grenade and blew himself to pieces, killing or wounding several of his adversaries also.

Believing the situation to have been cleared up, Easten joined hands with C Company, and on Laverty's orders took command of the sector. Just before the assault on the bakery Watts also had been wounded, but remained at duty till late in the day. To replace him in command of C Company, Laverty brought over Captain Tom Coath, from B Company. Coath, very steady and stolid, had joined the battalion as a private before the war and in later years was to rise to command it.

Laverty now had very few reserves to call upon and C Company had incurred sharp casualties, which were soon to become even more severe.

The Guns

Nothing, however, gave the garrison a greater sense of confidence this day (which was Good Friday) and for the remainder of the siege than the voices of their own artillery. Hill's 2nd Battery, under Peter Hartley, was already in action in the Jotsoma position behind them and 11th and 12th Batteries soon joined in. As soon as 2nd Battery was in action, Yeo abandoned all idea of using his own battery. He therefore dismantled his two Right Section guns, near Keene's bungalow, disposing the component parts in trenches, and manhandled

179

the Left Section nearly to the top of Garrison Hill as a provision against an emergency. Later in the siege they fired one shot. The Indian gunners henceforth served as infantry, a role in which some of them gave gallant service.

With himself, Kendall, Dickenson and Punia, Yeo was now able to deploy four OPs on all-round watch. All were manned continuously by day and two by night. Directed by these four officers, the guns of Hill's regiment, from now until the end, gave the garrison magnificent support. Hill had brought up an enormous quantity of ammunition in twenty-five three-tonners, far beyond the authorized scale. On the 6th and 7th his guns fired 803 rounds, and from then onwards until the 12th they averaged 525 rounds a day. After that date the rate fell, but, contrary to various reports, the regiment was never short of ammunition and never failed to respond to the infantry's needs, not only to those in Kohima, but also the rest of 161st Brigade, which was very soon having to fight its own battles as the Japanese cut them off from Dimapur as well as from Kohima and threatened them from the heights to the south of Jotsoma.

Kohima was, however, the guns' main task. Here the 3.7s very soon had the approaches to the Ridge 'recorded' with absolute precision. Again and again they broke up enemy attacks just as they were being launched, by day and by night. Their response to an infantry demand for 'defensive fire' was swift and exact. The DFs that had soon to be fired on the tennis court were as close to the infantry as twenty yards. Not once during the whole siege did a shell land on the infantry within the perimeter, despite frequent switches and alterations of range at night. This was due, not only to good direction of fire, but also to what Hill himself called 'the deadly accurate laying of our Indian gunners'.

At first Yeo kept his OPs with the infantry companies but very soon the company commanders themselves were able to order any DF they wanted and adjust it, speaking by telephone or wireless to Laverty's command post alongside Yeo's main OP.

Nor was this all. Before very long the ears of the gunner officers became so well attuned that they could tell from the Japanese noises just where and when assaults were to be made and were able to anticipate the infantry demands before they were made. On several occasions during a night Laverty would call:

'Gunner, D F No. 6,' and receive the quiet reply:

'It's on the way, sir.'

There can seldom, indeed, have been a better example of infantry-artillery co-operation. Thus, while it cannot be said that any one unit was the sole battle-winner at Kohima — for several were to play a vital part — it is none the less certain that 24th Indian Mountain Regiment was one of them and that without them Kohima could never have been held.

At first the gunners were much handicapped by the lack of large-scale, gridded, military maps and possessed only maps of 4 miles to 1 inch (1:250,000). After a day or two, however, there floated unexpectedly down on Hill's position from a RAF aircraft a bundle of new 1:25,000 maps, which the RAF cartographers had made and printed with remarkable speed from air photographs. Thenceforward gunners and infantry knew better what to do.

10: MOUNTING PRESSURE

(Night 7/8 and Day 8th)

Walking Wounded Cleared

THUS AS THE SUN sank in the distant mountains behind them and the chill of night of the 6th began to set in, the garrison felt a renewed confidence. The repulse of the Japanese at Detail Hill and the heartening voice of their own artillery gave assurance that they could hold their own till relief arrived. Tom Coath, on coming over to take command of C Company of the Royal West Kents, noted that the men 'had now begun to get a bit determined'. All knew now that they were not in for merely the normal holding action that most of them had expected, but that they were in for a stiff fight for at least a few days longer. They knew also that the enemy strength against them was mounting daily and Richards knew that at least 10,000 of Sato's division would soon be deployed, with another 5,000 available behind them.

It was on this day that Richards issued his orders for the rationing of water and his staff were kept at full stretch at this and other internal work. The most urgent administrative need, however, was to try to get the wounded away as quickly as possible. They already numbered 200. The risks were obvious but Young was confident that it could be done. Though the Japanese had blocked the road, it was unlikely that they had yet spread a curtain through the jungle.

Having obtained Richards's approval, he made a plan with 161st Brigade, the conversation being conducted in French between an officer of the RWK and Captain Cassematti, a liaison officer at Warren's headquarters. A route ordered by

Warren, by way of the steep valley that led away north-westward from Hospital Spur, was reconnoitred by a platoon of the Rajputs and found clear of enemy. This route, however, was far too rough for the stretcher-bearers, and accordingly, although the stretcher cases were obviously the more urgent, Young was obliged to limit the evacuation to those capable of walking the three miles of steep, broken, jungle country in the dark. He and Franklin then took order for the strange operation.

Three control posts were set up along the route, equipped with wireless sets lent by the RWK. The platoon formed an escort and a flank guard on the dangerous road crossing was provided by the Assam Rifles. The wounded, to the number of ninety-eight, were assembled in groups of about fifteen and each man examined by Captain Thomson, of the Parachute Field Ambulance, for his fitness to make the journey.

The first group started a little before 9 o'clock that night, moving very slowly down the steep Hospital Spur. John Corlett, of the Assam Regiment, slightly wounded but skilled in jungle craft, led the way accompanied by a Naga guide provided by Pawsey, with Franklin in charge. It was very difficult to maintain silence. The flank guard was engaged by fire and the evacuation halted, but resumed half an hour later with no further incident. Some of the wounded, however, could not keep up with their comrades, lost their way and had to be shepherded in again. In the words of Professor Crew, the official medical historian, 'the march in the dark over extremely broken ground by the enfeebled men was for many a continual anguish; there could be no halt though men stumbled and reopened their wounds'. It is not surprising, therefore, that the rate of progress seems to have been less than a mile an hour.

They were met at Milestone 42 by Major Richard Pilcher, Young's second-in-command, crammed into 3-ton lorries and rushed off to Dimapur before the Japanese cut the road, which they were expected to do (and did) next morning.

Young himself walked down in the deep river valley with the last group. Returning soon after midnight he saw about 100 non-combatants taking advantage of the walk-out and following in their tracks. Unaware that they were being evacuated by Richards's orders, he tried without success to turn them back, but at his request, Keene threw out a cordon of his Assam Rifles to prevent any further exodus.

On returning to his ADS, Young counted up the number of his lying patients. There were 104, of whom thirty-two were in a serious condition. By 8 o'clock in the morning he was at work amputating limbs infected with gas gangrene.

From Detail Hill, brought in hourly with great difficulty under heavy fire, there came forty new admissions.[43]

Lance-Corporal Harman

While the walking wounded were going out, C and D Companies on Detail Hill had again been threatened by attack. Tom Coath was now leading C Company, with Donald Easten in command of that sector. The rowdy jitter demonstrations on Jail Hill, however, gave Easten ample notice and the threat was firmly crushed by the guns at the call of the artillery FOO. For the rest of the night the enemy was heard prowling round the company position, keeping everyone on the *qui vive* but not making any attack.

Late on the previous day, when Easten had thought that the Japanese intruders at the northern end of the hill had been satisfactorily disposed of, he was surprised to hear that an enemy machine-gun post was still being manned close to the burning ammunition basha towards the rear of the hill.

Easten went out to see for himself with CSM Haines ('my super sergeant-major') and found the post to be a bunker that had been built for the original defences. After studying it a while, he said to Haines: 'They don't seem to be doing us any harm and, if they have any sense, they'll clear out tonight.'

As daylight slowly flooded in over the eastern mountain rim on the morning of the 8th, the Japanese were still there, however, and Easten decided that he must get them out. Accompanied again by his sergeant-major, he went up to a point not far from the bunker, to consider what to do, when he was approached by a remarkable young soldier in the person of Lance-Corporal John Pennington Harman.

Harman was a black-browed, strongly built youngster. He was the son of a well-known and wealthy City financier who had some slightly eccentric traits. At the beginning of the war Harman had enlisted as a trooper in the Life Guards, as he was fond of horses. When that regiment became mechanized, however, he did not like the change and secured a transfer to the infantry. He had joined the Royal West Kents in Arakan four months before Kohima, where he had become one of D Company's snipers.

His was in many ways a strange character. Easten, his company commander, found him entertaining to talk to, but the troops for the greater part thought him odd. When Easten asked him why he had not offered himself for a commission, he replied: 'Because I am an individualist; I would rather remain with my section.' He was devoid of any sensation of fear, and when he and Easten, in Arakan, had been caught in the beaten zone of a tornado of shelling, Harman had volunteered: 'You are quite safe with me, you know, sir. A man

I met in Spain told me I should live to be at least seventy, so I am quite all right and so are you as long as you are with me.'

He was now to give the first of two spectacular proofs of both his individualism and his fearlessness. As Easten was considering the most economical method of tackling the Japanese bunker, Harman came forward and said: 'I have worked out the right way to get at that bunker, sir. May I have a go?'

Easten, after a moment's thought, gave him permission and wished him luck. He and Haines then watched enthralled as Harman set out on his mission, which he had decided to carry out alone.

There was a distance of some thirty-five yards to cross, with no cover. They watched Harman crawl out, then, apparently impatient, get up and run right up to the mouth of the bunker and lie down. The machine-gun was firing at him furiously, but he had got underneath its fire and the stream of bullets was passing inches over his body. They then saw him take out a four-second grenade, throw away the clip, and clearly heard him count 'one-two-three' before tossing it into the embrasure. The explosion inside was instantaneous.

He then got up, ran round to the entrance of the bunker, found two dead Japanese inside and walked back carrying their machine-gun.[44]

Ordeal by Night

Evidence accumulated during the day of the enemy's increasing strength. The previous night Richards had seen a column of troops carrying lanterns, moving into Naga Village by the Phek track. He had called Yeo's attention to it, but the gunner did not consider it a favourable target. In the morning Richards observed five elephants on the same track, no doubt carrying artillery, and a few hours later Warren, back at Jotsoma, observed what were no doubt the same elephants and ordered Hill to engage them. These appear to have been the units that had been engaged and delayed by the Assam Regiment at Jessami and Kharasom.

Elements of Sato's division were thus known to be moving in the direction of Dimapur. Barred from the main road by the resistance at Kohima, they were obliged to move by forest tracks leading off the Merema road, but it was against Kohima, their fixed objective, that their main effort was concentrated. The importance of the Ridge lay in two facts — that its continued possession by the British denied Sato the use of the main road to Imphal, which he needed, and that, if continued to be held by the British, it would provide 33rd Corps with a springboard for a counter-attack. Sato therefore followed a policy of sending forward small parties to delay whatever relieving forces might arrive, while increasing his pressure on the Ridge as the rear elements of his division came up by their various routes.

During the day fresh Japanese artillery was mounted on the west along which ran the road to Merema, to the north of the Ridge, and the artillery already on Transport Ridge was Reinforced. The trees were quickly losing their foliage and branches were crashing down everywhere. Japanese guns were now covering the Ridge from all sides but the west. Almost every yard of ground was under observation. The enemy shelling on this Good Friday was severe, searching into crannies of the garrison's reduced stronghold and killing more wounded men in the ADS, where Glover noted in his diary: 'The casualties were awful.' Snipers had also moved in, many of them roped into trees at short range and extremely difficult to locate. The tree trunks still gave the garrison a fair amount of cover, but along the perimeter, and in many parts inside, the slightest movement brought a shot. Every shell or bomb that burst in the trees above ground level reduced the cover and the splinters from these tree-bursts caused severe casualties to men in open trenches below them. Many of the trenches dug before the arrival of the Royal West Kents had been provided with head cover, but some company commanders had had this head cover removed to prevent them from being used as mere shelters and to improve fields of fire.[45]

From now onwards the enemy adopted a regular routine in his attempts to reduce the garrison. At dawn and dusk there were steady bombardments by mortars and artillery, lasting sometimes for thirty minutes, sometimes for an hour and a half. As a rule, the rest of the day was relatively quiet, except when any movement was observed, but desultory fire by mortars was maintained from time to time to wear down the garrison and deny them any sleep. The enemy infantry, however, took their sleep securely during the day, abandoning daylight attacks as soon as the British resistance stiffened. Henceforward all assaults were made at night, when, in the absence of barbed wire, the Japanese had ample opportunities for infiltrating and could not be engaged by the British troops until very close. Indeed, what was impressive about the fighting during the Kohima siege was that virtually all of it was at a few yards' range, with the enemy 'suddenly appearing at the points of our rifles'. Before long, as Coath tells us, the British infantry developed a 'kind of instinct' of the proximity of the enemy.

Thus night became for the garrison a time of extreme strain, to which no one looked forward. The men in the perimeter trenches, staring out into the sombre void, heard strange rustlings and sounds of movement, but could see nothing when there was no longer any moon, except the spectral shapes of trees. In imagination these began to take human form and soon to move. All night long men were listening, listening and, when clouds obscured the moon and the stars, the ears became their only means of perception. With no visible contact with one's comrades to right or left, men became possessed by a sense of isolation, which was intensified by the bitter chill. When night gave way to day, they could never be certain that the occupants of the next weapon-pit were not Japanese. It needed guts to sit out there in the dark and to keep one's nerve, with the sensation that the enemy might be creeping up or getting in behind, and it needed good training not to loose off one's weapon at the vague shapes and sounds.

In the deep silence, a sudden outburst of yells, shots and grenades would tell of an attack coming in somewhere and all would be uproar, with the British artillery joining in. After a while the uproar would subside, another silence fall over the hills, and the strain of isolation return until the next outburst of violence. Thus the approach of each night took shape as the preparation for an ordeal and the dawn, though it brought bombardment, none the less brought light and relief from the tension of the darkness. 'The arrow that flieth by day' was more to be endured than 'the terror by night'.

All this was part of the Japanese technique of wearing down and unnerving his adversary. With their own numbers daily augmented, they were able to use fresh troops at will and to throw them against the thin-spread trenches manned night after night by the same troops, who could have no relief and little rest. To these tactical methods they added the crude 'psychological warfare' of the Jiffs, who set up a loud-hailer installation and who prowled round with their ridiculous attempt to seduce the British and Indians from their allegiance.

189

There were occasions when, with their long and difficult lines of communication through the jungle paths, the Japanese were short of artillery ammunition. They had not expected to need a great deal, supposing that, like the walls of Jericho, Kohima would fall at the blast of their trumpets. Of mortar ammunition, on the other hand, they had plenty. As the siege developed they made increasing use also of their grenade dischargers, which were small projectors held in the hand and capable of shooting a hand grenade a great deal farther than it could be thrown. Fired from under cover and fired in showers, they gave the impression of an enemy close at hand and were difficult to deal with.

All this noisy fire power was used to support attacks that were seldom of more than company strength. The steep, rough and wooded country (except on the Bungalow Sector) made it difficult to deploy larger numbers against the separate features of the Ridge, and the attacks were always concentrated on a small sector of the garrison's perimeter. But they were persistent, were pressed with an obstinacy that gave them impetus and power and, if one attack were repulsed, others would follow, usually throughout the night. Had the Japanese properly assessed the ground and the quality of their adversaries, they would have known that an attack by a battalion or more in silence on a wide front from the slope to the west of Garrison Hill would have been very much more difficult for the garrison to parry. This was a perfectly feasible manoeuvre and the one that Richards most feared, for it suited the Japanese infiltration methods, which could quickly have disrupted the defences. Barratt and Wilson-Hoole, lying in their trench in the middle of the ADS, with few or no troops to their immediate west, feared that any night they might find the Japanese swarming over the ADS and the appalling prospect kept their ears continually cocked.

Outside the Box, the Japanese on this day blocked the Dimapur road some six miles in the rear of 161st Brigade and cut the telephone line. Warren was thus himself isolated and he moved his headquarters southwards to higher and more defensible ground. The Japanese had also begun to occupy, not very strongly, the high ground to the west and south-west of Jotsoma. Warren, whose troops were very thinly strung out on difficult and broken hill-jungle, was therefore soon obliged to safeguard his own position, where he had now large quantities of transport and stores, and at the same time to be ready to assist the advance of 2nd Division's leading brigade as soon as it began, before he could attempt to relieve Kohima. The Jotsoma position became his essential 'firm base' from which he could operate to fulfil any of his several responsibilities, of which the one he was most eager to accomplish was the relief of Kohima.

Sato's purpose, on the other hand, was to tighten his grip on Kohima, prevent its relief and overcome its features one by one. He 'maintained his objective' in the Japanese rigid manner. He made no change in his method of doing so, never imagining that the paltry Kohima garrison could resist for long the mounting pressure of a soldiery that had never known defeat.

The Garrison Commander

No one, however, was under greater stress nor stood up to it with a quieter fortitude than the garrison commander and no report of these operations would be faithful which did not correct those accounts that have sought to belittle a gallant gentleman.

Knowing that in such a battle personal example was of the first importance, Richards made a point of visiting one or more sectors of the Ridge every day, unconcerned by fire or by the snipers who chased him. His command post became a dangerous spot, under fire from all weapons, and the entrance and the approaches to it closely covered by snipers. One of his staff officers, Lieutenant N. Oldrey, was killed by a sniper just outside it. Harry Smith, of the Royal West Kents, was later wounded by a grenade at the very entrance. At first, in the usual manner, Richards summoned the various unit commanders to a daily conference at his command post, but when he saw the dangers to which this exposed them, he cancelled the daily conference and went out to the units himself instead, running the gauntlet every time he did so.

He made close friends with a platoon of the RWK headquarter company posted close beside his command trench and joined them at the stand-to each dawn and dusk. As he approached his command post after his rounds each day, sprinting up the hill, often under snipers' fire, the men used to cheer him on, calling out 'Come on, Sir, you're winning', or some such homely encouragement. He got on well with troops and Private Wilson, his orderly, became his devoted servant and sometimes accompanied him on his rounds.

The tributes to his example come from many sides, not least from the Royal West Kents. Harry Smith, who was often in his company, was very much impressed and related that Richards 'was completely unmoved by bombardment and the continual snipers and seemed to be completely unaware of it'. Easten declared that both he and Borrowman 'were remarkably brave, always going round encouraging people'. Pawsey, with memories of the First World War in mind, declared that he was 'first class'.[46]

Borrowman himself, writing afterwards to the Cabinet Office historian, declared that Richards 'had a complete grip of things' and that he was 'quite fearless and when things were particularly sticky it was he who went to see for himself'. Elwell, of the Assam Regiment, noted similarly in his manuscript that Richards was 'under a nerve-racking strain, yet remained patient and understanding and was often seen laughing and joking under fire.' Rawlley, the Indian, noted likewise that he was 'always considerate and understanding and never rattled'.

Another figure that was to be seen walking about with the same quiet and reassuring demeanour was that of Pawsey. When all other civilians had gone, he had elected to stay, so that his Nagas should not lose faith in the British cause nor feel that he had deserted them. Each day, wearing civilian clothes, he walked about among the garrison, talking cheerfully to British and Indian troops and followed by his two Naga *dobashis* carrying their spears and *daos* and wearing the red blankets that denoted their status as interpreters. The British troops said: 'If this chap can walk about like a country gentleman, things can't be as bad as they look.' Life in a trench was no new thing to him and memories of the previous war, in which he had served with distinction as a young officer, came vividly back to him. It was all, he found, very much like that first war, except for the unfortunate absence of heavy artillery. Then he would go back to his trench among his friends of the Assam Rifles on Hospital Ridge and pass the time with 'Buster' Keene, listening to the Japanese broadcasts in English from 'Tokyo Rose'. Both Pawsey and Keene had their dogs with them throughout the siege, Pawsey's a mongrel, Keene's a shaggy little Tibetan lion dog, named Judy.

11: AT FULL PITCH

(*Night 8/9 to Day 10 April*)

Assam Rifles Attacked

HOW FORMIDABLY the enemy had increased his strength on the 8th was soon made painfully obvious and the scale of the conflict now rose to its full pitch.

That evening Garrison Hill, the Bungalow sector and Detail Hill were more heavily shelled and mortared than on any previous day. On a smudged page in his small diary, Glover, at the dressing-station, recorded: 'A terrible night. Two direct hits on the wounded shelter, killing several men.'

The bombardments were the preludes to three dangerous and critical attacks launched during the night and carried on into the next day, which was Easter Day. These attacks were against:

1. the Assam Rifles at the important 'back door' on Hospital Ridge,
2. the composite company of British Reinforcement Camp troops in the Bungalow Sector, and
3. C and D Companies of the Royal West Kents again on Detail Hill.

In the first of these Keene's men, armed with rifles and *kukris* only, were suddenly confronted in the darkness with ranks of shadowy forms emerging from the trees on the steep slope below them. Unaided by artillery or mortars, they shot them down at a few yards' range. Throughout the siege the Japanese never succeeded, in spite of repeated attempts, in getting within bayonet range at this important back door of the

Ridge, but the Japanese corpses with skulls cleft deep by the *kukris*, found afterwards on the hospital slope, were eloquent evidence that the Assam Rifles were not content to remain on the defensive.

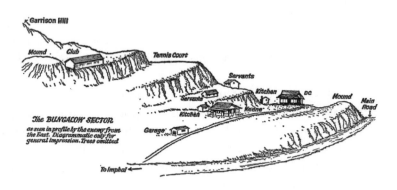

The Tennis Court Battles Begin

Farther to the right, apparently as part of the same Japanese operation, a much more critical situation developed.

Since the Bungalow Sector, and particularly the tennis court of immortal memory contained in it, were to become one of the fiercest close-quarter battlegrounds in history, we should pause for a moment at this stage to inspect it rather more closely.

As we have seen, the Bungalow Sector was a narrow spur of Garrison Hill projecting to the north-east like the pointed toecap of a shoe. The main road formed the welt of the toecap, with the Ladies' Mile running parallel to and above it, and at the hairpin bend that formed its pointed tip was the Traffic Control Post. From this sharp point the ground rose towards Garrison Hill in a series of terraces of irregular outline, like giant steps. At its lowest level a short drive led up from the main road, past a memorial to a former DC who had been murdered by the Nagas, on to a terrace on which stood Pawsey's garden. Another step up led to his bungalow among its eucalyptus trees, rhododendrons and cannas, commanding a superb mountain panorama to the north. In the rear of the bungalow were his servants' quarters and his outdoor kitchen in the colonial manner. On a different level, displaced a little on the south-eastern face of the hill, was Keene's bungalow, also with its servants' quarters and kitchen in the rear, and a garage in front.

Another giant step of about 35 ft led to the terrace on which the asphalt tennis court had been constructed by the Burmah Oil Company. The width of the terrace, measured athwart the side lines, was no more than about twenty yards. The court was aligned roughly north and south and was surrounded by the usual cage of tall wire netting and at its north-west corner Landor had installed a large tarpaulin water tank, which had been filled. About twenty-five yards south of the court and on lower ground was the somewhat larger and permanent steel cistern from which troops had been drawing their meagre trickle of water, and now to be very dangerously exposed.

Behind, or westward, of the court was another bank, about 8ft high, leading on to a natural terrace that overlooked the court. Here, before the main bulk of Garrison Hill swelled up towards its summit, there was a stretch of fairly flat ground sparsely clad with trees and therefore extremely exposed to enemy observation and fire.

On the northern and southern sides of this uppermost terrace the ground fell away extremely steeply to the main road that bordered the two faces of the Bungalow Sector. The northern end abutted on to the sector of Hospital Ridge held by the two Assam units. At the southern end and standing almost immediately on the edge of the terrace was the little club house, with its billiard-table and library, and close behind it was a prominent mound, about 20 ft high and 70 ft long, which was to have considerable tactical importance, for it commanded much of the lower ground on the eastern slope of the hill. Moreover, the loss of it would have made untenable what was to become known as the tennis court sector.

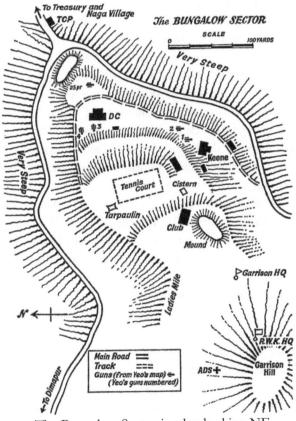

The Bungalow Sector in plan looking NE.

The total drop from the terrace on which stood the club and the mound down to the Traffic Control Post on the main road was nearly 100 ft in about 230 yards. It is to be noted that from any one terrace it was impossible to see down to the next except from the edge. Thus, whereas from the much higher ground of Richards's and Laverty's command posts most of the sector was visible, from the uppermost terrace everything below was dead ground.

The greater part of the sector was being held, as we have seen, by a composite company of British troops, but Yeo's gunners were also serving as infantry on the east face, near Keene's bungalow. His two Left Section guns lay there dismantled, with the lone 25-pounder not far away.

After the bombardment on the night of the 8th the Japanese put in a probing attack against these troops. The attack was repelled without difficulty. In the early hours of the 9th, however, there was a heavy concentration of mortar bombing from the tip of the spur as far back as Richards's command post. The bombardment was followed by a heavy attack in company strength from the direction of the Treasury across the road and up the shoulder of the hill on to Pawsey's garden, the enemy having assembled in the dead ground of the roadside.

At first checked, the attack was sustained and supported by continued mortar fire. The British and Indian troops were unable to prevent a lodgement by the Japanese, who penetrated between section posts in the dark. This lodgement the Japanese reinforced and the garrison troops were obliged to give ground. The two bungalows themselves were lost and the garrison troops withdrew through the trees and the scattered buildings up to the terrace on which the tennis court was situated.

Yeo's two dismantled guns left in the sector were lost but not until after some of their Indian gunners had fought stubbornly in their defence. Gunner Majhi Khan and Gunner Fateh Sher, both Punjabi Mussulmans, manned their bren guns to the last round before the Japanese overran and killed them.

The Japanese closed right up to the wire netting on the eastern side of the tennis court, bayoneting or shooting all but one (who shammed dead) of a British machine-gun post on the corner opposite the tarpaulin water tank. One or two sections of British troops, with considerable courage, dug themselves in along the parallel side of the wire netting, less than twenty yards from the enemy, one of their posts being close to the tarpaulin tank. The main body took post behind them on the upper bank overlooking the tennis court, in the club house and on the mound behind, where two stout-hearted old soldiers of mature years but unknown identities manned a well-sited bren gun.

Richards himself watched the latter part of these events and saw with regret many of the Indian gunners withdraw too soon; they came back, in fact, right past his command post. Together with Harry Smith, he could also clearly see the Japanese dodging from cover to cover beyond the main road, obviously assembling in the dead ground below to exploit their hold on the sector.

It was a very critical moment. The Bungalow Sector and Hospital Ridge, Richards appreciated, were vital ground; if completely lost, the whole of the Ridge would have been in jeopardy. He accordingly ordered a counter-attack by one platoon of the Assam Regiment and one of the Burma Regiment. The attack, hastily mounted, was commanded by Captain Patrick, of 1/7th Gurkha Rifles, who appears to have attached himself to Brown's battalion, and the platoon of the

Assam Regiment by Subedar Kapthuama Lushai. They were required to break through the enemy to a depth of 150 yards. This the Assam platoon did with great dash and few casualties under covering fire, reaching and occupying Pawsey's bungalow. The Burma platoon, however, was unable to make progress. Isolated and without supporting fire, Kapthuama's position became untenable and he was forced to withdraw.

It appears to have been intended that two platoons of the Royal West Kents also should have taken part in this counter-attack but, whatever the intention, it misfired.[47]

On receipt of this news, A Company of the Royal West Kents, which was in battalion reserve on Garrison Hill under the tall, strongly built figure of Tom Kenyon, was ordered to take over this critical new sector. This they did at dusk, at the very moment when the Japanese had begun another attack. They could be seen appearing beyond the tennis court and A Company was plunged immediately into the fray. On the right of the sector the staunch and reliable Sergeant G. W. Brooks, who had won the Military Medal in France four years earlier, was already holding the club and the adjacent mound, which were the key to the position. The next platoon to arrive, under Lieutenant Hinton, Kenyon sent to the other flank and the third platoon he posted in the centre. He took post himself at the forward end of the mound but later moved to a more central position. The British reinforcement troops who were already there attached themselves to A Company and seemed glad to find themselves back in the familiar matrix of a well-knit and well-led unit.

The Japanese attack then being made was hotly resisted and fizzled out. The remainder of that first night both sides spent digging in hard. The servants' quarters and the kitchens in Pawsey's and Keene's compounds were on fire and by their flames Kenyon could clearly see the Japanese at work. He resisted the temptation to engage them, knowing that to do so would bring instant retaliation before his own troops were ready.

By first light on the 9th all were more or less dug in. From Kenyon's trench a lone Japanese was to be seen standing up in the dawn light to the right of the tennis court, obviously thinking he was safely in dead ground. Kenyon's batman dropped him at the first shot. At about the same time the men in the lone post by the tarpaulin water tank had their first evidence of what might happen with an enemy so close. In the morning mist a figure leapt out of the machine-gun post at the opposite corner, where the Japanese had all but annihilated the British position, dashed straight across the court and, before a weapon could be levelled at him, jumped down into the West Kents' corner. He proved to be a British soldier, who had alone survived by shamming dead after a harrowing experience. The Japanese had trampled all over him and the bodies of his dead comrades during the night as they fortified their position. He proved a valuable recruit and was able to pinpoint the exact position of the enemy weapon-pit.

Like his numerous successors in that memorable position, Kenyon found that he could see nothing whatever beyond the tennis court, except from the mound, where there was a view down the steep slopes to the roof of Keene's bungalow. He also noted that the position was very exposed and under distant observation from Naga Village, but that it was possible to move about in the flat ground to the west of the tennis court as long as one kept well back from it. He was glad to see the bren gun dug in on the mound held by the two steady old hands. That day one of them was killed, but his comrade continued to man the gun alone until he himself was killed by a mortar bomb. So fell two gallant men whose identities are unknown and so began the immortal 'battles of the tennis court' in which, with superb gallantry, one unit after another held off repeated attacks at a range of twenty yards, with volleys of grenades crashing down where once the tennis balls had bounced.

The Japanese assaults were invariably preluded by prolonged and intense bombardments, mainly by mortars, from which the West Kents suffered grievous casualties. The steep bank on the enemy side of the court gave exceptionally good cover for an assault force to assemble unseen, but the bloodcurdling noises with which the Japanese always advertised their intentions gave the defence ample opportunity to call for defensive fire and the shells of 24th Mountain Regiment and the bombs from Sergeant King's mortars came crashing down among the Japanese as they formed up on the terrace below the court. So accurate was the fire of the guns that on many occasions they put down their curtain of shells just the other side of the court.

Occasionally, however, some of the enemy would escape or avoid the defensive barrage and at other times parties of enemy would attempt infiltration. Of these there was no warning until the silhouettes of the enemy took shape and substance in the dark on the far side of the court itself. There was no time to aim rifles, which were anyhow of limited use at night. Showers of hand grenades and a quick sweep with a ready bren gun alone served to stem the sudden rushes.

'A Bit Determined'

The third dangerous enemy offensive of the night of the 8th-9th was launched against the gallant remnants of C Company on Detail Hill.

Coath, on taking over the company after the loss of Watts, found a very taut and tricky situation. An ammunition shed was blazing and the Japanese were pressing hard on the company's front trenches, which, on the side facing Jail Hill, had a frontage of only twenty yards. It was impossible to manoeuvre, impossible to move except by sudden darts and impossible materially to improve the defensive works. Nevertheless, he found the NCOs and men in very high morale and it was then that he observed that they had 'begun to get a bit determined'. He mounted eight bren guns with interlocking arcs of fire, examined the stocks of ammunition and placed his faith in his men.

The evening bombardment crashed down and then came the first enemy assault. Again they could be clearly seen coming down Jail Hill and again Sergeant King's mortars bombed them accurately, but could not prevent strong parties evading fire and putting in their attack. They were fought off with coolness and skill.

The second attack came in and again the Japanese were repulsed by the sheer guts and determination of the men in the weapon-pits, who stood to their brens and rifles till either they or the enemy two or three yards away were dead. Sergeant S. J. Tacon, the very pattern of fearless and stalwart leadership, was severely wounded trying to bring in the wounded Corporal Rees. Very heavy casualties were inflicted on the Japanese but Coath's ranks were also further thinned.

A third attack came in later in the night. Once more every man left alive in the company stubbornly held his ground, but mounting casualties gradually opened breaches in the defences and over the dead bodies in the silent pits the Japanese pushed their way, and before dawn had established themselves in C

Company's front-line trenches which were at a distance of some twenty-five yards from their second line.

Easten (commanding the sector) thereupon brought up the reserve platoon of his D company to reinforce C on the right of the new front line alongside Lieutenant Phythian, and at the same time Laverty moved forward Mitchell's two platoons of the Rajputs to take over Easten's evacuated trenches at the foot of Supply Hill, which was in the sector under the command of Naveen Rawlley. Among those brought forward by Easten was Lance-Corporal Harman.

As the dawn of the 9th slowly crept over the hills, Easten himself crawled forward to a position from which he could observe and consider 'what the hell I could do'. There was a great deal of noise from shouting and mortaring and machine-guns. He saw five Japanese in one of C Company's old trenches digging away to convert it for firing in the reverse direction. As they worked, weapons in adjacent trenches and on Jail Hill gave them covering fire.

As Easten watched he saw Harman, twenty yards away to his right, suddenly jump out of his trench, rifle in hand and bayonet fixed. He saw him 'hurtle' down the hill through the trees and go straight for the Japanese. A machine-gun from Jail Hill opened up on him but did not stop his charge. He pulled up short a yard or two from the five Japanese and, firing from the hip, shot four of them and bayoneted the fifth.

He turned for the run uphill, with every enemy weapon turned on him. He had nearly got home when a burst caught him and brought him to the ground.

Easten, on seeing him fall, ran across to Harman's trench, and, with others of the section, darted out and pulled him in. Blood was spouting from Harman's body and Easten began to remove his equipment, but Harman said:

'Don't worry about that, sir. It was worth it; I got the lot.'

In less than a minute he was dead.

For this action, which materially helped ease the situation, and for his gallantry the previous day, Harman was posthumously awarded the Victoria Cross.[48]

A little later in the day, when Detail Hill was being heavily mortared, Easten was standing up and shouting above the din to Sergeant G. F. Boxwell to bring down counter-mortar fire. A bomb fell clean between them. Sergeant Boxwell was blown to pieces. Easten was flung into the air by the blast and fell into a trench, with his back dislocated and a wound in his arm.

Command of the sector now fell to Coath, and in D Company Easten was succeeded by Captain Fred Collett, a well-built Manchester athlete.

The 'Non-Combatants'

Easter Day was a severe testing-time for the garrison and they passed it with merit. Few men got any rest that day. Fatigue began to show itself in heavy-lidded eyes and slow responses. Unshaven and unwashed, officers and men had begun to get very dirty, imposing a further strain on morale. But the will to resist had stiffened throughout the garrison, spreading to many of the non-combatants. Numbers of these were sitting about rather helplessly, without officers, not knowing what to do or where to go, but having to be fed and to be cared for when wounded equally with all. Such were a liability to the garrison, but they were scarcely to be blamed, for they had not been trained to fight and should never have been expected to do so. There were one or two bad incidents; Landor had to draw his revolver on a Sikh who turned nasty when found looting some stores.

Barratt's mixed Indian company at the ADS, however, continued to do gallant and unselfish service under fire, constantly digging new trenches for the wounded, carrying away the dead and burying them, while the havildar's water platoon continued to go out every night.

While all this fighting was going on during the night of 8th-9th April, Young made another sortie outside the perimeter in the cause of the wounded. Though he recorded that his ADS was now 'running smoothly', he was short of supplies and tools, especially of blood plasma, which he needed badly. He resolved accordingly to search the abandoned buildings of 53rd IGH and the trucks down on the main road that had been abandoned by Lieutenant Aiappa, whom he had sent up initially with Laverty's column, but who had gone back to Milestone 42 with casualties and not returned.

It was a dangerous mission and Young undertook it himself. With a small escort of Indian sappers provided by Laverty, he led out a carrying party soon after dark, down the steep slope through the derelict buildings. He encountered no enemy and returned at midnight with ample supplies, including plasma and also 100 sorely needed blankets, which he had salvaged from the abandoned Royal West Kent lorries on the roadside. With the plasma he was now able to augment the three groups of his 'hospital' with a resuscitation group under Captain Hunter.

As a result of the fighting at Detail Hill and in the Bungalow Sector, the number of his patients jumped from the 104 of the previous day to 200.

In the perimeter fighting, where the ground was rocky and swept by fire, the problem of burying men who were killed was an acute one. Most were buried where they fell, but as a rule graves could only be dug at night. Men who could not be buried until after rigor mortis had set in presented a distasteful problem. In the shallow soil above the rock rigid arms and legs left in all the attitudes of violent death stuck out of the ground unburied. The burial of the dead mules was an even more serious problem. There were fifteen of them in the garrison, of which eleven were killed. They required large graves, which they did not get. At each extremity of the perimeter Japanese corpses lay rotting. The stink of putrid flesh began to pervade the air; so, too, did odours of the Japanese burning their own dead.

A little light relief appropriate to Easter Day was provided by a small incident that Richards witnessed on Kuki Piquet. A hen appeared, leading a brood of chicks. A British soldier pounced on the hen, stuffed her into his shirt and vowed that no one should have the chance of dividing her up into convenient portions.

A special class of non-combatant were the 'line boys' of the Assam Rifles on Hospital Ridge. These youngsters never turned a hair and Keene had the greatest difficulty in making them stay under cover. Whenever they had the chance, they liked to sit out on top of their trenches to see what was going on in the mad world around them.

Rain

After a fairly quiet afternoon on the 9th, the enemy artillery and mortars burst into life again in the evening. So also did the elements. An overcast, pitch-black night descended, with heavy rain. It beat down on the trees and the roofs of the remaining bashas with a din that matched that of the machine-guns, blanketing all signs and sounds of enemy movement, increasing the troops' discomfort, adding to the dirt with which they were already coated and drenching the wounded in their shallow trenches. The resourceful Private Wilson, however, brought a quantity of rain water that he had collected in a waterproof sheet to Richards and invited him to share it, but Richards laughed and told him to take it to the dressing-station.

At the two extremities of the Ridge — the tennis court and Detail Hill — the enemy put down a very heavy concentration of fire at dusk as the rain came down and there followed a long night of bitter and continuous fighting, with no let-up. The enemy was now at full strength and poured in his troops in what seemed like successive waves.

Along and above the western length of the tennis court Kenyon's A Company of the RWK and the Reinforcement Camp troops with them stood up in the pelting rain as soon as the bombardment stopped and braced themselves for an attack. It came in shortly after dark, while the rainstorm was at its height. The enemy, having swarmed up the bank on their side of the court, suddenly appeared on the crest and, with shouts and yells, tried to dash across the court. Another of the fierce grenade battles took place. Kenyon's company threw off the first wave of the attack with confidence and skill. He called for defensive fire and in a minute a curtain of shells of Hill's mountain regiment crashed with immaculate accuracy just the other side of the court.

This, however, was but the first of a series of attacks that went on all night. There was never more than half an hour's space between the enemy's repeated attacks to break in or to infiltrate at one point or another. To Kenyon, it was a night full of crises. The darkness of the night, the rain and the din made it difficult to know what was going on. He felt some discomfort on his left flank, but soon had to turn his attention to his right, where a dangerous attack was launched from the direction of Keene's bungalow and pressed hard against the club house. The building was a snare and a magnet for enemy fire, but had to be held. Sergeant Brooks and his platoon held it stoutly enough, but were soon running short of grenades as they hurled them down the slope again and again. All along the line the call was for grenades and more grenades.

By the next morning's light, A Company and the reinforcements which had joined them, bruised, tired but unshaken and their morale extremely high, still held all their line unbroken.

To the left rear of A Company, another attack was made this night against the Assam Rifles and Assam Regiment guarding Hospital Ridge. It was thrown off with remarkably efficient small arms fire at point-blank range and the morning light showed the slopes of Hospital Spur below to be once more thickly strewn with enemy dead. Their corpses brought further identifications of Sato's division and showed that the whole of 31 Div was now deployed against Kohima and Jotsoma. All three of Sato's brigades were now represented around the perimeter of Kohima Ridge itself and it is probable that some 8,000 Japanese were now trying to get at the throats of Richards's little garrison, while the remainder of the enemy division was working down the Dimapur road.

C Company's Last Ditch

At the other extremity of the ridge, however, where Coath was commanding the decimated C Company on the battered tip of Detail Hill, a more serious situation arose on the night of the 9th-10th. Coath had just buried the remains of the gallant Harman and what he had left of his new company now found the Japanese at close quarters for the fourth night in succession in the pelting rain and the utter darkness. With one platoon in the rear, he posted another right forward, covered by his bren guns with interlocking fire.

This night, however, with the enemy now at full strength, the attacks were more or less continuous and they were supported by showers of discharger-launched grenades. In the rain and the black darkness no enemy preparations could be heard or seen. At such close quarters there was nothing to stop the enemy but brens, rifles and grenades; with these the handful of C Company threw off one attack after another. Individual fights took place on the very parapets of the trenches and even inside them.

As the long, wet night drew on, however, the casualties went on mounting until, shortly before dawn, every man in the forward trenches was dead. No one retired; they were killed, at their posts, weapon in hand, by the incessant rain of fire. Coath, left with about twenty red-eyed, soaked and exhausted men, watched the Japanese come forward in the damp, grey dawn of Easter Monday, pour petrol over the bodies of his dead men and set them on fire before occupying the trenches themselves.

He decided that it was hopeless to try to recover the lost trenches and that he could not exist another night. They were at the last ditch. Unless they could be reinforced, they must either withdraw or else stay to be overrun to no purpose. He explained this to Laverty on the radio and asked that he or his second-in-command should come and see the position for himself. Laverty sent Franklin, who had one look at the position and declared it quite untenable. Laverty had very few fighting reserves in hand and could not afford to incur further heavy casualties for ground that was not vital. He sent Coath a small reinforcement from headquarters and told him that he must hang on for the rest of the 10th, but was to withdraw that evening.

Coath accordingly began to thin out in the afternoon of the 10th, disguising his action by simulated activity, laying booby traps and destroying all the stores he could in the bashas. Yet another officer of C Company was lost in the process when Gordon Inglis was mortally wounded by a sniper. The company had been reduced to fifteen men, less than half the strength of a platoon. Detail Hill was not vital ground, but the company's heroic resistance, supported with no less valour by D Company, had held off a greatly superior enemy in a disadvantageous position for four vital days. They had done so by the sheer guts of the individual soldier and junior officer, fighting a series of night battles at a few yards range that would have tried the nerves of any troops in history. Detail Hill, no less than the tennis court and the dressing-station, was one of the heroic spots of Kohima.

Increasing Strain

It was the seventh day of operations and the fifth since the enemy had closed the ring. The officers and men of the Assam Regiment from Jessami and Kharasom, indeed, had been almost continuously in action for fourteen days, with only one full night's sleep. A heavy, wet pall of mist lay over all the hills after the night of rain, dulling all sounds. The strain had begun to show on all, except for the hard-as-nails Young, who seemed impervious to fatigue and hardship — a 'soldier by day and surgeon by night' in Barratt's words. No one could sleep except in short, uneasy snatches, fully clad and with boots on, and even in their sleep men were always listening. Fatigue was evident in every face and movement and reaction. All were sprouting beards. The ground had begun to be very foul with excreta.

In the dressing-station the lying wounded were in a deplorable state. Those of the original garrison had been lying in their open, shallow trenches for six days without any covering against the bitter cold of the nights. Unwashed and unshaven, they had now been drenched with rain and many were suffering severely from shock. On the 10th the ADS experienced its first shelling and bombing. It was not serious but several wounded men were hit again. Glover recorded in his little notebook: 'This type of war destroys all one's thoughts.' He noted that he and others had become indifferent to the daily horrors and sufferings and he commented: 'What a smell putrefying flesh has.'

Though the doctors and medical orderlies went round as often as possible to dress wounds, other needs could not be properly attended to. There were no bedpans. Elwell, going there to have his eye dressed, found the stench of the place 'horrible' and was repelled by the clouds of flies that settled on men's wounds.

In the operating-pits Young and his British and Indian doctors worked round the clock in reliefs attending to terrible wounds and carrying out amputations in the most primitive conditions, very soon with shells and mortar bombs bursting around them. There were at first ample supplies of anaesthetics and dressings, but conditions were such that many operations failed. Many wounds turned pussy with sepsis. Gas-gangrene was maintaining its dangerous attacks.

Yet in spite of all, as Barratt and two of the doctors who survived testify, the fortitude of those blanched and recumbent forms was exemplary. Wattison, who did no operating but spent his time attending to the men in the trenches, said: 'They were magnificent.' No complaints passed their lips. To help his neighbour keep his end up seemed by a common instinct the first thought of everyone. They talked quietly to one another and helped each other when they could. Of Shaw it was said that, even when grievously and painfully wounded, his example of cheerful courage was inspiring to all. When he was not talking to other people, he spent most of his time reading the Bible or a little pocket Shakespeare.

If morale was high in the dressing-station, it was no less so among the men who were still fighting. Dirt and fatigue were submerged by a determination in all ranks to fight it out and by their confidence that they could lick the Japanese as long as they could stand on their feet and hold a rifle. The typical little back-chat of British troops and their homely jests were evidence to those who understood that breed that all was well. What lay deep down behind this inner firmness was the absolute determination at all costs to save the wounded from falling into the savage hands of the Japanese. All knew too well the terrible fate that would fall upon their comrades if that should happen. Everyone who visited the dressing-station came away stiffened in his resolve not to let the Japanese get at them. Tactical features and blasted strips of foreign soil weighed less with them than that simple human appeal.

It was therefore heartening to receive on this day a message from Warren on Laverty's wireless with hopes of speedy relief. This hope derived from the fact that 2nd British Division was now mustering in the Dimapur area and 5th Brigade, under Brigadier Victor Hawkins, was poised to advance. As soon as he could join hands with Warren, Warren would be free to relieve Kohima. On this day, the 10th, accordingly, Stopford ordered General Grover, the commander of 2nd Division, to take over operations from General Rankin, and Grover ordered Hawkins to march forthwith for Kohima.

But Warren's message of hope was merely the first of many that were to follow almost daily for yet another week and to be received with diminishing credit each time. For between Hawkins and Warren and between Warren and Richards the Japanese had already interposed several of those road-blocks by which they were so skilful at delaying forces much larger than their own. Warren tried to send a bren-carrier patrol into the garrison on this day, but it was ambushed and failed.

12: PRIVATE BROWN AND HIS KIND

(Night 10/11 to Day 12 April)

The Tennis Court Held

AT DUSK on the 10th the reinforced Japanese shelled. and mortared the whole Ridge with increased severity. They began to employ some captured British 3-inch mortars and in the space of ten minutes they put down 100 bombs in the forty yards between the ADS and Laverty's command post.

The bombardment was heaviest and most continuous against Kenyon's company at the tennis court, who received a severe battering from mortars and artillery which splayed open the newly dug trenches, blew in the head cover of the quickly built bunkers, smashed weapons in men's hands and inflicted severe casualties. The weapon-pit on the mound received a direct hit. Dazed but undismayed, the West Kents clung to their trenches, expecting to be attacked as soon as the bombardment ended.

In the brief intermissions Kenyon went round his platoons, restoring confidence where it was needed and adjusting his dispositions to fill holes torn by casualties. There was a steady stream of wounded back to Young's dressing-station, itself a perilous journey.

No attack followed the bombardment but when one was launched later in the night, with what the battalion War Diary calls 'grenade discharger fire in profusion', the bruised West Kents and the guns at Yeo's command were ready for it and forced the Japanese to retire after a very stiff fight at close quarters. Kenyon spoke to the adjutant on the telephone and asked for a relief. 'I do not know,' he said afterwards, 'how the men stuck it nor how any of us was left alive.'

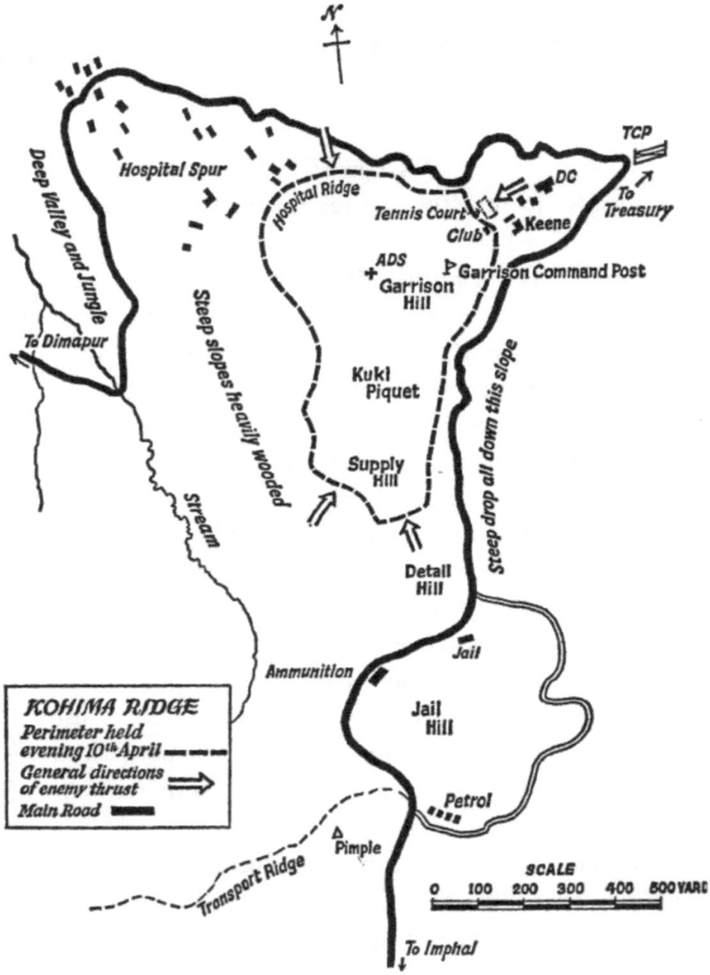
N
TCP
Hospital Spur
Hospital Ridge
DC
To Treasury
Tennis Court
Club
Keene
ADS
Garrison Command Post
Garrison Hill
Deep Valley and Jungle
To Dimapur
Steep slopes heavily wooded
Kuki Piquet
Steep drop all down this slope
Supply Hill
Stream
Detail Hill
Jail
Ammunition
Jail Hill
KOHIMA RIDGE
Perimeter held evening 10th April
General directions of enemy thrust
Main Road
Petrol
Pimple
Transport Ridge
SCALE
0 100 200 300 400 500 YARDS
To Imphal

Situation at dusk on April 10th.

On the other hand, Detail Hill was at last lost when Coath withdrew the remnant of C Company on the evening of the 10th. Its loss at once exposed Supply Hill, on which Naveen

Rawlley's composite Indian company was established, with Mitchell's two platoons of Rajputs apparently in front of them on the south and the Indian platoon believed to have been commanded by Lieutenant Kuriyan towards the western flank. The Kuriyan platoon seems to have stood fast almost to the very end of the story, often at grenade range, but the Rajputs were temporarily upset by the death of Mitchell, who was killed by a shell-splinter in the head at about the time that Coath withdrew from Detail Hill.

It was a tense and critical moment. The Japanese were expected to press a new attack on the remnants of Coath's retiring company and Mitchell's sepoys were much shaken by his death. Subedar Sultan Singh, however, took command and rallied the platoons. Thereafter until nearly the end the Rajputs fought a close-range fight with great spirit and determination until exhausted and decimated.

During the 11th intermittent mortar fire went on more or less all day and the enemy snipers crept closer in, but no fighting took place and no new enemy threat developed, thus bringing hope to the garrison that their friends to the west were beginning to relieve the pressure.

Their friends at Jotsoma, indeed, were this day themselves under considerable pressure as they awaited the advance of Hawkins's Brigade from Dimapur. That day Hawkins reached Milestone 32 and overcame an enemy road-block there, only to encounter another a few miles farther on. But the War Diary of the Royal West Kents recorded next day: 'Never for one moment did anyone doubt in successful resistance against the strong Jap forces.'

Up in his command post trench on Garrison Hill, Laverty, at his best in a tight corner, kept his fingers on the pulse of the battle as reports came in from his companies, adjusting their movements as the changing situation demanded, seldom resting by day or night and, like everyone else, always listening. There was a heavy responsibility on him, for his battalion was at this time bearing the brunt of the fighting and setting the tone for the rest of the garrison. He was beginning to feel fatigued, but was alert to every emergency and his loyal and devoted adjutant, Douglas Short, now sprouting a flamboyant red beard, did what he could to take some of the strain off his CO. Laverty was at all times splendidly served by his battalion signallers, who never failed to keep alive the aerial life-line with Warren's headquarters. Towards the end of the battle his signals officer, Captain Topham, was mortally wounded.

On the side lines of the tennis court Kenyon's company had now broken a series of attacks on two nights, had sat tight under a fierce bombardment and had accomplished the first of many memorable feats at that heroic spot. Under firm and steady leadership and with the immaculate support of Hill's mountain guns back at Jotsoma, A Company had given the second of the most positive repulses to the Japanese. Laverty now ordered John Winstanley, whose B Company on Kuki Piquet had not yet been closely engaged, to relieve Kenyon.

Winstanley was a medical student (of St Thomas's Hospital, London) of strong physique and was the only remaining officer of the pre-war establishment, having served with the battalion for some six years. As we have seen, he had just lost his captain, Tom Coath, to command C Company. He was left with two subalterns, Victor King and the Scot, Tom Hogg. The company included a strong element of Welshmen, including the sturdy Sergeant Glyn Williams, who commanded a platoon. The Welshmen were, in Winstanley's words, 'absolutely first-class fighting material'.

B Company had recently endured a gruelling experience at the notorious Tunnels of Hanaya's Golden Fortress in Arakan where they had incurred severe casualties, which had not been replaced, and where Winstanley had won the Military Cross. They had been plucked straight out of that fiery battle, packed into aircraft and flown at once to the scene of the new crisis. They were thus the thinnest of Laverty's companies.

Winstanley now took over smoothly soon after dark on the 11th and Kenyon's company retired to Kuki Piquet. B Company was disposed with Victor King's platoon on the right, covering the mound and the club house, Hogg's in the centre and Sergeant Williams's on the left. They were soon put to the test. In the dark void beyond the tennis court a jabbering and shouting and blowing of bugles told their tale of the enemy mustering for the attack. As the noise began to increase in pitch and tempo, Winstanley called by telephone for defensive fire. In less than a minute the first salvo from Hill's guns and the first bombs from Sergeant King's mortars were plunging down into the bank beyond the tennis court. The attack was broken up before it could be launched. Only a few Japanese struggled up the bank and, as their forms were silhouetted against the night sky, they were met by the fire of bren guns and by showers of grenades bursting at their feet. The stock of grenades ran low and Winstanley had to call urgently upon battalion headquarters for replenishment.

Two or three more similar attempts were made during the night by a persistent and stupid enemy and each time they were repulsed in a similar manner, but the company was forced to endure galling fire from mortars and grenade-discharger volleys in profusion. Typical of the fighting spirit and devotion of the fighting soldier was the example of Private Brown, a small, tough, bandy-legged Glaswegian with a heavy brogue.

219

Although he had served in the company for some time, Winstanley had never had reason to rate him very highly until this moment of trial.

Brown was the bren gunner in a section manning one of the exposed forward posts right on the edge of the tennis court. Almost as soon as the company relieved Kenyon's this post became extremely active and under pressure, but Brown completely dominated the tennis court right from the very start, under an almost continuous deluge of grenades; indeed, his was one of the posts constantly calling for more ammunition, both ball and grenade.

One by one every man in the section was killed and Brown, seeming to bear a charmed life, was left alone. He hung on, undismayed, standing up to the fire and engaging the enemy on every possible opportunity. Winstanley was therefore distressed to find, on his next ammunition round, the little soldier slumped over his gun, having just been shot by a sniper.

Brown, like Harman in a different way, was typical of many soldiers who never revealed any special qualities until they came to such a situation. By such humble men battles are often won. As this was a key post, Winstanley was concerned about whom to entrust it to. It was a death-trap to the unwary, yet Brown had shown that it was possible to hang on and dominate the vital tennis court.

The man he sent for was Corporal Richards, an ex-miner from Wales, who had served in his company for a long time, and whom he knew to be a tough and loyal character. From the way in which Richards responded to this dangerous assignment, Winstanley knew that the post would be safe in his hands as long as he could survive. And so it proved, for, when in due course the company was relieved, he was able to hand over his post intact.

Throughout this and the following night, the enormous bulk of Colour-Sergeant Eves was to be seen calmly going from trench to trench with dixies of warm food, which the men ate when they could between the bouts of fighting. The smaller parties of other men not in organized units and the maligned 'non-combatants' elsewhere in the garrison were less fortunate and had to fend for themselves. Thanks to Richards's foresight, there was ample food, but the means of heating in view of the enemy were almost non-existent, though most men in the organized units managed somehow to brew a little tea occasionally from the meagre water ration.

Supply Hill's Turn

As Stopford was to say later, the Bungalow Sector was the key to Kohima. Richards had made the same appreciation and so, no doubt, did the enemy commander also, for he continued to hurl his troops against it nearly every night in deadly encounters at close quarters. With their ant-like industry, the Japanese also began to fortify the ground they had taken, defensively and offensively. They dug a series of formidable bunkers at vantage points, which were later to take weeks of hammering to subdue, and they posted snipers and observers who made movement above the tennis court extremely dangerous.

While trying to seize this key, Sato, using Miyazaki's brigade, also maintained his pressure against the southern end of the box, which he now grasped as in a vice. With Detail Hill in his hands, he brought severe pressure on to Supply Hill, where Rawlley's troops now stood guard, with the Rajputs and the Kuriyan platoon manning the perimeter. Behind Supply Hill there now remained only the little Kuki Piquet and the dominant Garrison Hill.

Supply Hill therefore now came in for a severe hammering, particularly from mortars and from a 'beastly little infantry gun' on Jail Hill firing at a range of a bare 500 yards. This plastering was the overture to the inevitable attack. It came in sharply on the morning of the 12th in company strength and fell mainly on the two Rajput platoons and apparently on the Kuriyan platoon.[49] The veteran Subedar Sultan Singh and the young subaltern held their ground resolutely and on the front of the Rajputs twenty-eight Japanese corpses were counted after the attack had been repulsed. So close were the opposing trenches in some places that Punia, the Sikh observation officer of 2nd Mountain Battery, from an OP on Hospital Ridge, was bringing down the fire of his guns with extraordinary accuracy on targets scarcely fifteen yards from the troops he was supporting.

At about this time in D Company of the West Kents the gallant Sergeant-Major Haines was blinded by a burst but, with extraordinary fortitude, he remained at his duty, being led about by a private and doing all he could to encourage and sustain the NCOs and men.

Appeal to the Air

Conditions at the dressing-station on the 12th gave cause for mounting anxiety. At dawn that morning it had experienced the first of its deliberate bombardments by both artillery and mortars. Thirteen wounded men had been killed as they lay and sixty re-wounded. The whole place had become a scene of horror.

The contracted perimeter had brought the enemy nearer to it on two sides, while at the same time Barratt's little shallow trenches were rapidly expanding outwards as the numbers of the wounded multiplied every hour. They were scarcely 200

222

yards from the tennis court and were now under fire from snipers as well as by high explosive. The defoliated trees now gave little cover from observation. There was scarcely any more room to dig trenches. The swollen numbers and the enemy fire made the feeding of the patients increasingly difficult, but Young was able to arrange with Laverty that the British patients should be fed from the RWK cookhouse, while the Indians continued to be fed from his own. Young's supply of rations fell very low but he appealed to Barratt, who at once surrendered the greater part of the rations of his non-combatants. Young also appealed to Laverty for more blankets and the men of the Royal West Kents gave up 200 of their own.

On top of all these problems, Young was worried about his dwindling medical stores. He was running short of plasma, morphia and anti-gas-gangrene serum and needed more water than Barratt's platoon could supply. He therefore walked over the shoulder of Garrison Hill, reported his difficulties to Richards and asked for replenishment by air. As the Royal West Kents were running short of mortar ammunition and grenades, Richards summoned a conference at his command post and it was arranged that Laverty should ask 161st Brigade for an air drop. Richards, who was experienced in air supply and knew that an air drop would be very difficult, required that demands should be kept to a minimum, so that the medical supplies in particular could be dropped by light aircraft if necessary.[50]

The difficulties for pilots were enormous. The area was very constricted and covered with trees. The hill conditions, with their air currents, made low flying not very safe. The aircraft would be subjected to small arms fire, though not to anti-aircraft guns. There could be no niceties of a cleared and marked dropping zone. There were (contrary to some accounts) no ground strips to guide the aircraft. All that could be done was to give the pilots a map reference on a small-scale map and trust to their skill and judgement.

A drop was promised for the next afternoon.

13: THE BAD DAY

(Night 12/13 to Day 14 April)

Supply Hill in Danger

THERE FOLLOWED a very bad twenty-four hours. Sato's division was doing its utmost to liquidate the stubborn garrison, now reduced to less than 1,000 fighting men, while holding off the relieving forces. Hawkins's brigade was only eight miles away, but was obstructed by one road-block after another. Unequipped and untrained for jungle warfare, with enormous columns of motor transport, they were having to discover for themselves the technique of fighting the Japanese.

Their whole operation was being conducted astride a single road built on steep hillsides, with hairpin bends, precipitous drops into the valleys below, sharp rises to the hills above and densely wooded down to the very verge of the road. Not a single side road existed to relieve the strain on movement, which was frequently forbidden by deep nullahs not shown on the map. Only in a very few places was it possible for artillery to deploy or for vehicles to get off the road. Thus artillery had often to fire from the side of the road, which was also lined with dumps, parked vehicles, camps and parties of men trying to sleep or cook.

Supply Hill in Danger

At Kohima the night of 12th-13th was made hideous by increased jitter tactics by the Japanese all round the Ridge after the habitual evening bombardment. Another attack developed on the steep slopes of Hospital Ridge, but the Assam troops again threw it off. More dangerous was another attack against the weakened Rajput platoons on Supply Hill under Subedar Sultan Singh. This was an infiltration attack, but the Japanese were spotted and seen off. At a second attempt, however, having located the gaps in the Rajputs' thinly held posts, they succeeded in establishing themselves in a basha right in among them.

The morning light of the 13th disclosed a brittle situation and Laverty asked Richards for troops to clear it up. Richards sent in a platoon of the Assam Rifles, led by Subedar Uttam Sing Chettri. The platoon went in in good style, met the Japanese hand-to-hand, and wiped them out. They then came under heavy flank fire from machine-guns on Transport Ridge. Uttam Sing was wounded but hung on until increasing casualties forced him to withdraw.

An anxious day followed. The fate of Supply Hill was in the balance. The Japanese were pressing strongly against it and their guns from Jail Hill were firing straight into the exposed British and Indian trenches on the forward slope. The situation on the hill appears extremely confused and becomes increasingly difficult to follow. Elements of several units were on different parts of the hill, without coordination. The Sector commander appointed by Richards was Rawlley, but, according to the RWK War Diary, their D Company was also on the hill, without Rawlley's knowledge.[51] Kenyon, who began to move in next night with A Company, was only vaguely aware that there were 'some troops on my right' but had no positive knowledge of the existence of Rawlley's troops.

Except when a relief was required, the Royal West Kents virtually ignored other units. On Supply and Garrison Hills they occupied trenches where other troops were already in position, but usually dug new trenches for themselves right in among the sitting troops and without any regard to them.

Some of these troops could by no stretch of the imagination be called combatants, but others were, or had the will to fight if not the knowledge. No effective attempt at coordination seems to have been made. 'We were inclined,' wrote Kenyon afterwards, 'to hold each feature with little regard for others who might be able to help or who were in fact helping.'[52]

Language created an awkward barrier. The West Kents did not speak Urdu or Gurkhali and probably none of the Indian composite troops spoke English, except for their few officers. Had there been better cooperation, it is quite possible that Supply Hill would never have been lost.

'The Black 13th'

In all high drama there is a moment when events pile up to a point of crisis and the *denouement* hangs in the balance. To the garrison at Kohima the moment came on this Thursday, which, as the War Diary of the West Kents records, became known as 'the black 13th'. To the historian of the Assam Regiment it was 'a tedious agony of anxiety and misfortune'. In the more restrained language of Richards, it was 'a very difficult day'.

Of the several factors that made it so, none was more severe than the terrible events in the ADS, filling the whole garrison with horror.

In the dawn bombardment a heavy and continuous storm of high explosive fell among the wounded, lasting for an hour. Twenty-one were killed where they lay and thirty re-wounded. Four direct hits were sustained on or close to one of the operating-pits. Two of the doctors, Captains Moti and Sadiq, were killed and Young himself slightly wounded. Glover ran out on hearing the screams and found a scene of desolation, with human limbs strewn about the ground. Medical

227

equipment was scattered far and wide by blast and the whole dressing-station put out of action.

When the shooting subsided at 7 o'clock, Young at once began reorganizing and reconstructing the place and recovering and cleaning the medical equipment. At 3.30 in the afternoon he was able to report to Richards that things were fairly satisfactory, except for water, of which he had lost his reserve by damage to the container. The dressing-station reopened and more wounded began to come in.

In the evening bombardment at 6.30, however, the harsh tale of slaughter was repeated, beginning with a salvo from 3-inch mortars. Ten more patients were killed and an unspecified number re-wounded. Of the medical staff, Lahiri and three orderlies were killed and Captain Majid severely wounded. The whole medical staff worked throughout the night at dressings and at salvaging the scattered equipment. The ADS had now become one of the most dangerous places in the garrison, a regular target for the dawn and dusk bombardments. Young therefore walked down to the Garrison command post and asked if he might take over some of the State battalion's well-constructed trenches. Richards willingly gave orders accordingly. By 4 o'clock next morning Young was able to report to Richards that all was once more in order but that the medical staff were becoming exhausted.

Of that 13th Glover recorded in his diary: 'a terrible day', and he went on: 'the preservation of human life appears useless. Our operations very unsuccessful, most of them dying on the table or very shortly afterwards.'

This was one of the very few occasions when Young's buoyant spirit, which had so heartening an effect on all who saw him, suffered a set-back. The loss of his three doctors and of much valuable medical equipment, but, more especially, the sight of his patients dying so soon after he had operated on them affected him keenly and for once he looked very down in the mouth. He told Barratt that, because of the impossibility of proper nursing, the men died from post-operation shock following upon wound shock.

Other disappointments and trials contributed to making the 13th a black day. Things went wrong. The air drop was a distressing failure. The prospects of relief remained as far away as ever. Supply Hill was in great danger. The enemy pressure reached its highest pitch, sustained and seemingly inexorable. The bombardment increased in intensity and duration. The Japanese snipers multiplied and pressed closer in. Most of the trees had been stripped of their foliage and had become gaunt skeletons, so there was little cover left and any movement drew immediate fire.

The stand-to normally mounted at dawn became that day continuous and in most sectors was rigidly adhered to. Men had the feeling that they were being relentlessly squeezed by a giant fist. Officers were beginning to ask themselves how much longer they could expect the men to stand up to the physical and nervous strain. Their exhaustion showed in sluggish movement and in dulled perceptions. Coath and his orderly, sitting together in a trench on Supply Hill, found that both were showing one of the manifestations of fatigue — an uncontrollable trembling. They laughed at themselves but could do nothing to stop it. To Coath and many others the battle had become not only a physical trial but also a test of nervous tensions, against which each man had to fight inwardly. The close-quarter fighting of the previous night had kept all the perceptions continuously stretched, but the daylight hours of the 13th brought no relief and as new trials and disappointments took shape the prospects grew hourly a little darker.

Thus the 13th was a stiff test of morale. The garrison passed it with their will to fight unimpaired. They were infused by what Laverty, quoting Sir Douglas Haig, described afterwards as the 'backs-to-the-wall spirit'. The British troops remained steady and lost nothing of their native humour.

Of that spirit, Elwell was given proof after returning from a visit to his Assam CO, Bruno Brown, on Hospital Ridge. There had been a storm of mortaring and when it subsided he saluted and dashed off round the hill, pausing occasionally to recover his breath. Approaching Kuki Piquet, he was picked up by a Japanese machine-gun and took cover. Each time he tried to move there was a flight of bullets and the flash of tracers disagreeably close. He flung himself down, rolled, rose and dashed, flung himself down again and slithered along. A burst came too close and he lay in the dust with the tracer bullets kicking up the earth a foot from his nose. He wondered how long he would have to lie still before daring to move again, when a friendly voice said quietly:

'Why don't you come in, instead of cluttering up the doorstep?'

A corporal of the West Kents was lying in the entrance of a dug-out which he had not noticed. Elwell slid in as two mortar bombs burst outside, sucking the air from the little dug-out and returning it filled with dust.

'Thanks,' he said.

'Think nothing of it,' replied the corporal. 'Have a cuppa char?'

'Thank you very much; I could certainly do with it.'

'Sorry the missus isn't in, sir. Here, Charlie, pass the mug.'

A tall soldier in the back of the dug-out passed a chipped and battered mug filled with hot, sweet tea. Seldom, thought Elwell, had any beverage tasted so good, but it was not more refreshing than the cheerful calm of this Kentish soldier.

The corporal wanted to know what news there was, but there was little Elwell could tell him except that relieving troops were on the way.

The corporal nodded sagely in a manner which plainly implied that he had heard it all before and remarked: 'Well, that's a good thing, sir. Meanwhile, here we are and here we stay. That's it, sir, isn't it?'

The Air Drop

The first aircraft were heard coming in on time at 2.30 in the afternoon. All eyes, British, Indian and Japanese, turned to watch them. They were three American aircraft. They came in low and straight, disregarding the small-arms fire from the ground. They passed on and began to circle, but did not see, or could not recognize, the green Verey lights shot up by the Royal West Kents. With chagrin the garrison watched them circle the wrong hill, saw their hatches open, the coloured parachutes fall, billow out and drop their loads of ammunition to the enemy.

A little later a second flight appeared. They were RAF aircraft. After circling, they came in accurately and dropped their loads with precision. The parachutes settled and stretched out along the ground or were caught in the trees. These also were ammunition loads, but they were the wrong ammunition; they were 3.7 inch howitzer ammunition that should have gone to Hill's guns at Jotsoma.

A third flight appeared and again dropped straight and true. Most of the parachutes caught in the trees and the garrison could see water cans dangling tantalizingly before their eyes but out of reach. They were two-gallon petrol tins tied together in bunches of eight, like metal grapes. The Japanese could see them, too, and began to shoot holes through them, the water running out. Other parachutes, improvised from jute, failed to open, their loads crashing heavily, killing and maiming several of the garrison. One load, missing Lieutenant Punia by a foot as it sailed past his OP, struck two Indian gunners, who became 'mere lumps, as if without bones'.

No attempt was possible to recover what was left of the loads until after dark, while the enemy swept the area with fire. The stalwart Sergeant Clinch, from the RWK pioneer platoon, led one of the parties. They recovered a little water and were still more pleased to find all or most of the medical stores that Young so urgently needed.

But there was no mortar ammunition for Sergeant King. That had all gone to the enemy.

The Cromwellian Touch

Richards, as he moved about the stricken scene that afternoon, the tenth of the battle, and beheld the tired, unkempt figures and the strained, unshaven faces, sensed the tension in the air and knew that the day of mental crisis which so often supervenes in all such ordeals had arrived; if it could be overcome, all would be well as long as men's reserves of physical strength could last. It was, he reflected, like the third act of a play or the second innings of a cricket match, when, after a superb performance so far, the players seem suddenly in danger of cracking.

Keenly affected, he went back to his command post, dodging the snipers, and, in response to a suggestion by Laverty, wrote out a Special Order of the Day. It had a true Cromwellian touch and is still treasured by many of the old garrison today. Then he walked along the trench to his clerk, telling him to type out a copy for each unit, and gave orders for its distribution. It was taken out perilously by men who crept out among the splintered trees and handed to arms cautiously outstretched from the trenches. It read:

1. I wish to acknowledge with pride the magnificent effort which has been made by all officers, NCOs and men and followers of this Garrison in the successful defence of Kohima.
2. By your efforts you have prevented the Japanese from attaining his object. All his attempts to overrun the Garrison have been frustrated by your determination and devotion to duty. Your efforts have been in accordance with the highest traditions of the British army.
3. It seems clear that the enemy has been forced to draw off to meet the threat of the incoming relief force and this in itself has provided us with a measure of relief. His action now is directed to containing us by harassing fire, while he seeks to occupy odd posts under cover of that fire.
4. The relief force is on its way and all that is necessary for the Garrison now is to stand firm, hold its fire and beat off any attempt the enemy may make to infiltrate among us.
5. By your acts you have shown what you can do. Stand firm, deny him every inch of the ground.
6. I deplore the sufferings of the wounded; every effort is being made to alleviate them at the first opportunity.
7. Put your trust in God and continue to hit the enemy hard wherever he may show himself. If you do that his defeat is sure.
8. I congratulate you on your magnificent effort and am confident that it will be sustained.

The premonitions of the 13th seemed to be fulfilled that night, when bitter fighting took place as the Japanese again tried to break in. On Supply Hill the exhausted and hard-tried Rajputs suffered another severe battering by mortars and high-velocity shellfire. When it seemed that they could no longer possibly hold on, Subedar Sultan Singh, with one of his platoons reduced to seven men, and the remainder at breaking point, felt obliged to withdraw. Kenyon, whose A Company of the Royal West Kents was then on Kuki Piquet, accordingly moved in the platoon commanded by Lieutenant Jack Faulkner to plug the dangerous gap. The rest of the company, together with the remnants of Coath's C Company, now only fourteen strong, followed. Rawlley himself briefed the Kentish officers and while he was doing so a Rajput sepoy was shot by a sniper as he ran from one trench to another.

As far as could be judged in the dark, Kenyon's companies were separated from the Japanese by only the length of a cricket pitch. A little later, Kenyon and Coath were together in a front trench when the dark forms of some Japanese were observed occupying a basha twenty yards away. Kenyon ordered Faulkner, a youngster of spirit, to dispose of them and Faulkner decided to do so alone. Having been provided with a Molotov cocktail made by the sappers, he dashed out into the night, lit the fuse and threw the bottle at the hut. It failed to ignite. He ran out a second time, right up to the hut, lit the fuse again and threw the bottle through the window opening. The hut went up in flames and a bren gun was waiting for the Japanese as they ran out.

Thus the black 13th passed unregretfully into the 14th. The whole of this sector of Supply Hill was thoroughly unwholesome in every sense. Several weapon-pits a little forward of Kenyon's position were really open graves, crowded with dead, and as the day grew warmer on the 14th, the stink grew worse. He decided to recover them, clear them out and at the same time make his position more secure. He ordered an attack under Cover of a smoke screen from the Company's own 2-inch mortars, but the mortars failed to produce an effective smoke screen and the attack was called off. The only result was to provoke defensive fire by the enemy.

The companies stuck it out, very uncomfortable but very determined.

Vantage Striker

On the tennis court there was another series of attacks on Winstanley's B Company on the night of the 13th, lasting the greater part of the night and continuing well into the 14th. There was an almost continuous rain of grenades from dischargers and frequent showers of mortar bombs. All the attacks were repulsed with the same determined spirit and the same excellence of artillery support as before. The tennis court itself and its surroundings were now strewn with Japanese corpses, but heavy casualties were also suffered by a defence that took a severe buffeting but would not budge an inch. There were some dangerous moments when, by a rush attack, a party of Japanese gained entry to the club house, but Lieutenant Victor King attacked them with grenades and liquidated them.

On another occasion Private Williams and another soldier manning a machine-gun on the mound behind the club were attacked by two or three Japanese sneaking up along the side of the club; the bren jammed and the Japanese rushed them, but

Williams, seizing a shovel, felled the leading Jap and the remainder fled.

Laverty now asked Richards for a relief of Winstanley's company. In spite of the restricted perimeter, Laverty was hard put to it to effect any reliefs within his battalion. His casualties had by now amounted to about 150 killed and wounded out of the original 444 (the total casualties of the garrison being so far some 400). Besides the decimated C Company, D was down to about 30 out of its initial 75. All troops in the garrison were now desperately tired, but the Royal West Kents had borne the brunt of the fighting since the 6th.

Richards accordingly, dodging the snipers covering his command post, made his way to Bruno Brown on Hospital Spur and gave orders for Winstanley to be relieved by a composite force of the Assam Regiment and the Assam Rifles. To this command was appointed the remarkable figure of Major Calistan of the Assam Regiment. Calistan, who had served in the ranks in the Guards and who had recently married an American nurse in Assam, was a tall, dashingly handsome man, black-haired and moustached, slim and wiry, hard as nails, hot-tempered, fastidiously correct and smart in his turn-out, a severe disciplinarian, insisting on the meticulous performance of duties under no-matter-what conditions, and of great personal courage.

The relief, carried out by day, was a dangerous one and several casualties were suffered from snipers. One of these was Major James Askew, of the Assam Regiment, who, after having handed over to Winstanley on Hospital Ridge, was shot dead by a sniper near Richards's command post. Eight others of the Assam troops were killed or wounded when dashing over open ground to occupy the forward bunkers. So risky was this relief that it was not completed until dusk. On the loss of Askew, the defence of the left wing was taken over, in spite of a slight wound, by Peter Steyn, the very tall, cool-headed young South African.[53] The Assam Rifles platoon, under Cleland, held the mound and the club on the right.

The Assam troops found well-made bunkers and weapon-pits left by the RWK. They found other evidences also of a stout-hearted and unyielding defence. Steyn, making his way into a trench in the dark that evening, found three or four figures leaning on the parapet in firing positions and told them to move over. When they refused, he pushed them, to find that they were all dead. Many other dead of the previous night's fighting were found and the Assam troops set about burying them.

Looking sprucer than anyone else, Calistan, by force of personal example, kept the vital tennis court sector unbroken for five days, twice as long as any others. When offered relief two or three days later, he refused it, because of the risk of unnecessary casualties. From the start he adopted methods of aggression as far as the situation allowed, and, lacking the support of Sergeant King's heavier weapons, made shrewd use of his own little 2-inch mortars, cocking them up to extreme elevation so that the bombs fell not twenty yards in front of his own troops. He never, however, lacked immediate and accurate support from the artillery at Jotsoma, which he could call for by his telephone line to Richards, kept open by a gallant Sikh linesman.

Having failed so often to overcome the Royal West Kents by violent assault, the Japanese began during Calistan's tenure to attempt penetrating by sneaking up in very small parties with fused and primed slabs of guncotton. Such methods, however, had no terrors for the keen-eared hillmen. On Calistan's orders, one man in each section post lay out on the parapet and every now and then a single rifle shot told its story.

Throughout the whole of the 14th the garrison was pommelled by mortar fire. Lieutenant Oldrey, one of Richards's staff officers, was shot by the sniper who was keeping the command post covered. Landor and another officer ran out and brought him in, but he died very soon afterwards. His place in Richards's staff was taken by Maclachlan, of the Burma Regiment.

The same morning there was another air drop, this time much more accurate, but again the ropes of several jute parachutes broke and caused further casualties, and one of the aircraft crashed on Transport Ridge.

14: HOPE DEFERRED

(Night 14/15 to Day 17 April)

Respite from Assault

NO SOONER had Young returned from reporting to Richards at 4 AM on the 14th that the ADS was now working normally again than another violent assault fell upon it. At 5 o'clock it was once more bombarded. A direct hit on a shelter containing ten patients killed them all. Once more the operating-pit was hit, by three shells this time, killing two patients on whom Young had carried out amputations during the night, together with the orderly nursing them. Twenty other patients were re-wounded.

Once more Young repaired and reorganized and salvaged his scattered equipment. He decided also that a new operating-pit was vital and set Barratt's men to work on a new site. Barratt himself took charge and by 9.30 the new 'theatre' was finished. It was 6 ft deep, 10 ft long and had a strong timbered roof. Before midday it received a direct hit from a 3-inch mortar bomb, without any serious damage.

Two nights and days followed in which the garrison continued to be attacked by fire but no major assault developed. Probing attacks on the tennis court were seen off by the alert Assam troops. The Japanese pressed heavily against Supply Hill, blasting the exposed trenches with high explosives. On the first night some Japanese succeeded in infiltrating into Kenyon's A Company position but were vigorously cleared out.

To the northward, a Japanese battery that had come into action some days before on the Merema crest was pounding the Assam troops above the tennis court, Richards's command post and the dressing-station. Volleys of discharger grenades continued to pour in and in one of these Harry Smith was wounded in the face while talking to Richards just outside the garrison command post. Perhaps most galling of all, however, was to be bombarded by the 3-inch mortar ammunition that had been dropped to the enemy from the air, especially as the British bombs were far more lethal than the Japanese, detonating with a vicious crump. Smoke bombs were mixed indiscriminately with high explosive. One of the worst sufferers was Barratt's burial party, who were also under small-arms fire, but they remained very steady, responding to Barratt's orders for evasive action.

There were two more air drops, one successful but the other falling again to the enemy. Fresh medical supplies were received and all Young's patients, to the number of some 300 now, were injected with morphia and anti-gas-gangrene serum. More heartening was to see Allied aircraft out for the first time strafing the enemy among the hills.

During these last few days repeated messages had come in from 161st Brigade promising early relief, but there had been no fulfilment. The advance of 2nd British Division from Dimapur was being obstructed by road-blocks every mile or two and, until they joined hands with 161st Brigade, Warren could not move to relieve Kohima. The sounds of the distant fighting could be clearly heard by the garrison, but seemed to come no nearer. On the afternoon of the 14th an officer patrol of the Rajputs skilfully made its way into the garrison. It went out again soon afterwards, reporting to Warren that the garrison was 'utterly exhausted'.

The situation remained difficult as the Japanese strove to prevent the relief. Not till the 15th did 5th Brigade dispose of the last road-block, when Hawkins himself made his way over a damaged bridge and met Warren. At this point Brigadier Shapland's 6th Brigade took over the baton from Hawkins and Warren was at last able to turn to the relief of Kohima. He at once moved forward his Punjabi battalion, to the command of which Harry Grimshaw had been appointed only the day before.

'Damned, Lonely'

In spite of the relief from actual assault, the condition of the garrison was now becoming very serious indeed. Officers and men were beginning to be groggy on their feet, but were bolstered up by the determination to protect their wounded. In the ADS more men died or were killed. Gas-gangrene and sepsis were spreading. Young had lost two more of his doctors; Captain Ribeiro collapsed from nervous prostration and Glover was shot in the leg on two separate occasions by snipers.

Elwell, visiting the ADS again, was asked by one of the doctors to go round and talk to the Indians, as he spoke Urdu. Carrying his rifle, wearing a piratical black patch over his injured eye and with his other eye puffed up, he wandered round the slits and bays, some open to the sky, some covered 'with all manner of rubbish', where the wounded lay. Some moaned and were incoherent but most were amazingly calm. He saw that they were drinking out of ration tins and using other tins for urination. The once thick trees that had been their canopy had been stripped by fire and were here and there festooned with parachutes. The smell of death hung over the whole area and, as he walked round, the bombs were still falling, but they no longer worried him.

In one bay he found some British orderlies removing bodies. A haggard and sweat-stained orderly said to him: 'Poor devils; lying here wounded and a bomb dropped right in the middle of them.' He wiped his face on his arm and bent down to pick up an empty stretcher.

In one hole Elwell found an officer of the Royal West Kents, his revolver lying by his side. Seeing Elwell's bearded and swollen face and his eyepatch, he grabbed his revolver, pointed it at Elwell and asked: 'Who the bloody hell are you?' For the one thing all the wounded feared was to be taken by the enemy.

Elwell told him, but the officer continued to hold out his revolver until Elwell leaned his rifle against the side of the hole. The officer relaxed and said: 'I thought you were a bloody Jiff.'

Elwell asked if there was anything he could do for him and the other replied:

'No, not much. It's damnably lonely though; will you stay for a bit and talk? What's happening?'

Elwell told him cheerfully about the promised relief, but the officer shrugged in disbelief and said:

'No, we've heard all that before. What's really happening?'

Elwell told him what he knew and said that both their regiments were holding out well on Supply Hill and the tennis court but were pretty tired. The RWK officer commented:

'It's damned awful, isn't it? One can't help wondering how much longer it can last. Another night or two, I should think, and then — finish.'

'Another night or two, as you say, and by then Daddy Warren's chaps will be here.'

'The Japs will do their damnedest to stop them. Let's be realistic. There's, one promise you can make me. If you do get out, take me with you. If not, make sure I'm dead.'

Elwell, feeling very much impressed that a man in his condition could still have so aggressive a spirit, tried to reassure him and left him lying very much alone in the midst of death and desolation. He noticed that nearly all the wounded officers who were not too far spent had their revolvers beside them.

In a square pit he stopped to talk to four sepoys who lay silently looking up at the sky through the lattice-work of the torn trees.

'*Kaisa hai*?' ('How is it?') he asked.

One was too far gone to notice. The other three, with the fine discipline of the good Indian soldier, struggled to a semblance of attention on their stretchers till he told them to lie down. He told them about the relief force fighting forward. One sepoy beamed but the other two shook their heads. 'They will not be able to reach us, sahib; there are too many Japanese.'

They chatted awhile light-heartedly and Elwell was able to raise some smiles. As he left them, they said: 'Come and see us again, sahib.'

He heard them chattering among themselves and felt a queer mixture of emotion. Nearly all the wounded he spoke to were quietly waiting for what seemed to them the inevitable end. He went back later in the day and found the pit where the four soldiers had lain, empty and stained with blood.

The evening mist was filling the valley below. On the prominent ridge east of Jotsoma, which was to become known as Punjab Ridge, he could see heavy fighting going on, with the shells of the British 25-pounders of 2nd Division detonating in black clouds, but over Kohima Ridge a brooding silence lay as the tired garrison waited for the night and made their preparations for what might well be the final assault by the enemy.

On the night of the 15th, after Hawkins and Warren had met, Laverty was advised by radio that relief could be expected on the next day, which was Sunday, the 16th. Accordingly the garrison began to make early arrangement for the evacuation of the wounded, which was the first of all priorities. All were warned and Young made orderly dispositions of what was a difficult and dangerous operation. It was a dismal, overcast night, with the mountain mist denser than ever.

As on other such occasions, men's first thoughts were of those at home and the wounded who were to be taken out asked those remaining to give them any letters that they wanted got away. Of this moment, Elwell recorded:

> Returning to my slit trench, I sat down to write to my parents and to my fiancée, but what was there to say? Censorship forbade us to say anything of the fighting. So we just wrote that we were well, we hoped that they were well, we would write at length in the near future and we sent our love. It seemed a poor little letter, written with the stub of a pencil on someone else's paper and saying nothing. I folded my cap badge into Pauline's letter and thought it might be the last thing that I would ever send.

The promise of help, however, proved to be only another instance of hope deferred. No sign of the relief materialized. The Japanese knew perfectly well what 161st Brigade was up to and did their best to stop them. It was unfortunate that the troops had got to hear of the message. Glover, himself at the point of collapse from wounds and fatigue, recorded in his diary that a few of his patients and some elements of the troops were beginning to become demoralized. But the men in the perimeter trenches took their disappointment philosophically and no thought entered their heads but to fight on as long as they could stand on their feet.

Richards accordingly walked up the hill to Laverty's command post to discuss the situation with him and found him speaking to Warren on the radio about the serious plight the garrison were now in. Richards himself also spoke to Warren and said that unless relief came quickly it would be too late. Warren replied that he was doing all he could, but intended to make 'a proper job' of it.

A Flash of Spirit

A certain amount of tension developed on the 16th from deferment of the expected relief and down on the tennis court Calistan's composite Assam troops had been plagued by a Japanese machine-gun post among some trees behind Keene's old bungalow. Movement in the tennis court sector had been severely restricted and casualties incurred. Calistan had tried first to suppress the enemy post by 2-inch mortars, but with only temporary success.

Accordingly, acting on the best precepts of the offensive defence, Calistan decided to attack the post, and to attack it moreover, with the maximum economy of force. It was a very small operation, but a model of its kind.

As the light was failing, four men, led by Naik Dilhu Angami, who was a local Naga, got out of their trench on the terrace above the tennis court and dashed down the steep slope to the shouts and cheers of their comrades. Each clasped in his hands grenades from which the pins had already been withdrawn. They had about forty yards to go. Two bren guns opened fire to cover their attack — one from Calistan's extreme left and the other from the shattered club house, in which Sepoy Wellington Massar boldly mounted his gun on the billiard

245

table. This exposed him to the full view of the enemy but gave him better command.

The Japanese were taken completely by surprise as Dilhu's grenades burst among them. The machine-gun was destroyed and the detachment wiped out. Adjacent Japanese weapons sprang to life and opened fire on the little band as they darted back, triumphantly carrying an officer's sword, seven rifles and some signal equipment. All got home safely, but Sepoy Wellington was less fortunate. Covering Dilhu's withdrawal, he was badly wounded and fell off the billiard-table. With a great effort he climbed up again and continued to fire until the raiders were home.

After dark Wellington was carried from the club house. He asked not to be taken to the dressing-station, but to remain among his comrades. His wounds were accordingly dressed at Calistan's headquarters post and there, he stayed until the end. He died soon afterwards in hospital.

The little offensive, watched throughout by the admiring Harry Smith, was a great stimulus to the Assam troops and the enemy machine-gun was not replaced. Moreover, so completely had the garrison now attained ascendancy in the tennis court sector that no more serious assaults were launched there by the enemy, though they never ceased attacking it by fire and frequently made tentative movements towards it. Calistan maintained strict and offensive vigilance, opening fire on the slightest signs of enemy movement and continuing to use his little mortars aggressively at very short range.

Supply Hill under Pressure
The night of the 16th was dark and foggy, with rain supervening. The ghostly shapes of dripping parachutes hung from the leafless trees in queer and distorted shapes. The

troops, bearded, chilled, dizzy with fatigue, very dirty, footsore from continuously wearing their boots for nearly a fortnight, many wounded, leant against the wet parapets of their trenches, staring into the black void and listening. That evening they had seen Warren's troops fighting forward from Jotsoma supported now by the 25-pounders of 2nd Division, whose shells were bursting about the Treasury and the Naga Village also. Would tomorrow really be the last day? The garrison was quite determined to go on sticking it out, but they wished devoutly that 'the Duke of York's Own' would hurry up.

That night Keene's Assam Rifles were again attacked on Hospital Ridge and again the attack failed, twenty-four enemy bodies being counted the next morning. An attempt against Calistan's force above the tennis court similarly failed.

The northern door of the box thus stood as firm as ever, but the southern door was gradually cracking under insistent pressure. this night there was further penetration, following heavy bombardment, into the positions occupied by the combined A and C Companies of the RWK on Supply Hill. Both were now seriously depleted and very tired. Many were suffering from wounds, having returned to the firing-line after quick treatment at the dressing-station. All had got very thin. On the morning of the 17th they were heavily attacked, suffered casualties and stubbornly gave ground.

Laverty had now no troops left who were fit to relieve them and again asked Richards for assistance. Richards, in his turn, could now only call upon the Assam troops once more. Again a mixed force was hurriedly made up of two platoons of the Rifles and the transport platoon of the Regiment, consisting of seventeen mule-leaders and drivers, whose only experience of arms was two practice courses of musketry and who were under an officer strange to them. None of the platoons possessed automatics. The scratch force mustered and moved forward towards Supply Hill to attempt a mission for which neither unit had had any training whatever. They were no less fatigued than the West Kents, but had not had to endure continuous close-quarter fighting nor such severe bombardment. They now received their full share as the Japanese mortar bombs cascaded on them when they approached A and C Companies' trenches. The relief operation failed and the Assam troops, severely shaken, withdrew more or less simultaneously with the Royal West Kents.

By the personal leadership of Rawlley, however, the positions were regained and, although lost twice more, were twice more recovered. The citation for his subsequent Military Cross says that 'he personally led troops back into vacated positions on three occasions'. Supposedly these were Indian troops.

Kenyon had withdrawn A and C Companies to the south of Garrison Hill. But the day was far advanced before the troublesome business was completed and the 17th ended with the situation on Supply Hill very tense and difficult. The only heartening fact was that Major Gavin Dunnett's company of 1/1st Punjabis could now be plainly seen in occupation of Piquet Hill, only half a mile to the westward, and when a patrol from the garrison went down the steep slope of Hospital Spur the only Japanese to be seen were the putrid accumulations of their corpses that gave evidence of how securely the Assam units had held the back door.

That day there had been a more firm promise of relief the next morning, with special emphasis on the evacuation of casualties. It was to be covered by heavy concentrations of artillery fire on the adjacent enemy-held features. So much Laverty learnt by radio from Jotsoma and he passed the news on to Richards and Young. Richards visited Young at the ADS during the afternoon and an hour later Young saw him at the Garrison Command Post and received approval of the plan he proposed. The evacuation was to be from the foot of Hospital Spur and was to be carefully controlled, but he would need the maximum possible numbers of stretcher-bearers. He saw Richards again after dark and informed him that everything had been tied up with Warren's headquarters and again received Richards's confirmation. But this time, in case hopes should again be dashed, the wounded were not informed.[54]

15: THE LAST DITCH

(Night 17/18)

ON THE evening of April 17th, the main dispositions of the formed bodies of troops were apparently as follows:

> SUPPLY HILL. The composite Indian company, the mixed Assam force and the Kuriyan platoon (Rawlley).
> KUKI PIQUET. D Company RWK (Collett) and what was left of the Rajputs.
> GARRISON HILL. A and C Companies RWK (Kenyon and Coath) on Southern slopes; HQ company of the State battalion.
> GARRISON COMMAND POST AREA. Platoons of HQ Company RWK (Harry Smith) and some mixed troops.
> TENNIS COURT. Calistan's mixed Assam force.
> HOSPITAL RIDGE. B Company RWK (Winstanley), with remainder of Assam Rifles (Keene) and Yeo's gunners.

In spite of their buffeting, the spirit of most of the garrison remained remarkably high. 'The proven warriors of the West Kents', as Elwell had called them, had set all a magnificent example. Red-eyed, bearded, dirty, they were still vigilant and aggressive, still capable of cracking a joke, always clinging to their positions till the last possible minute, using their weapons skilfully. But their ranks had been torn by casualties and those who remained were making heavy demands on their reserves of endurance; all had lost a lot of weight. This night their fatigue very nearly resulted in disaster as the Japanese launched the most powerful assault they had yet made.

Unaccountably, Sato had left Piquet Hill, the high, knobbly feature just to the west of Kohima Ridge, untenanted and

Harry Grimshaw, ordered by Warren to capture it as his first task on taking command of 1/1st Punjab, had beaten the pistol and sent Dunnett's company forward to seize it. It was therefore imperative for Sato to overcome what remained of the garrison before Warren's brigade broke through from that feature. If he could gain possession of Kohima Ridge within the next twenty-four hours, Sato would be in an immensely strong position to hold the advancing British 33rd Corps at bay. If Imphal fell, he could be quickly reinforced by the main road and the great mountain barrier of which Kohima was the key would be secure against whatever strength might be brought against it. He therefore redoubled his efforts.

Above the tennis court Calistan's Assam force still dominated the scene. His strict personality imposed itself almost visibly. An aggressive defence kept the howling Japanese at bay and another attempt at penetration was seen off. All attempts against that sector having failed, the enemy once more made his main effort this night against Supply Hill, sensing a slackening in the hitherto stiff resistance.

The evening began with a particularly heavy bombardment of that hill. It went on for five hours without respite. Garrison Hill also was very severely punished. There were long and heavy concentrations on the areas of Richards's and Laverty's own command posts and it was miraculous that neither received a direct hit. Smoke and incendiary shell were mixed with high explosive. The bashas on Supply Hill were set on fire and the men crouching in their trenches dazed with the deluge of fire.

On the top of Supply Hill, Rawlley, with his orderly and signaller, stood in his trench at the corner of a basha wondering when the bombardment would end. It did so at about 9.30. Knowing that this was the dangerous moment,

Rawlley got out of his trench with his two men to go round his posts and alert them for the expected attack. He looked round and saw all his trenches empty. He began cautiously to walk down the hill. At fifteen yards range he beheld a solid phalanx of Japanese, shoulder to shoulder, advancing up the hill, with two more waves behind. He and his small party turned and ran, escaping capture by a hair's breadth as the Japanese 'breathed down our necks'.

He made his way towards Kuki Piquet behind him, but on approaching it was firmly challenged by D Company of the Royal West Kents and fired on. He took cover, shouted out who he was and received the unequivocally hearty reply:

'You ——, Major Rawlley was killed three hours ago.'

Wishing for once that the West Kents were less alert and aggressive, he and his companions lay in the little valley between the two hills for half an hour, in the cross-fire between the two armies. At length an officer who knew him, and who he believed was Fred Collett, came forward, admitted him and politely asked him if he wished to take command. Rawlley, however, thanking him for his courtesy, made his way through the ravaged night across the little hill, stumbled over the hard going of Garrison Hill and so to Richards's command post and asked for orders. Richards, understanding and calm as ever, received him kindly and told him to find somewhere to rest.

Meanwhile, however, Kuriyan and his small band of Indian infantry were still holding out, alone, on the shattered south-west slope of Supply Hill. Not until he realized that he was cut off and the enemy already behind him, did he think of withdrawing without orders. He then collected his men and stole out in good order and unbeaten.

In spite of his outward calm, Richards was now seriously concerned. He had no news of Brown's Assam force on Supply Hill, and it was very important that he should have a more complete picture than Rawlley had been able to give him. He therefore telephoned to Hepworth, at the headquarter dug-out of the State battalion, where he knew the injured Donald Elwell was likely to be. Calling for Elwell to speak on the telephone, he asked him where Brown was and when Elwell replied that he did not know, Richards said:

'Then you will have to go and find him.'

Taken aback, Elwell said:

'Where do I look, sir?'

'I don't know, but possibly still on Supply Hill. The Japs seem to have overrun the place, but Colonel Brown has not returned. He may be cut off. You must find him and bring him back to Kuki Piquet.'

'That will be difficult, sir. I can hardly see.'

'I am sorry, but that can't be helped. You are the only officer I have to spare who knows Colonel Brown. You must go immediately and report back to me as soon as you have definite news.'

Elwell picked up his rifle, called his faithful orderly Ymtongsau Lotha and set out into the night. At the best of times he would not have relished the task of penetrating the Japanese lines and now, half-blind and the night dark, he would have to rely on the eyes and ears of Ymtong.

They wound their way round the side of Garrison Hill into the gulley that separated it from Kuki Piquet, where he had hitherto spent most of the siege with his transport platoon. All was quiet, but he knew that eyes were watching them somewhere in the darkness and hoped that some trigger-happy soldier would not shoot at them. They went on down the path that they both knew. Three mortar bombs burst and then all was quiet again. They knelt in the shadow of some scrub for a while, watching and listening. Knowing that D Company of the West Kents were on Kuki Piquet, Elwell thought it wise to let them know that he would be wandering about their front. Telling Ymtong to wait, he began scrambling up Kuki Piquet alone calling out in English not to fire.

He was stopped suddenly at a slit trench and found himself looking down the barrels of two rifles. He had a moment's horror when he saw that the owners of the rifles were not British, before recognizing them as Rajputs. He felt profoundly thankful for their fire discipline, for they could not have understood a word he said. A young jemadar crept forward and pointed out the direction of D Company's headquarters. Thanking him, Elwell said: 'We are going forward to do a little reconnaissance of Supply Hill. Tell your men to be good enough not to shoot us and pass the word along to D Company.'

A gleam of white teeth showed in the darkness as the jemadar smiled. Elwell dropped back to the path where Ymtong was waiting, his rifle at the ready, and said: '*Age chalo, bhai*' — 'Forward, brother.' He slipped forward the safety-catch of his rifle and moved on, Ymtong three paces behind, stopping occasionally to stare out into the darkness and listen. The night around them seemed to breathe and to be watching them. Small rustling sounds came from the scrub. The ground glittered with a million phosphorescent particles, the remains of burst grenades, making the stars seem dull.

They crept on up the slope of Supply Hill, but were brought up short when, a few feet away, a dozen men were heard quietly pulling open packing-cases and muttering among themselves. The two crept closer still and listened again, trying to identify the muttered language.

'*Japani*,' whispered Ymtong.

Elwell longed for a tommy-gun or a few grenades, for rifles were useless. Ymtong's murmured word or the click of his safety-catch was enough warning for the Japanese, for they dived at once for cover behind the cases and all was quiet again.

Elwell and Ymtong crept back a little, then moved off left-handed, hoping to swing round the Japanese party, but had not gone twenty yards before they heard another group muttering in the same way behind some bushes. They turned about and manoeuvred to the right of the first party.

There were Japanese everywhere — behind every clump of bushes, behind the trees and in the garrison's old slit trenches. Elwell reflected that if his CO was on the hill he must have been killed or captured by now. More than that, it seemed to him that this concentration of enemy so near to the base of Kuki Piquet must import an early attack on it. The best thing he could do was to get back with the news as soon as possible.

The night wrapped itself round them like dark-blue velvet as they moved like shadows, one at a time, back to the point where they had seen the party of Japs by the packing-cases. Suddenly Elwell stumbled over a kerosene tin, which clattered and banged down the hill. A man rose up at his very feet. Elwell pressed the trigger of his rifle and the man fell as silently as he had risen.

The Japanese behind the boxes buzzed into activity like a disturbed wasps' nest as the shot rang out. Half a dozen grenades came bowling over, to burst all around as Elwell flung himself on the ground. Other grenades followed, the fragments whizzing over his body. Then there was silence. He waited for what seemed to be an age, then slithered his way to the gulley between Supply Hill and Kuki Piquet. Ymtong had disappeared.

As he waited to get his breath back he wondered how, having escaped the Japanese, he was going to escape the vigilance of the Royal West Kents. Ignoring the Japanese behind him, he called out: 'West Kents, I'm coming in. For God's sake, don't shoot. Think of Maidstone and the Medway and the apple blossom blooming now.'

Then he got up and climbed Kuki Piquet at what he hoped looked like a casual speed.

All was silence. Not a head was to be seen silhouetted against the night sky. Gasping for breath, he had nearly reached the top without seeing a sign of British troops, when suddenly a rifle cracked in his face. The flash blinded him, the blast hit him in the face and the bullet missed him by an inch. He dived under the bayonet, shouting:

'What the bloody hell are you doing? Didn't you hear me?'

Two rifles were covering him. 'Didn't you hear me?' he repeated angrily. 'Where the hell do you come from?'

'Nottingham,' one of them said. 'Don't know anything about Maidstone.'

At length Elwell was taken to D Company headquarters, where he learnt that Brown had now arrived at Kuki Piquet himself. Having found him, in company with Hoyt, the junior SO of the State battalion, Elwell reported that there were at least two companies of Japanese near the foot of Supply Hill, so probably there was the best part of a battalion on the hill altogether. He thought they were certain to attack Kuki Piquet soon. Brown astonished the two junior officers by saying:

'Then we must counter-attack at once.'

Though the force that remained to him there numbered only ten men, he was dissuaded with difficulty. He accordingly made his way through the night to Richards's headquarters to ask for orders.

Elwell, as he returned to Hepworth's dug-out on Garrison Hill, observed that there could not be more than thirty or forty bayonets left to hold Kuki Piquet, the last defended post before Garrison Hill itself.

Worse was to follow and to follow immediately. Brown and Elwell had scarcely left when a tumult broke on Kuki Piquet, with the crash of mortar bombs and the darts of tracer machine-gun-fire ripping through the trees. The British artillery and mortars added to the din as D Company called for defensive fire. When a silence followed, the atmosphere on Garrison Hill grew very tense. A West Kent soldier with a shattered arm staggered up towards Elwell, looking for the doctors. Elwell got up to help him and found him looking 'ghastly and haggard'. The soldier was almost in tears as he said:

'We couldn't do a thing, sir. We didn't have a bloody chance. The Japs were simply all over us. Hundreds of them. They've got Kuki Piquet now.'

The news shook everyone. Supply Hill and Kuki Piquet gone in one night. Only Garrison Hill remained. The last ditch had been reached. The walking wounded on the southern slopes got to their feet, preparing to go into the battle again and do what they could in the desperate situation. Donald Easten crawled painfully down the hill to rejoin D Company and was shocked to find his gallant sergeant-major, the blinded Haines, lying dead.

Farther round the shoulder of Garrison Hill, A and C Companies were seriously alarmed. If the Japanese should press their success, there was now very little to stop them. There would be a running fight, which was the one thing they did not want. It would be impossible to distinguish friend from foe in the darkness. They fixed bayonets and stood ready, determined to fight to the death to protect the wounded in the ADS, which was now less than 200 yards from the enemy.

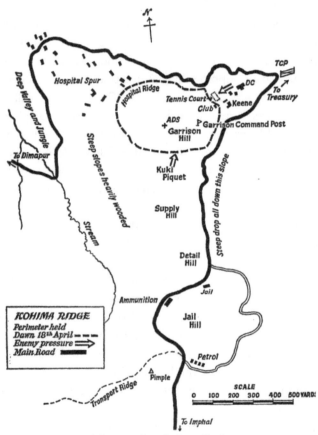

The garrison's last ditch.

Sergeant King, the gallant mortarman, came through. His jaw had been smashed by a shell-splinter during the attack on Kuki Piquet but, holding up his jaw with his hand, he had refused to quit as long as he could support his friends of D Company. It was with difficulty that he was persuaded to go to the dressing-station, where he was blown unconscious by a shell-burst.

To Richards the sudden and unexpected losses of both features was a severe blow. Until then he had felt confident that the garrison could hold out until help arrived, which could not now be long delayed. But with Kuki Piquet gone and the cohesion of the Royal West Kent companies impaired by the confusion of the night's events, he felt that nothing but the intervention of Providence could prevail if the enemy was to press his advantage that night. A very young private soldier standing beside him as they stood-to all night outside the command post asked him in a shy voice:

'Sir, can I ask you a question?'

'Of course, what is it?'

'When we die, sir, is that the end or do we go on?'

16: RELIEF

WHAT WAS left of the garrison on the night of that April 17th stood at bay on the foul ground of Garrison Hill and along the side line of the pitted tennis court, ready to make one more stand. Into that space — only some 350 yards in length and width — all were now crowded: combatants, non-combatants and the recumbent wounded. Those in the best shape were the fighting troops in the trenches; they had the means and the spirit to fight, which they were determined to do. For the passive non-combatants however, it was a harrowing experience and for many of the wounded it was a night of horror. It was scarcely possible for a shell to burst anywhere without killing someone. For the remainder of the night the enemy bombarded the diminished keep with great violence, and nowhere more violently than on Richards's and Laverty's command posts. On the darkened hill, strewn with debris, filth and desolation, pitted with trenches and shallow graves, scarred with blackened rock and burnt-out bashas, its shattered trees festooned with the ghostly shapes of parachutes, its air contaminated with the smell of decaying corpses, the garrison waited stoically for the yells and bugles that would herald another assault by the enemy.

The long night dragged on but no attack came. The dawn light rimmed the mountain-tops high above them, but still there was no attack. The chill morning mist dissolved and the men in the trenches relaxed. Richards looked round the trenches of the Royal West Kent's headquarters company close to him and found that in the night's bombardment many had been filled with dead.

As the light improved he saw to the westward the thin lines of Dunnett's company of the Punjabis moving on the crest of Piquet Hill half a mile away. Soon afterwards he heard the sharp, imperious crackle that denoted the beginning of a timed artillery programme and a few seconds later cascades of shells from the guns of 2nd Division were showering down on Detail and Supply Hills, on the Bungalow Sector and on Transport Ridge.

A little later he saw the hard shapes of tanks emerge round the bends of the mountain road, stopping every now and then as flashes leapt from their gun muzzles, for the Japanese were still in occupation of the Merema crest across the valley to the north. Then at last, up through the wreckage that had once been 53rd Indian General Hospital, picking their way through the litter of rotting Japanese corpses which testified to the record of the Assam troops, came Major Tom Ware's company of the Punjabis and with them, Harry Grimshaw, their new CO.

They had come just in the nick of time. The tension in the garrison was suddenly relaxed but there were still urgent things to be done and the position was still critical. The garrison had been reinforced but not yet relieved. Grimshaw, brisk and businesslike, began to take over some of Laverty's responsibilities and he posted Ware's company on the dangerous flank of Garrison Hill facing Kuki Piquet, alongside Kenyon and the remnants of A Company, RWK, and near some bunkers still occupied by the State battalion.

Grimshaw found Laverty 'dead beat' and Yeo showing the strain of his long day-and-night vigil, but the companies on the perimeter struck him as being in 'remarkably good shape', considering all that they had gone through. Indeed, what struck the Punjabis most was not the squalor and the desolation, to

261

which they were not unaccustomed, but that the badly bruised garrison were still ready to put up their fists for one more round.

Richards, asked if he considered that it was necessary to continue holding the tennis court, replied emphatically that it was vital. At this stage it could scarcely be hoped to effect a daylight relief there without incurring casualties, but the risk had to be taken. Accordingly, Dunnett's company, who had now followed Grimshaw in, was sent charging down the hill at the double right across Richards's command post to take over from Calistan's Assam troops, who had held the court with gallantry and skill for nearly five days. Dunnett found Calistan 'in very good heart indeed, sticking his neck out' as he took his relief round the position, and his Assam troops 'bloody but unbowed'. At the main artillery OP, Yeo was shortly relieved by Major T. H. H. Harrison, who was second-in-command of 24th Mountain Regiment and who was very soon to be killed.[55]

Second only in importance to holding the position was the evacuation of the wounded, itself a difficult and dangerous operation in the face of an enemy who was devoid of humane instincts. Apart from those with minor injuries, there were 320 still alive who had to be got away. On the day before, Young, by wireless, had been informed by Richard Pilcher, second-in-command of his field ambulance, of the plans made by 161st Brigade.

As soon as the Punjabis had cleared the road, a column of thirty ambulance cars and ten 3-ton lorries, commanded by Colonel George Collingwood, second-in-command of Warren's brigade, accompanied by Pilcher, assembled at Milestone 42, ready to move up to Kohima along the serpentine mountain road. Collingwood and Pilcher reconnoitred ahead in bren carriers. Ignoring the omen, they selected a point near the mortuary of 53rd Indian General Hospital, near the foot of Hospital Spur, where there was a little defilade and where vehicles could turn. Here also Pilcher set up a light dressing station. Then, signalling to Captain Tom Howat back at Milestone 42, Pilcher began calling forward the ambulance cars, two at a time, while tanks stationed themselves at each bend in the road facing outwards across the valley and engaging the enemy the other side of it from time to time.

Pilcher himself took command of the loading party, assisted by Sergeant D. H. Dalby and 12 Indian orderlies. In their clean and starched uniforms, they watched with astonishment as the thin, bearded and bandaged scarecrows, some on foot and some on stretchers, under spasmodic but deliberate fire, came painfully but cheerfully down the long slope of Hospital Spur past the ruined buildings, to the background of the continual trumpeting of the guns. The loading point was very soon under fire and three of Pilcher's men were wounded at the first shelling. Out of the fourteen in the loading party, eleven were killed or wounded before the end of the long operation, which went on for four hours. In the afternoon Pilcher himself was wounded in the thigh and hand and Howat came forward to take his place.

Up on Garrison Hill Young supervised the departures, all of whom were first given half a grain of morphia. There were 140 stretcher cases. They were carried down coolly and steadily by 600 'non-combatants', led by Barratt and his own makeshift company, who thus fulfilled the last duty of their long spell of devoted service. Half an hour after the operation had begun Barratt was able to report to Young that all was going well.

As Elwell made his way down the long slope of Hospital Spur 'the air above our heads was full of the song of bullets, which seemed to come from another world that we were leaving behind'. Soon after midday there was some light shelling and mortaring of Hospital Spur, but the evacuation was not impeded. A little later Young himself went down to the mortuary and met the senior medical officer of 2nd Division, Colonel Bush. He was tired but still remarkably resistant and it was he, indeed, who, together with an orderly, loaded the wounded Pilcher into an ambulance, making Pilcher feel very shamefaced.

Then, later in the afternoon, Young climbed back up the hill again and reported to Richards, and to Warren by radio, that the evacuation was satisfactorily accomplished.

The reinforced garrison stood to its arms that night refreshed in spirit, but the situation was still extremely dangerous and again they stood-to all night, the while Richards's command post was again heavily mortared and grenaded. Two attacks were made. One was a series of heavy attacks with grenades and slabs of explosive on the tennis court, in which the Punjabis suffered twenty-two casualties, but once more, and several times during the night, the mountain guns came down with impeccable accuracy to break up the attacks when Dunnet signalled his SOS.

The other was a dangerous penetration up Garrison Hill itself from the south. Here Kenyon's company was occupying some weapon-pits very close to the bunkers of the State battalion. At stand-to on the morning of the 19th, they found that the bunkers had been abandoned by the State troops during the night and were now occupied by Japanese. They were within forty yards of Laverty's command post, twenty yards of Kenyon and about the same distance from Grimshaw. A spirited attack by a platoon of the Punjabis, with supporting fire from Kenyon's company, cleared them out. In one of the bunkers all but one of the Japanese intruders were burnt alive when some kerosene went up in flames and set off their own phosphorus bombs. The lone survivor ran out screaming with his cotton clothes on fire. The brisk little assault delighted the hard-tried West Kents, who afterwards counted twenty Japanese dead.

In the afternoon, however, the Punjabis suffered a reverse in an attempt to recapture Kuki Piquet. A concentrated bombardment by the artillery of 2nd Division having first blotted out the little hill, Ware's company of the Punjabis then went in and gained the summit, but were later forced to withdraw by the flanking fire of the Japanese machine-guns on Transport Ridge which the Royal West Kents had had to endure for so long. That night the Japanese once more made an attempt on the tennis court, but it was held as firmly as ever, and once more they bombarded and grenaded Richards's command post. But it was for the last time.

Outside, some sharp fighting was still going on, but 2nd Division was now coming up strongly and at last, at dawn on April 20th, 1st Royal Berkshire Regiment, spearhead of 6th Brigade, under Lieut-Colonel Wilbur Bickford, marched in and Shapland took over the baton from Warren.

Richards had received orders to evacuate the original garrison and to hand over command to Grimshaw, though the two did not meet. Bearded and tired, Richards made his way for the last time up the-smoking hill-top and then down to Keene's headquarters, whence he watched the relief going on. He saw the smart new troops march in and then the magnificent remnants of the Royal West Kents, the Assam troops, the composite companies of Indians, the devoted doctors and their orderlies, the long-suffering non-combatants and all the odds and ends of his memorable garrison file steadily out. He noticed how thin they all looked, but how full of spirit even now, soldiers still in spite of their outward look of bearded brigands, and he wished that there could have been someone there to give them a cheer. When he had seen the relief completed at about 4 o'clock, he walked thoughtfully down Hospital Spur, leaving behind the dust, the din and the stench, and was driven to 2nd Division headquarters, where he made a report to General Grover.

The gallant Young also remained to the end, when he handed over to the CO of 6th Field Ambulance. Such was the physical resilience of this remarkable 'tactical doctor' that he even returned next day and acted as guide for the divisional commander.

The garrison marched out to the plaudits of the whole army and the acclaim of the world's press. Few men had deserved it more. In the words of the official historian of the Cabinet Office, 'The heroic defence put up by Richards and his small garrison against overwhelming odds thus played a small but very vital part in the defeat of the Japanese in the decisive battles in South-East Asia'. And Slim recorded: 'Sieges have been longer but few have been more intense and in none have the defenders deserved greater honour than the garrison of Kohima.'[56]

Other commentators, even a left-wing Indian newspaper, aptly described Kohima as 'the Stalingrad of Burma'. It was the 'hinge of fate', in Churchill's phrase, by which at last the gates were opened for the British and American forces to have one victory after another until the final triumph. Had Sato been able to seize the whole Ridge, the success of the Japanese plan in forcing Slim to commit his reserves in Arakan would have had its full effect. The war in Burma would have been much prolonged. Fourth Corps, still shut up in the Imphal Plain, would have become much straitened. Stopford would have been even more hard put to it than he was to dislodge the Japanese from a position in which every advantage of ground lay with them. Though it was itself commanded by higher ground, Kohima Ridge was as vital to both armies as the Pass of Thermopylae had been to both Xerxes and Leonidas in the days of old. But, unlike the Greeks and Spartans, Richards and his doughty company held their pass securely. Garrison Hill and Hospital Spur became the nodal point, the pivot, the toe-hold from which Stopford fought the bitter and sanguinary battles of the next few weeks, in which both armies were simultaneously engaged in offensives against each other for possession of the Ridge. Second Arakan and the first Chindit operation had marked the resurgence of the Army's morale and had proved the new methods of overcoming the Japanese, but Kohima Ridge was tactically the turning point of the Burma war, after which all movement was forward.

For this the fundamental credit was due to Richards's decision, when left on his own, to select what he judged to be the vital ground and to abandon all the other 'boxes', which the rag-bag of troops on the spot were quite incapable of holding. With no artillery, virtually no defence stores, poor communications, only a handful of officers with any knowledge of infantry action and not one single complete unit fit and equipped for battle, he might quite well have considered the outlook hopeless and taken advantage of the authority that Rankin had given him to withdraw altogether.

Instead, though never knowing from one minute to the next what troops were to be left him, he decided to make a go of it, concentrated what he thought to be the best available troops on the one piece of ground that the enemy could not possibly afford to be denied and hurried away as many as he could of the poorer fighting material. Even so, what he was left with up till April 5th was poor indeed. The seven platoons of the Assam Rifles, though of good material, were unequipped and untrained for a pitched battle and the remnants of the Assam Regiment, after their own private battles at Jessami and Kharasom, were exhausted and dismembered before ever the siege began. His great disappointment was in the State battalion, who, he was entitled to think from their origins and training, would provide good fighting material.

The second provision that made the long stand possible was Richards's forethought in stockpiling each sector with ample supplies of rations and ammunition. With the exception of defence stores, everything was on the spot; he assumed authority for drawing on them and made provision in every sector for supplies that were calculated to last at least a fortnight. Not that he anticipated to have to fight for so long, but he appreciated that, once battle was joined, the normal issue of supplies would be impossible, and each sector, whether held by his own troops or their successors, might have to be called upon to hold out on its own. No one could have foreseen that such an enormous quantity of hand grenades would be used and it is probable that supplies of both grenades and mortar ammunition in fact existed in the Field Supply Depot on Supply Hill.

Thus ground, ammunition, rations and water (which was not completed in time) were the essential bases for withstanding the siege. Neither, however, would have availed without troops of an exceptionally high fighting spirit, skilled in the use of arms, unshaken by the ordeals of close-quarter combat night fighting against 'savages with modern weapons', determined to fight until they dropped. Richards and Laverty had exceptionally difficult tasks and handled their emergencies well, but the chief glory was the portion of the officers and men in the companies and platoons. Shelled, bombed, grenaded, machine-gunned, sniped, short of water, short of good meals, desperately short of sleep for a fortnight, seeing their pals shot down all round them, fighting nearly every night at a range of a few yards, the best of them faced the enemy at the last hour with as much determination, if with less strength, as at the first. There has seldom been a fight in which so much depended on the private soldier and his personal devotion to duty in a lonely trench in the dark.

Without doubt, it was the Royal West Kents, under an able CO, who saved the situation and bore most of the brunt of the fighting. Their outstanding company commanders, their superb NCOs, their experience of fighting, their good communications, their cohesion and the steady nerve and cheerful disposition of the humblest soldier showed Laverty's battalion in its finest hour. They were severely mauled but never shaken. Easten's company lost fifty men out of the seventy-five with which it began the action and one platoon was reduced to a single private; but that private was still able to grin and crack a joke.

If the RWK were the dominant unit, the Assam troops were little behind them and many of them not in the least behind in valour. The Assam Regiment saved Kohima by its resolute defence at Jessami; when it got back to the Ridge it was dismembered, short of officers, without heavy mortars and signal equipment and was no longer fully effective as an organic battalion, yet, together with their friends of the Assam Rifles, they extemporized successfully in many an emergency, held the back door securely and, under Calistan, held the tennis court in a fine example of soldierly conduct.

Even such fine infantry, however, could not have held their own through the murderous and incessant night fighting without artillery support of the highest order. Though Hill had only twelve guns left in his regiment, their precise and instantaneous fire, skilfully directed by Yeo and his fellow FOOs, frustrated enemy assaults time after time, caused heavy casualties and, together with Sergeant King's mortars, was one of the battle-winning factors of the siege.

Accurate official figures of the casualties sustained do not exist. From the information collated on the spot and immediately afterwards by Richards's staff, the Garrison War Diary records that, for the period April 4th to 20th, they 'were somewhere in the region of 600, of whom 250 may be assumed as killed'. On analysis this seems to be a very reliable estimate. To these have to be added the casualties of the Assam Regiment at Jessami and Kharasom, which formed an essential part of the defence of Kohima. The losses of the Royal West Kents, as recorded in the battalion War Diary, amounted to 199, of whom 61 were killed.[57] In percentage, the heaviest casualties seem to have been in the gunners of 20th Mountain Battery, who lost 41 out of 80.

To Richards there came congratulatory letters or signals from Mountbatten, Giffard, Stopford and Grover. To him and the men he commanded the last tribute is paid by Major-General Rawlley, as he is now. 'I would like to give full credit,' he wrote, 'to all those officers and men, from different units, who fought together so magnificently under the guidance and leadership of Colonel Richards. I do not think he has been given full credit for the simply magnificent job of work he did in holding Kohima against such odds. I saw him frequently, both at his headquarters and when he visited me on many occasions. At no time did I see him upset, flustered or worried. He had a humane and understanding outlook. He won the affection, respect and admiration of all of us in those short three weeks.'

Well-deserved honours flowed. In addition to Harman's posthumous Victoria Cross, the DSO went to Richards, Laverty, Young, Yeo and Bruno Brown. Other decorations went to some of those who deserved them and the list of awards was curtailed only by the official rules of rationing and, as in all battles, by the fog which cloaks many an act of unwitnessed heroism and self-sacrifice.

17: VICTORY

The Second Phase

THE RELIEF of Richards's garrison was but the end of the
first phase of the great Battle of Kohima, which raged for
another six weeks, while the twin Battle of Imphal was being
fought out with no less severity.

As all three brigades of Grover's division came forward they
found themselves confronted with immensely strong mountain
defences some five miles long astride the Imphal Road, with
Naga Village approximately in the centre and clasping Kohima
Ridge within two threatening arms. The steep, commanding,
forest-clad hills had everywhere been strongly fortified by the
Japanese and the approaches to them were across the most
arduous terrain, over much of which all loads had to be carried
by men on their feet. With the exception of the Ridge itself, it
constituted, in fact, the ground that Sato had been required to
seize as part of the great mountain barrier that the Japanese
intended to hold to guard their conquest of Burma. Few armies
in history have ever been required to assault a position so
formidable.

The greater part of the vital Ridge itself was now in enemy
hands. Burrowing industriously, they had constructed a series
of well-sited, well-concealed bunkers, with mutually supporting
fire, from Transport Ridge to Kuki Piquet and in the bungalow
area. The most formidable of these positions was Jail Hill, in
which a great underground redoubt had been tunnelled out, its
loopholes and exits barred with steel plates taken from the jail.
Of all their planned conquests, Garrison Hill alone still eluded
them. Sato, from his eyrie in Naga Village, looked down and

saw 2nd Division advancing and he ordered Miyazaki's 58th Brigade, reinforced by a fourth battalion, to intensify their efforts to capture it.

Just before the Siege of Kohima was raised Mutaguchi had sent orders to Sato to dispatch a brigade group southward to assist 15th Division, whose attempt to capture Imphal from the north and north-west had been brought to a halt and against whom Scoones had begun a counteroffensive. Sato gave order accordingly. On the very day of the Kohima relief, however, a copy of Mutaguchi's order was captured on Imphal Plain and on the following day an officer of the Cameron Highlanders shot a Japanese cyclist carrying Sato's orders on a track north-west of Kohima.

Slim thereupon ordered 2nd Division to exert the fullest possible pressure in order to prevent Sato from complying with Mutaguchi's order. Accordingly, Grover and Sato simultaneously began offensives against each other on Kohima Ridge. The inevitable result was a series of hot and murderous clashes, in the course of which Shapland's 6th Brigade punished the Japanese with savage casualties. The greater part of one of the battalions ordered to go south was wiped out. At the same time 4th Brigade under Brigadier Goschen and 5th Brigade under Brigadier Hawkins were dispatched on wide flanking movements, over appalling country, on the south and north. The result was that, within four days, in direct disobedience of Mutaguchi's orders, Sato countermanded the move south of his 124th Brigade.

The Battle for the Ridge continued remorselessly. Near Pawsey's ruined bungalow, in what even the aloof Official Historian describes as 'superb gallantry', a company of the 2nd Dorsets, to secure a way forward for tanks, seized a small knoll and held it for five days, emerging on relief with only thirty-two officers and men out of their original 100. In these and the subsequent operations all three-of Grover's brigade commanders were killed or wounded, so also was the fourth who succeeded one of them.[58] The Japanese, under the sustained and accurate fire of the British artillery, suffered even more crippling losses, but clung to their bunkers with tenacious bravery.

The rains came and the British troops, drenched to the skin, slipped and slithered on the steep hillsides, where their tracks were turned into treacherous mud-slides, or floundered in water-logged trenches, like their fathers of a generation before.

The Japanese assaults were held at almost every point by 6th Brigade and, little by little, all three British began to eat into the enemy strongholds. Transport Ridge was slowly regained and attacks began to develop on the daunting Jail Hill. At this moment Messervy's 7th Indian Division began to arrive from Arakan and their 33rd Brigade, under the commanding leadership of Brigadier Loftus-Tottenham, after two days of desperate fighting in rain and mud, were brought to a halt just short of the conical summit with 400 casualties. After a second night of crouching in muddy holes, Loftus-Tottenham called upon his bedraggled men for one more effort and, as they stumbled to their feet in the cold, wet dawn on May 13th, the enemy broke at last all along the Ridge.

Last of all to be overcome were some bunkers in the Bungalow Sector, where the tenacious Japanese were not disposed of until explosive charges had been thrust into the embrasures or until tanks had been winched up the slippery slopes to fire into them point-blank.

So ended the battle of the Ridge. It had lasted five and a half weeks. It had been fought over a narrow strip of ground little more than a mile long. How many men of both sides were killed for the possession of its scarred and ravaged features, how many maimed for life are questions that cannot be answered accurately, but what is certain is that their total would have been far higher if the Royal West Kents, the Assam Regiment, the Assam Rifles and the odds and ends of troops who took post with them had not clung fast to their precarious foothold and if 24th Mountain Regiment had not sustained them with such remarkable address.

The Break Through

The third phase of the Battle of Kohima began with the assaults upon the heights in and around Naga Village and on the lofty eminence of pine-clad Aradura. They were made under the most gruelling conditions and in torrential rain. As Messervy's division moved up in full strength and joined hands with Grover's, the odds were heavily turned against Sato. Pounded by the British guns under Brigadier 'Hair-trigger' Steevens, the fire-eating commander of 33 Corps artillery, bombed heartily by the combined Allied air forces, subjected to the daily attrition of infantry attacks, the Japanese continued their sacrificial resistance for a little longer and, when their bunkers had been smashed by Steevens's heavy artillery or by bombing from the air, the garrisons still emerged from the wreckage to meet the ensuing infantry attacks.

Gradually, however, their fighting spirit was broken down. To the blows from Stopford's troops were added the miseries resulting from their own negligence. The folly of their administrative risks began to bring its punishment. The supplies which they had calculated they would capture from the British had been denied them. They became critically short of ammunition, food, and medical supplies. Few reinforcements arrived to replace their punishing casualties.

The withering diseases of the tropics widened the ragged gaps in their ranks. No aircraft or tanks came to their support.

For Sato, therefore, the capture of Kohima had by the middle of May become a vanished dream. He asked his Army Commander for permission to withdraw but Mutaguchi, who considered that Imphal was about to fall to his other division and contemplated moving Sato southward to reinforce them, refused. By the end of the month, however, Sato saw a nightmare image of total annihilation confronting his tottering division. Naga Village, the heart of his defence, had become a stinking mess of mud, corpses and ruins. The Chindits of Perowne's All-British 23rd LRP Brigade,[59] having forced a way through fierce jungle from the distant north in one of the most rigorous of marches, had now cut his main route back to the Chindwin. On the 31st, again disobeying orders, bitterly accusing 15th Army of incompetence, and lamenting that 'I cannot see the enemy through my blinding tears', he began to steal away through the mountain mists that enveloped the sodden jungle.

Still desperately trying to reinforce failure and to save face, Mutaguchi gave *ex post facto* approval to the withdrawal, ordering Sato's crippled remnants to join hands with 15th Division for a final assault on Imphal, which he deluded himself was still within his reach. In a Special Order of the Day, Mutaguchi declared to his troops:

> After a month's desperate and courageous fighting we surrounded the strategic position of Kohima. In three months we had the enemy hemmed in round Imphal and the battle situation stabilized. Still all this has not been fully up to the expectations of our nation. This is indeed a most regrettable matter.

Withholding my tears, painful as it is, I shall for the time being withdraw my troops from Kohima. It is my resolve to reassemble the whole army and with one great push to capture Imphal…

This forthcoming plan of operations will be the army's last. You must fully realize that if a decisive victory is not obtained we shall not be able to strike back again.

On this one battle rests the fate of the Empire. Each and all must unswervingly serve the Throne and reach the ultimate goal so that the Son of Heaven and the Nation alike may be forever safeguarded.

Mutaguchi Renya.

The desperate appeal was of no avail. For a few days longer the remnants of Miyazaki's brigade on Aradura Ridge continued to block 2nd Division's attempt to advance southwards along the road to Imphal, but as soon as they had been ejected the pursuit was on. Stopford directed 2nd Division to push down the road and join hands with 4th Corps and he sent 7th Indian to sweep south-eastwards through the jungle tracks of the Somra Hills, while Perowne's Chindits menaced the enemy's rear.

The monsoon was now in full force but Slim, defying all historical precedent and teaching, ordered that there should be no remission. The 'campaign season' must know no limits. In appalling weather, with the mountain slopes turned into mud-slides and the valley bottoms into racing torrents, with even the sure-footed mules sliding and tumbling down the treacherous slopes, Stopford's sodden divisions, pushing through the steaming jungle, harried a defeated enemy whose withdrawal soon became a rout. Enfeebled, half-starved, filthy, stinking, diseased and dispirited, the soldiers of the Son of Heaven, who had never known defeat and whose creed had taught them that the only alternative to victory was death, threw away their arms and staggered through quagmires made foul by their own rotting dead, while the unforgiving rain poured down in solid sheets and the expectant vultures waited for their opportunity. The Retreat of 1942 had been more than avenged.

The Last Act

All this time 4th Corps' battle on the fringes of the Imphal Plain had been going on with only such intermissions as were necessary for one side or the other to recover its breath in the constant buffeting. Since the cutting of the main road of March 29th the maintenance demands of Scoones's troops had been unfailingly fulfilled from the air until the monsoon began to create flying difficulties, when troops were put on reduced rations and there was a period of acute anxiety for artillery ammunition. On the very day that Jail Hill had fallen 17th Indian Division and their old enemies of 33rd Japanese had, like Grover and Sato, launched simultaneous offensives against one another, each cutting in behind the other's lines of communication. Once again Ronald Cameron's 48th Gurkha Brigade distinguished itself in a brilliant exploit, but it availed little. Both divisions were fought to a standstill. But the heavy slaughter and the cruel conditions, in which the Japanese were reduced to eating grass, leaves and roots, began so to shake the enemy's spirit that General Tanaka, now commanding the division, was constrained to order that officers should not shrink from using their swords on their own men who showed unwillingness to fight.

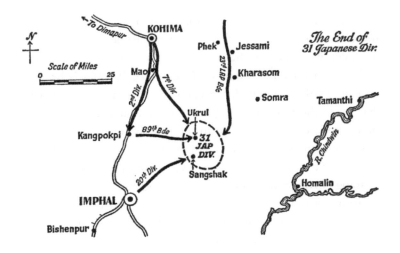

On the Palel Road sector 20th and later 23rd Indian Division, clinging grimly to the heights of the Shenam Pass, administered equally severe punishment against an enemy who continued to bruise his head against an unshaken defence. North of Imphal and on the avenues to Ukrul, Scoones's counter-offensive was making slow progress in the appalling weather, but at long last, on June 22nd, a patrol of 1/17th Dogras of 5th Indian Division (James Barratt's regiment), accompanied by some tanks of the Carabineers, at a point some twenty-six miles north of Imphal, saw some infantry and a troop of tanks advancing towards them down the main road from Kohima. They were the 2nd Durham Light Infantry and 149th Royal Armoured Corps from 2nd Division. Grover himself immediately motored through and met Briggs. Within a few hours the two Corps commanders had also met and planned the enemy's destruction. The Battle of Imphal, which had lasted for more than three months, was virtually over.

The last act was played at Ukrul, the main Japanese forward base, strongly guarded by their 15th Division.[60] Thither were making the sick, starving and emaciated enemy troops, hoping there to find some relief from their miseries. Thither also, however, were making the converging columns of 7th and 20th Indian Divisions and the hardy Chindits of Perowne's brigade, passing, as they marched, the enemy's guns and vehicles lying derelict in the mud and long trails of emaciated corpses, many of whom had been drowned in the muddy ooze that filled the pot-holes into which they had stumbled and from which they did not have the strength to save themselves. By July 7th, pushing through downpours of blinding rain, crossing valley bottoms steaming with sub-tropical heat, then clambering up to mountain-tops wreathed in cold mists, the British columns had ringed the town and captured it.

Almost as if by joint consent, Slim and Mutaguchi both called off the battle simultaneously. Mutaguchi, realizing bitterly at last that all hope was gone, ordered his shattered divisions back across the Chindwin, where he, Kawabe and his divisional commanders awaited their inevitable disgrace. Of the 84,000 troops (exclusive of the useless Jiffs) with which he had begun the battle, 30,502 were dead and 23,000 wounded more than lightly.

Slim, with total casualties of only 16,700, had different reasons. To continue the pursuit would have meant plunging into the malarial Kabaw Valley at the most dangerous season. The morale of his troops was on the top line, but their health was not. Physically exhausted, suffering from malnutrition on short rations in the cruel conditions, their numbers were slowly being eaten into by dysentery, scrub typhus and skin diseases. Many had been fighting almost continuously for nearly a year. There was no need to make any further call upon their fortitude. They had done their task. Not only had they recovered the lost ground, but they had also destroyed 31st

Division, shattered two others and shaken the enemy's belief in his own invincibility.

Except for those who were necessary to keep watch and ward, Slim sent off his hard-driven troops to rest, refresh their vigour and gird themselves for the Last Battle.

APPENDIX A: A NOTE ON THE INDIAN ARMY

SINCE THE dust of time is beginning to obscure many landmarks once familiar to most of us, it will be helpful to the general reader to outline a few facts concerning the Indian Army, so far as they concern an understanding of the events in this book. The reader is reminded in the first place that, as observed in Chapter 2, there was at this time no distinction between 'India' and 'Pakistan', which were formed as new states after the grant of independence in 1947, and that the term 'Indian' applied to all in the sub-continent.

Indian Army formations and units were organized and trained in precisely the same way as those of the British Army. British officers and men formed a very large part of Indian Divisions. At the beginning of the war virtually all the officers in all units were British. With little exception, all the field artillery, Officers and men, were wholly British, though not the very distinctive Mountain Artillery, who were the crack troops of the Indian Army and of whom we have seen a good deal. Moreover, in each infantry brigade (of three battalions) there was one wholly British battalion.

As the war progressed, however, a considerable degree of Indianization took place in officers of all arms, including the newly raised Indian Air Force, and the increasing difficulty of providing reinforcements in the British infantry battalions resulted in a few brigades becoming all-Indian, except for officers. Before the end of the war one or two Indians had risen to the rank of brigadier.

In the combatant units, with a few exceptions, all the Indian rank and file were recruited from two sources only — the Gurkhas (who were not Indians, but Nepalese) and a few martial races of Northern India — Mahrattas, Dogras, Punjabis, Rajputs, Jats, Sikhs, Garhwalis and Baluchs. They came from village communities, very often from families that had served the Indian Army for generations; they were tremendously proud of their regiments and were held in considerable honour in their villages. Soldiering was in their blood and they had a deeply founded loyalty to the British Raj. Indeed, in any part of India a man who had served in any kind of military unit had a considerable status.

Prominent among units not recruited from the northern martial races were some of the engineer units, which retained their old name of Sappers and Miners, by which the Royal Engineers of the British Army used also to be known; of such were the Bombay and the Madras Sappers and Miners. These sappers were, of course, very much combatant troops.

The Indian soldier was known as a sepoy, an old Anglo-Indian word adapted from the Urdu. The non-commissioned officers were havildars (equivalent to sergeants), naiks (equivalent to corporals) and lance-naiks. Above them was a grade peculiar to the Indian army known as Viceroy's Commissioned Officers (VCOs), who were junior in status to the King's Commissioned Officers. Except in the cavalry, their ranks were those of subedar (wearing two stars) and jemadar (one star). A very special VCO was the subedar-major, who was a man of great influence in the battalion and the CO's right hand man in all matters concerning the sepoys. VCOs were usually men of long service, who had risen from the lower ranks. They commanded platoons and the equivalents of platoons in other arms.

British and Indian units trained and fought side by side and performed exactly similar tasks. They were on the most cordial terms with one another, but, if there was one man for whom Thomas Atkins had a particular affection, it was for 'Johnny Gurkha', the nimble little mountain soldier with the ready smile and the boyish spirit.

Behind the fighting division were a great many lines-of-communication units composed of men who were merely civilian labourers in uniform, entirely untrained in arms and indeed, mostly unarmed, but not deficient in discipline. These ministered to the forward units in repairing roads, driving vehicles, issuing stores, baking bread, driving cattle and so on.

Note must also be taken of a special sort of unit, which was not of the Indian Army, but served with it in the campaign. Of such were the battalions or cavalry regiments raised and maintained at their own expense by the Indian (and other) princes, such as Patiala and Hyderabad. These princes ruled their own territories and were not part of 'British India', but in the two great World Wars unhesitatingly offered their troops to the King-Emperor. They were known as 'State' or 'Native State' troops. To them were attached a few British Senior and Junior Supervising Officers, whose main duties were training and liaison and who did not command the units, which were officered entirely by Indians or Nepalese.

APPENDIX B: AUTHORITIES AND SOURCES

Maps: Asia 1:1,000,000 Assam, aeronautical edition.
  India 1:126,000, 83K/N W.
  India 1:250,000, 83K.
War Diary of the Kohima Garrison.
War Diary of the 4th Bn, Royal West Kent Regiment.
War Diary of 75th Indian Field Ambulance.
War Diary of 53rd Indian General Hospital.
Report of the ADMS (Colonel F. K. Bush) in War Diary of HQ 2nd Infantry Division.
Unpublished MS of Lieutenant Donald Elwell.
Papers of the late Lieut-Colonel C. G. Borrowman.
Papers of Sir Charles Pawsey, Kt, CSI, CIE, MC.
Papers of Brigadier H. U. Richards, CBE, DSO.
Diaries of Colonel R. K. Pilcher and Dr F. R. Glover.
Yeo, Lieut-Colonel R. de C: *The Gunners at Kohima* in the Journal of the Royal United Services Institution (India).
General Staff 33rd Corps: *Account of Operations* (unpublished).
Steyn, Major P.: *History of the Assam Regiment.*
Cabinet Office Official Historians: *The War Against Japan, Vols I and II.*
Combined Historical Section, India and Pakistan: *The Reconquest of Burma 1943-45, Vol. 1.*
Slim, Field-Marshal The Viscount: *Defeat Into Victory.*
Evans, Lieut-General Sir Geoffrey and Brett-James, Major Anthony: *Imphal.*
Barker, Lieut-Colonel A. J.: *The March on Delhi.*
Giffard, General Sir George: *Dispatches* in the London Gazette

Supplements of March 13th and March 30th, 1951 (together with prior dispatches by Field-Marshals Wavell and Auchinleck for earlier operations).

Maclachlan, Captain W. P. G.: *The Kohima Box* in the National Review, July 1944.

Other War Diaries and Regimental and Divisional histories have also been consulted.

The personal narratives, written or interlocutory, of:

Mr J. P. Barratt, MC.

Lieut-Colonel T. C. Coath, TD.

Colonel D. F. Easten, MC.

Mr D. S. Elwell.

Lieut-Colonel P. H. A. L. Franklin, DL.

Dr F. R. Glover, MC, MB, BS, DPH.

Major-General E. H. W. Grimshaw, CB, CBE, DSO.

Lieut-Colonel M. Hepworth.

Brigadier R. H. M. Hill, CBE.

Lieut-Colonel G. A. E. Keene, MBE.

Major T. Kenyon.

Dr S. R. S. Laing, MA, MB, MRCS.

Lieut-Colonel J. W. N. Landor.

Colonel H. J. Laverty, D SO, MC.

Major D. E. Lloyd Jones, MC.

Sir Charles Pawsey, Kt, CSI, CIE, MC.

Colonel R. K. Pilcher, MC, MRCS, LRCP.

Brigadier J. S. Punia (Indian Army).

Major-General N. C. Rawlley, MC (Indian Army).

Brigadier H. U. Richards, CBE, DSO.

Major P. E. M. Shaw.

Major J. D. K. Short.

Major H. C. Smith.

Major P. Steyn, MC.

Major P. E. Watts, MC.

Major W. G. Williamson.

Major J. Winstanley, MC, TD, MB, FRCS.

Lieut-Colonel R. de C. Yeo, DSO.

Information on various minor points has also been kindly provided by:

Colonel S. W. K. Arundell, MRCS, LRCP; Major J. C. Breaden, MBE; Major W. G. Dunnett, MBE; Lieut-Colonel P. Hartley; Captain W. P. G. Maclachlan; Mr P. J. Mountstephen; Captain John Nettlefield; Mr M. K. Smith; Major T. S. Ware; Dr Alec Wattison, MB, ChB.

A NOTE TO THE READER

If you have enjoyed this book enough to leave a review on **Amazon** and **Goodreads**, then we would be truly grateful.
The Estate of C. E. Lucas Phillips

Sapere Books is an exciting new publisher of brilliant fiction and popular history.

To find out more about our latest releases and our monthly bargain books visit our website:
saperebooks.com

[1] Putao in the vernacular.

[2] Pronounced approximately *Myi-chin-ah*.

[3] Pearl Harbor December 7th, Siam and Malaya December 7th-8th, Hong Kong December 8th, Philippines December 9th, North Borneo December 17th, Sarawak December 25th, Celebes December 26th, Dutch East Indies January 10th, New Guinea January 25th. Related to Greenwich Time, the attack on Malaya actually took place 1 hour 35 minutes before that on Pearl Harbor.

[4] *Defeat into Victory.*

[5] 1st Gloucesters, 2nd Duke of Wellington's, 1st Cameronians, 1st Royal Inniskilling Fusiliers and 2nd King's Own Yorkshire Light Infantry. Most were very much under strength.

[6] 7th Hussars (Lieut-Colonel F. R. G. Fosdick), 2nd Royal Tanks (Lieut-Colonel George Yule), 414th Battery (Essex Yeomanry) RHA (Major B. de H. Pereira), 'A' Battery 95th Anti-Tank Regt RA, 1st West Yorkshires, 13th Light Field Ambulance and 65th Coy, RASG.

[7] Previously by Lieut-General N. M. S. Irwin, who then became commander of Eastern Army.

[8] The commander of this column was not Tanahashi, as stated in other works, but Major-General T. Sakurai, the divisional infantry commander who personally led it. Tanahashi commanded one of the brigades in the column. Sakurai, T., is not to be confused with Sakurai, S., formerly commander of 33rd Division and now commanding 28th Army.

[9] Styled an Indian division at that time for deception purposes.

[10] The force, officially designated 3rd Indian Division, but more usually called Special Force, also included 111th Indian Infantry Brigade and 3rd West African Brigade.

[11] Also known as Manipur Road.

[12] See Appendix A.

[13] See Appendix A.

[14] Short for Phakekedzumi; or, to the troops, 'Fake'.

[15] His promotion to captain had not yet been gazetted.

[16] Subedar Karindra Rajbongshi.

[17] After much investigation, it has not been possible to fix the date and time of this call (known to only a few people) with any certainty; but, as events recorded in the next chapter will show, it can scarcely have been later than the 28th or early on the 29th (the date when the Imphal road was cut).

[18] The War Diary of the Kohima Garrison records this aircraft as having been sent on the 29th.

[19] He was also a keen hunter of butterflies and, when in command of the bren-carrier platoon, issued a butterfly net to every carrier.

[20] Lieut-Colonel R. A. Stanley, of the retiring V Force, appears to have assumed command for a brief period.

[21] *Defeat into Victory*, p. 310.

[22] This meant, in effect, Naga Village, the Treasury and Merema.

[23] The text of Richards's order ran: 'From OC Kohima Garrison to OC 1 Assam Regt. It has been decided to withdraw to a closer defence of Kohima. You will withdraw from your present position not repeat NOT before night 31 Mar/1 Apr and preferably on that night. Rajputs have formed a firm base at MS 44 and you will meet patrols of Rajput East of MS 44. You will withdraw along road Jessami-Ghizami and MT will take you to Kohima. Phek and Kharasom are also being withdrawn at the same time.' The message was intentionally sent in clear.

[24] On his return to Dimapur, Rankin telephoned 14th Army and Slim confirmed that the whole brigade must be withdrawn to Nichugard Pass as soon as possible.

[25] Captains J. Ribeiro and Abdul Majid and 2nd Lieutenant N. C. Lahiri.

[26] Respectively, 2nd Lieutenant S. W. Ghose-Dastidar and Lieutenants G. S. Sarin and S. S. Sapre.

[27] Captains L. N. Budhraja and J. A. Roy.

[28] Others, cut off from their companies, could not reach Kohima before it was invested and made for Dimapur.

[29] The official Order of Battle of the Kohima Garrison is not reliable.

[30] One Company 5 Burma Regt and a Garrison Company Burma Regt (second line troops).

[31] Aradura Spur was not 'lost', never having been occupied.

[32] Aiappa, however, never reached Kohima.

[33] Unlike a field battery, a mountain battery had only four guns instead of eight.

[34] 'Where Destiny and glory lead.' Indian officers and men had a different motto.

[35] Laverty considered that he was too young for the majority to which he would otherwise have been entitled.

[36] When he appointed Lieutenant A. J. Hoyt to command them in succession to Lunn.

[37] Map reference: RE 466676.

[38] I/138 and III/58. The latter had in fact entered the village two days earlier but, believing that the Kohima Pass had already been captured, had pushed on for another six miles by the northerly track to Cheswema.

[39] War Diary 75 2nd Fd Amb. Not on the night of 6/7th, as given in other accounts.

[40] Lt-General D. R. Thapar.

[41] This and the subsequent accounts of operations on Detail Hill are based mainly on the joint narrative, co-ordinated by Lieut-Colonel Coath, of himself, Colonel Easten and Major Watts, together with the battalion War Diary, a brief narration by Major Shaw and a few other sources on points of detail.

[42] Stories much publicized of Easten's men going round the bakery and dropping grenades into ovens in which Japanese were still concealed are fictitious.

[43] The evacuation of the walking wounded is entered in the War Diary of 75 Ind. Fd Amb. under the apparent date of 9/ 10th April. The WDs of both Kohima Garrison and the RWK record it under 7/8th April, as given above. Colonel Pilcher's diary makes it 8/9th April.

[44] The accounts of Harman's two exploits here and in the next chapter are based on the personal narration of Colonel Easten.

[45] Yet it was complained afterwards by some commentators that no head cover had been provided as a protection against overhead bursts.

[46] All these comments were made to the author.

[47] The battalion War Diary says: 'In the afternoon an attack with artillery and mortar support by carrier and No. 8 platoons and a further officer-led Gurkha platoon was arranged to clear the DC Bungalow spur. It did not materialize successfully.'

[48] The citation is in the Supplement of the *London Gazette* of 20th June 1944. In this the dates of Harman's actions are given as the 8th and the 9th, but the War Diary of the RWK enters them on the 7th and the 8th.

[49] The notes on Kuriyan's actions are based on the personal narrative of Major-General Rawlley, but it has not been possible to obtain other accounts.

[50] Young relates these facts in detail in the WD of 75 Ind. Fd Amb.

[51] 'D Company at FSD were reinforced.'

[52] To the author.

[53] Steyn's Military Cross, won at Kohima, was awarded on the recommendation of the CO of another unit.

[54] Detail condensed from Young's WD. He was always very correct in his dealings with the Garrison Commander, consulting and reporting to him regularly and always asking for approval of his own proposals.

[55] He exchanged appointments with Yeo, Yeo becoming 2 i/c of the Regiment.

[56] *Defeat into Victory*, page 317.

[57] The statistical tables of 33rd Corps give the figures as 115 in all, but this is clearly not correct.

[58] Killed: Brigadiers W. H. Goschen (4 Bde) and his successor, J. A. Theobalds. Wounded: Brigadiers V. F. S. Hawkins (5 Bde) and J. D. Shapland (6 Bde).

[59] 60 Fd Regt R A, 12 Fd Coy RE, 2 Duke of Wellington's, 4 Border, 1 Essex.

[60] Now commanded by Lieut-General Shibata.

Made in United States
Troutdale, OR
09/23/2024

23086832R00166